Eyes Right!

Geoffrey Morlet was born in Perth in 1932. He studied Medicine at Adelaide University, and went on to specialise in Ophthalmology, following his father's footsteps. Prior to specialising, he worked in the Northwest Medical Service and the Royal Flying Doctor Service for two years, and then spent a year in a rural general practice. He furthered his studies in the UK, having worked his passage there and back as a ship's doctor. He practised Ophthalmology in Melbourne for some years before returning to Western Australia.

He is married to Elisabeth, with three children and nine grandchildren. He is still in practice, together with his son Nigel.

Geoffrey Morlet has published two novels, *The Journey* and *Spinifex*.

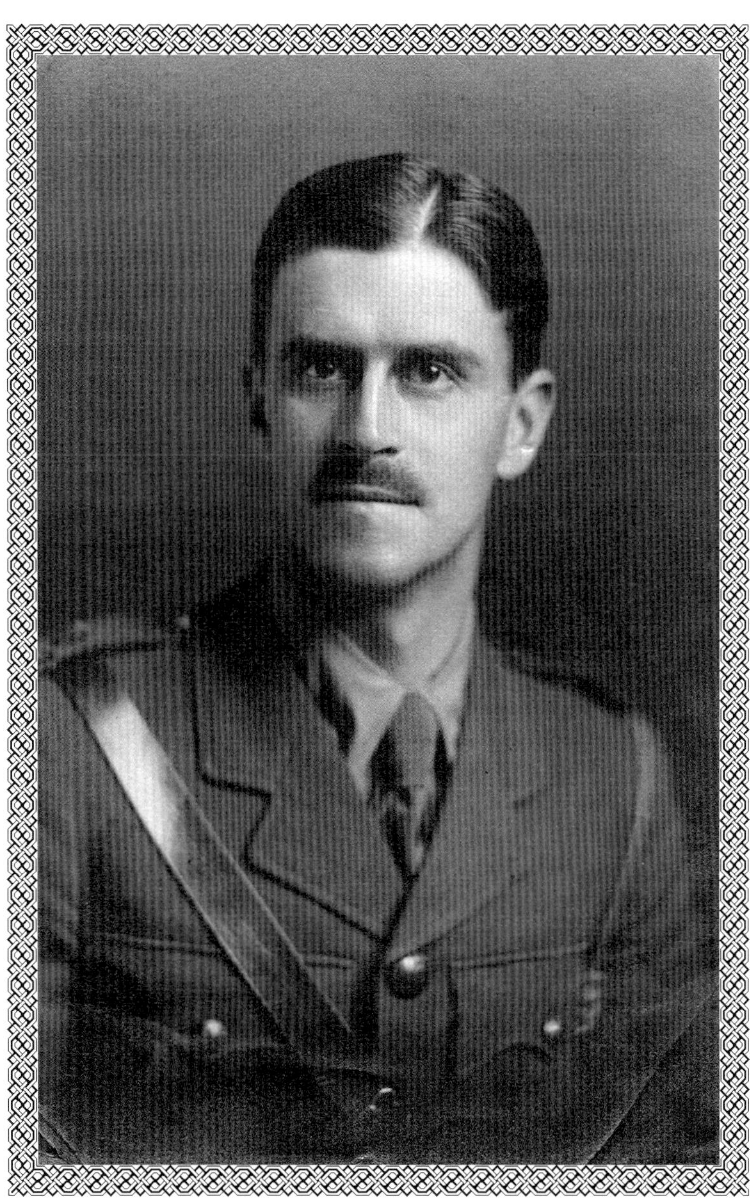

Lieutenant-Colonel Claude Morlet, 1918

Eyes Right!

The Life of Claude Morlet, DSO
Eye Surgeon and Soldier

Geoffrey Morlet

Lythrum Press
Adelaide

Published in 2007 by

Lythrum Press
PO Box 243 Rundle Mall
Adelaide SA 5000
Australia

www.lythrumpress.com.au

ISBN 978 1 921013 15 7

Cover design by Stacey Zass, Melbourne
Designed and produced by Lythrum Press, Adelaide
Printed by Hyde Park Press, Adelaide

Foreword

Recently in Australia there has been much discussion, and indeed argument, on the question of what it means to be 'an Australian'. What are our values? What do we mean by service, duty and being part of the wider aspects of our nation? Views have been given that indicate the importance of such things as language, our flag, our sport and our form of government, but it seems to me that this falls short of what the average person means when describing what it is to be 'an Australian'.

Eyes Right! by Geoffrey Morlet tells of his father's life during the two world wars, and is a book that shows us some of the complex values, attitudes, strengths and weaknesses that have influenced the 'Australian way' through our history in both peace and war.

Morlet writes a very moving book based on the diaries and letters of his father Claude Morlet, a medical graduate from Melbourne in 1913.

When war was declared in 1914 he enlisted in the 1st AIF, and saw service in North Africa, Gallipoli and the Western Front. Most of his war service was in the forward area, being first a Regimental Medical Officer in Gallipoli, and later in command of a Field Ambulance in France. For his outstanding service he was awarded both a DSO and a 'Mention in Dispatches'.

After the war he specialised in Ophthalmology, and returned to practise in Perth, Western Australia, where he married, and raised a family of three children.

Once again, when war was declared in 1939, he felt that he should serve his country, and at the age of 52 he enlisted.

In those desperate days of the early 1940s, he was soon in the thick of battle in the fearful Siege of Tobruk, serving as an Ophthalmologist with the 4th Australian General Hospital. Later he served with the 4th in Jerusalem and Colombo.

With the collapse of the Allied Forces in Singapore in 1942, he, with fellow Australians feared for the safety of their young families, and waited anxiously for their return home to care for them.

The author writes proudly of his father's service and puts life into the story by dealing with the history of the Morlet family and their French origins. He tells of their early days and dedication to Christianity, the family's life in Melbourne, and their attitude of service to their country which at that time was very much part of the British Empire. England was still the 'Home Country'.

Although his father died when he was an infant, Claude grew up in a protective loving family, aware and willingly understanding that he was expected to contribute to mankind, and that duty, service and loyalty to the nation were part and parcel of daily life.

His enlistmentment and early days in the AIF, however, were not without difficulty. The rugged Australian soldier was something new to him, and although the harshness of war, the horror of battle casualties and shellfire ultimately became his way of life, it was not easy for him. It was not the way he knew. His diary details his fears and concerns, and is an excellent account of what is now recognised as a common experience of all Australians who go to war.

There is pathos in his writings over and above the essential detail of his work as a doctor caring for sick and injured soldiers in combat, such as on his departure for war in 1940 on a troopship from Fremantle, when his son Geoffrey, aged 7, said to a bystander 'We are waving good-bye to my Dad, who is going to the war'. And Claude's reason for going to that war, he recorded as 'Doing my small part and making sacrifices to help my country'.

Here is a book that I recommend to all wishing to read of an Australian and his family. It provides a mosaic of some of the characteristics of an Australian. It presents a moving account of a successful Australian doctor who served his country magnificently in both peace and war, who faced personal triumph and success, and also tragedy.

Digger James
Brisbane
6 May 2007

Major General W.B. Digger James AC AO(Mil) MBE MC (Retd)

Former Director General of the Australian Army Health Services,
and Past National President of the Returned and Services League of Australia

To my sister Pamela,
our late brother Neville,
and the descendants
of Claude Morlet

Prologue

It is a characteristic of my family not to throw things away, and thus, a great number of family papers and documents have accumulated. By default, they have come to me.

Claude's mother Mary Alice kept a diary, as was the custom, and Claude was brought up to write regularly to his mother when away from home.

He kept a diary of the First World War, but unfortunately, the part covering the war in France is now lost. However, the first part, covering Egypt and the Gallipoli campaign, and all his letters to his mother – more than fifty, remain.

His diary of the Second World War was complete, but lacked the detail and passion expressed in his first war diary.

He wrote other diaries, one titled 'Leave in Paris 1917' in which he described his brief flirtation with a French girl. Another was a description of his honeymoon with Mildred in 1928, when they sailed to England and Europe for six months. Regrettably, both diaries were destroyed, however some letters survived to tell of their travels.

From this rich source of information, I have pieced together the interesting story of my father, Claude Morlet.

******

During the French Revolution, many family records were destroyed or lost, and so it was with the ancestors of Claude Morlet. The Morlet name is scattered about the pre-revolution records, however no direct lineage can be established. It is said that in the reign of Louis X1, an ancestor was the Grand Provost who carried out all the King's cruel decrees. (Hence John Marie Morlet's joke that he was 'descended from the hangman'.)

Claude's great grandfather Firmin Marie was born in the Champagne district in their ancestral 'Chateau de Museau' before the revolution of 1789, and though of a Catholic Royalist family, Firmin broke ranks and joined the Revolution, and served in Napoleon Bonaparte's army. After the war he settled in Brittany and married Mlle Aguar, an orphan, brought up 'as a daughter' by an old Royalist nobleman.

Their son John Marie was born in 1800 in Rennes, and like his three brothers, he was educated for the army. However, after the fall of Napoleon's Empire, they turned to a life in Commerce.

John Marie came to England in 1826, and taught French and Latin at a school in Staplehurst while he learned English. His three brothers remained in France.

He became a General Commission Merchant in London, in partnership with another young man, and traded as 'Morlet & Horne' at 2 Philpot Lane, EC. They traded mainly in wine with Spain and Portugal, and records show that John Marie frequently plied between France and England.

He became associated with the firm of Winteler & Verdier, long established General Merchants of Lisbon Portugal, who had a London branch, and thus he met, and in 1837 married, Rosina Winteler, the daughter of Gaspar and Helene Winteler (nee Verdier) – a well-to-do Portuguese Lutheran family.

Of their nine children, the second last was John Stanaslas, Claude's father. John Marie (or 'Jack' as his wife Rosina called him) died in 1860 when John Stanaslas was only 5 years old, leaving in his will the sum of £6,000 to his wife.

As a child, John Stanaslas (also called 'Jack' by his mother) was known to have a 'weak heart', possibly following an attack of rheumatic fever, though this is not certain. His early days are not recorded, but in his twenties, and probably on the recommendation of his doctor, he decided to take a long sea voyage to Australia to visit his mother's relatives, the Langmores, who lived in Victoria.

He was met in Melbourne by the Langmore brothers, and taken to their home 'Coonil,' in the suburb of Malvern, where he stayed for many months, and ultimately decided to settle in Australia.

He spent a good deal of his time in the north of Victoria and in New South Wales, where he made a number of friends, and stayed on their properties, joining in their active social life.

Among the early settlers of the North East of Victoria, he met the Docker family of Bontharambo, near Wangarratta, who settled in 1838, and also James Lindsay Brown, who squatted at Gooramadra in 1839, close to Bontharambo, and who planted the first vines in the Ovens Valley.

Lindsay Brown fell in love with Josephine, the daughter of the Rev. Joseph Docker, though at first her parents had opposed their marriage, as Brown was more than twenty years older than Josephine. They sent her for a holiday to England, probably in he hope that she would '*meet someone else and forget this middle aged man*' who was Rutherglen's first settler and close friend of Thomas Clarke, who was married to Josephine's older sister Mary. Ultimately, they married in 1859.

Lindsay Brown sold off a large part of his property to George Morris (whose family and descendants became a successful wine makers) and built a home in Beechworth, which he named 'Whaitber' after his family home in England.

John S. Morlet with his wife Mary, and children Lucile and Claude

On 9 February 1860, at Bontharambo, their daughter Mary Alice was born. In May 1861, Lindsay and Josephine with baby in arms, set out in their buggy to visit her family at Bontharambo. On the way, the horse shied at a snake and bolted, tossing Josephine and her baby out of the buggy. Josephine, then aged 27, was killed instantly but baby Mary Alice was unharmed.

Lindsay Brown went on to bring up his baby daughter, with help from his elderly in-laws the Dockers. Thus, Mary grew up in an atmosphere of early Victorian morality and deep Christian values.

When John Stanaslas, or 'Jack' as he was known, and Mary met, they fell in love at first sight. Mary's father however, was very much against the prospect of their marriage, probably on the grounds of Jack's ill health.

By this time, Lindsay Brown was elderly, had become very deaf, and found it difficult to understand Jack's rapid manner of speech when he tried to plead his case.

Ultimately, after receiving a long and impassioned letter from Jack, and

Bontharambo. The photograph is annotated by Mary Morlet
'Where I was born Feb 9th 1860'

after Josephine's brother George Docker had interceded on their behalf, he gave his consent and blessing, and they were married on 11 March 1886 at Bontharambo.

The following notice was recorded in the *Ovens and Murray Advertiser*:

Marriage at Bontharambo

On Thursday afternoon at the residence of the bride's uncle (Mr F.G. Docker), Bontharambo House, near Wangaratta, Miss Mary Alice Brown daughter of Mr J Lindsay Brown of Beechworth, and niece of the Hon Fredk. Brown MLC was united in bonds of matrimony to Monsieur Jean Stanaslas Morlet (sic) of the Prairie Station, Toowoomba Queensland. The Rev. G.F. Cross, incumbent of Christ Church Beechworth officiated …

Over the six months prior to their wedding, Jack spent most of his time in Queensland on the property he had purchased in the Darling Downs near Toowoomba. There he designed and built their future home, which they named 'Prairie'.

After their honeymoon in Tasmania, they returned to 'Prairie', and settled in to their isolated rural life. They had a cook and a housemaid, and lived comfortably, with Jack in seemingly good health.

By the end of that year, and with the first baby nearly due, Mary's cousin Maggie came to stay, and remained to help Mary until after the baby was born. Muriel Lucile arrived on New Year's Day 1887. The birth was easy and uncomplicated, and when the baby was three hours old, Jack came in and read prayers of thanks.

When the baby was eight weeks old, they travelled to Victoria to visit old Lindsay Brown, who was nearly blind, but to Mary's great joy he could recognise her, and distinguish the baby by looking very closely into their faces.

Jack returned to 'Prairie' after a couple of weeks, for there was work to be done, and Mary accompanied her old father to Melbourne where '*he had the cataract removed, and his sight restored in five weeks*'. Jack rejoined them in Melbourne, and they spent a few weeks visiting relatives, then returned home, after an absence of four months in Mary's case. After their return, their servant left them, leaving only the old Chinese gardener to act as cook. They had no nurse, and Mary had difficulty coping with baby Lucile who was a big heavy baby, and was very restless at night. Jack would come in from the fields after a long day's work, and '*instead of having the quiet rest he so much needed, he was frequently up and down half the night trying to pacify our tyrannical little daughter*'.

By autumn 1888, with Mary again pregnant, Jack's health started to fail. He spent long days in the fields, shearing and haymaking, and came in at dusk exhausted. He became breathless and giddy, and suffered from severe indigestion and headaches. When he developed severe pain in his side, Mary felt helpless and frightened, having no experience in nursing. At a neighbour's suggestion, she applied hot bran poultices to his side, which seemed to give him relief.

After a few days he felt well enough to visit the doctor in Toowoomba, and insisted on driving in alone. When he returned the next day, Mary was surprised to learn that instead of suffering from 'his liver' as they had thought it was his heart, and that he must take things quietly. Jack improved, and his doctor was pleased with his progress on the next visit, but soon after returning home, he caught a cold, and became breathless, coughing and spitting blood, which terrified Mary.

The doctor called, and pointed out to Mary, now eight months pregnant, that she could no longer cope with nursing her husband, and arranged for a Mrs D'Arcy MacDougall to come and stay for the next three weeks. During this time Jack made a good recovery, and although weak, he could lie on a couch on the veranda and from there, give orders to the workmen.

Claude and Jack

Claude

Chapter 1

Early Days

'On the 11th of August, my darling little Claude was born, and very thankful I was that he was a healthy little fellow, tho' very thin and small …' Mary wrote in her diary.

The nurse had not arrived, and the doctor was many miles away, but fortunately, Mrs Mackie the ploughman's wife assisted, with Jack helping in the background.

Mary soon realised that Jack could no longer manage 'Prairie', and so it was decided that they should move to Victoria. Jack was to leave first and spend a week in Toowoomba with Mrs D'Arcy, while Mary travelled south with young Claude. They reached Beechworth uneventfully, and after a week's rest at her father's home, they set out for Melbourne to join Jack, who had travelled in Mrs D'Arcy's care. Eventually they settled at Dromana.

Mary's third baby was born on 9 January 1890, a healthy boy with a shock of black hair, whom they named Jack. His father was delighted, though weak and bedridden as his health declined. He died only a few weeks later, on 26 January 1890.

Jack was buried in Dromana, leaving written instructions that there must be no mourning or black clothes, and no funeral procession. He was to be buried in a simple pine coffin. Mary, dressed in the white 'washing dress' that she had worn on the day they were married, followed the wagon bearing Jack's remains to the little cemetery on the hillside above Dromana. Jack was buried with a simple reading of prayers, in a peaceful setting of wild myrtle and gum trees that he would have loved. The grave was surrounded with a little railing and marked with a small headstone bearing a short inscription that he had chosen himself. Each summer for some years, Mary and the children spent a few weeks in Dromana, and kept fresh flowers on his grave.

CHAPTER 2

In March after Jack's death, Mary and the children left Dromana, and spent a short time with Aunt Jeanie in Melbourne. She then travelled to Beechworth to her old father. The children were a delight for the old man, and they remained there for the next three years, travelling to Melbourne and Dromana for their summer vacations.

In spite of her general observance of Jack's last wishes, Mary followed the example set by Queen Victoria, and after the accepted period of mourning continued to wear 'widow's weeds' for the rest of her days. Likewise, she resolved to never marry again, as this would be disrespectful to her late husband. She went on to bring up her children with her strict beliefs and deep religious principles.

Lindsay Brown died on 10 April at the age of 81. Reverend Joseph Docker had provided well for all his children, and Josephine's inheritance had been passed on to Mary. This, together with Lindsay Brown's legacy left Mary well endowed for the rest of her life.

'March 1894. After my dear old father's death, it seemed to me the right thing to do to take my children home to see their Grandmother in England. So after having a sale of furniture, etc. at Whaitber, and leaving a caretaker there, we packed up and started on our journey.'

They boarded the French ship *Polynesian* bound for Marseilles, and had a grand send off party. Mary found it strange to hear French spoken around them, and thought it peculiar that wine should be served with every meal. On the first night at dinner she *'modestly poured a little into a small wine glass, but afterwards found that these were only used for either liqueurs or for holding tooth picks, and that everyone took their wine in tumblers. There were no salt spoons, and we were expected to use our knives ... The meals seemed strange altogether to me.'* They travelled First Class, and a nurse, Ellen, cared for the children, having her own meals with them.

At Aden they watched with amusement as the Arab boys around the ship dived for coins, while others came aboard and sold baskets, embroidered scarves, silk cloth and trinkets to the passengers. At Port Said once again a number of Arabs came on board selling Turkish delight and trinkets, while a conjurer entertained the children with sleight-of-hand tricks. Lucile and Claude were taken for a donkey ride, but they had not gone far when they wished to get off. They were frightened by the horde of chattering Arabs around them. Many years later Claude recalled this occasion as he sailed on a troop ship through the Canal on his way to the war.

'The Morlet Widows and their children'

They disembarked at Marseilles just four weeks after leaving Melbourne, and travelled by train to Avignon where they stayed a week, then to Lyon and finally on to Paris. After five days of shopping and sight-seeing, they travelled by train to Calais, and crossed the Channel by steamer to Dover. They reached London by train on 12 April 1894, and were met by Jack's oldest brother Auguste and his wife Maria, and they lodged in Blackheath village, close to Granny's home.

The next day Jack's sister Lucile took them to Granny, who welcomed them with open arms.

In August, Claude turned six. He received a great many presents and had a party with Aunt Goldie's family. A family photograph was arranged, and Goldie and her children all came for lunch, after which they posed for the photographer, together with old Granny. (The photograph was later annotated by Claude: 'The Morlet Widows and their children'.)

In September, Mary and the children travelled by train to Edinburgh, where they spent two weeks sight seeing and touring. Mary then sent the children back to London with Nurse Ellen and set out alone to explore the countryside of her ancestors, finally arriving back in Blackheath at the end of October. Mary had a portrait photograph taken of herself with the three children, and as Christmas approached and the days grew shorter, she spent her time shopping or visiting relatives. Throughout her time in England she had been a regular churchgoer and often attended twice on Sundays, usually taking Lucile with her.

Mary Alice Morlet, with her three children, Jack, Lucile and Claude

On 20 March 1895 they left England for the long journey home. Once again they crossed the Channel, and arrived in Paris about seven in the evening. From Paris they took the train to Lyon and stayed overnight, then travelled on to Marseilles. They reached Cannes on 23 March and drove to the Pension de la Tour, which was on a hillside overlooking the bay. It was so delightful that they decided to stay until the end of the month. On Sundays, the boys went to the seaside with Nurse Ellen while Mary and little Lucile went to church, after which they all met on the seashore.

On 1 April, they left Cannes for Marseilles, and spent two nights at the Hotel de Louvre before boarding the *Ville de la Ciotat* for their final voyage home. The passage was calm and uneventful, and they arrived in Melbourne on 4 May, where Aunt Jeanie and her family met them. They were invited to stay at Coonhil with the Langmores and spent a fortnight comfortably surrounded by friends and family. At the end of this time, having said farewell to Nurse Ellen, who joined the Victorian Children's Aid Society, Mary went to Bontharambo with Lucile, while Daisy, who had stayed with them, took the boys to Shrublands in Beechworth.

After six weeks in 'the bosom of her family', Mary returned to Melbourne where she took possession of her new home in Stanhope Street, Malvern. After living in the empty house for a week with deck chairs and a trunk for a table, all of the luggage and furniture from Beechworth, and from England arrived at once. With Daisy's help, they unpacked and made the house comfortable.

CHAPTER 3

For the next seven years they lived quietly in Stanhope Street. The children had a daily Governess – first Miss White, and later Miss Wingrove – until the boys were old enough to go to Melbourne Grammar School, which they did when Claude was nearly thirteen, and Jack was eleven. Lucile was sent to Lauriston, where she completed her schooling and passed the matriculation examination.

Claude dressed as a 'Spanish Cavalier', aged 11

At Melbourne Grammar, the boys were known as 'Tweedle Dum and Tweedle Dee' as they looked alike, and there was little difference in their ages. Also, Jack was a burly fellow, and Claude though older, was slightly built. To add to the confusion, they were in the same class, Jack being ahead of his age group, and Claude a little behind.

When Lucile went to university, Mary sold the house in Malvern, and she and Lucile moved to South Yarra. Mary had been unwell, suffering from lumbago, and was advised to store her furniture and move into lodgings until her health improved. The boys went to live at 'The Grange' in Domain Road, a boarding house close to Melbourne Grammar, where they stayed for the remainder of their school days. By the time they matriculated, Mary had shown no inclination to move back to her own house, even though she had recovered her health, as she thoroughly enjoyed her lodgings, with the constant company it provided. Her abode was on the other side of Domain Road, opposite The Grange where the boys lived.

In 1907 the boys commenced Medicine at Melbourne University, but continued to live in The Grange to be close to their mother. At university they were in the same academic year and studied together, continuing their close brotherly relationship. Jack became an excellent tennis player, competing in Pennant Matches, while Claude played lacrosse, apparently without distinction. Both brothers passed their first year without mishap, and in the long summer vacation at the end of first year, Claude and his friend and fellow medical student George Cole embarked on a walking tour, of which Claude kept a diary.

'About December 1906, a tourist track was opened up by the State Governor, Sir Reginald Talbot. The track commenced at McVeigh's Hotel on the Wood's Point coach road, and followed the Yarra river valley for about fifteen miles, reaching a point just below the magnificent Yarra Falls. Here a small wooden hut was built, consisting of two rooms and a stable. It contained frying pans, billies, spoons, plates, etc. for the convenience of tourists, and also five spring mattresses, though tourists had to provide their own blankets.

The track then left the Yarra, crossing over the dividing range, and down the other side to the Thompson River, which it also crossed. From there onwards for about eighteen miles, the track steadily rose, ascending Mt Whitelaw where there was another shelter house. It then ran over what is known as the Baw-Baw Plateau. A branch track led to the top of Mt Baw-Baw itself.

The track continued over Mt St Philax, between the peaks of Mt Talbot and Mt Erica and then descended precipitously to the mining town of Walhalla.'

On Thursday 13 February 1908, Claude and George set out on their tour. They carried swags weighing 25-30 pounds, with their clothes, bedding and provisions for the trip divided between them. They reached the first shelter hut just below Yarra Falls at dusk, and after a meal of German sausage, bread and jam, they stoked up the fire, and slept soundly, rolled up in their blankets. Claude described the first part of their trip in his letter.

Exchange Hotel [M. Berry. Prop.]
Walhalla
Tuesday, 18 February 1908

Dear Mum
As you see, I'm at Walhalla!

We have done the trip – over the Baw-Baw, Mt St Philax, Mt Talbot and Mt Erica, and up the Yarra Falls. We have entirely changed our plans since we left. We intended, as you know, to go to the top of Mt Baw-Baw and then to return by the same way, without going down the other side in to Walhalla. However, as we found the walking a great pleasure instead of being a drawback to the trip, and as we just love camping out, we changed our plans altogether.

When we got to the top of Baw-Baw, 5130 ft above sea, we thought it would be too slow going back over our tracks, so we have come down into Walhalla, a distance of 18 miles from Baw-Baw. We're not going back to Warburton by the Baw-Baw track, but are going to take a wide circuit round the country, through Aberfeldie, Mount Lookout, BlueJacket, RedJacket, Jerico (on the Jordan Creek), Matlock, and along the coach road to McVeigh's hotel again and back to Warburton.

The last 20 miles we will take the coach, which will cost five shillings and sixpence. We are keeping a diary, or rather George is, which I shall copy when I get back. The scenery coming over was something to see and die for! The most glorious views you can imagine! The shutter on the camera got jammed with crumbs of a biscuit in the swags, so I could get no photos of the Falls, as the 'instantaneous' would not work.

We intend to get back to Warburton next Tuesday evening, though if we get at all 'knocked up' we shall spend a day longer on the road. Our food lasted splendidly, and we have a lot left over. In future we pass through little villages with stores nearly every day, so we won't have to carry much now.

We always have a heavy breakfast, carry a light lunch in our pockets, and have a heavy three-course dinner at night (soup, meat and boiled rice).

We saw three snakes on the track and killed two. The other one got away!

It is too late, and I am too tired to write a description of the trip, but it was absolutely glorious and wonderful.

The country we now propose touring was 'rushed for gold' some 50 years ago, and was just as quickly deserted. Now, the whole country is quite empty and dead, but the scenery is beautiful. We could see it all from the mountaintops, and we shall now see the mountains from below. Where we were this morning is now an enormous blue mountain away in the sky, indeed you cannot see the top from here.

Well, goodnight Mum dear. We enjoy every minute. We have now walked 81 miles and are not in the least bit footsore or done up.

Love to Jack and Lucile and lots to you dear old Mum.

From Claude

Contrary to his description of the trip to his mother, they reached Walhalla about six in the evening, tired, thirsty and hungry. Their dried beef had gone bad and had been thrown away, likewise the biscuits, which were soggy and stale. Their water supply, too, was exhausted. Their decision to stay at Walhalla however, proved costly, as they had to pay for accommodation, and purchase some cooking utensils, which caused Claude some financial anxiety. His second letter summarised the rest of the journey:

'Sunnydale'
Warburton
24 February 1908

Dearest Mum
Here I am safe and sound at Sunnydale again, two days before we intended. When we got to Walhalla and decided to go home via Jerico and Matlock, knowing that we would be camping in the open for about six nights, and only passing a few small villages on the way, we laid in a new stock of provisions, there being not much of our original supply left.

We bought a tomahawk and a large six-quart billy for baking in. – Oh I forgot to tell you about our baking. At one of the shelter houses on the Baw-Baw, we found two workingmen encamped who were repairing part of the shelter house. Seeing that we had to put up with their society for the night we made ourselves out to be pleasant. They met us halfway, and we were soon fast friends. They were making bread when we arrived, and were thorough bushmen, both of them. They taught us to make bread in a most professional way, and made us a loaf to go on with it. They also showed us how to make 'bush scones' or 'Johnny cakes', the latter being much the same as damper, only nicer.

We made our own bread for the rest of the tour until the flour ran out, and then on the last two days we had to buy our bread, which, on my honour, was not as nice as our own.

Well, we were deadbeat when we got to Walhalla, and decided to spend the night comfortably in a hotel and have our tea and breakfast cooked for us for a change. We spent a most comfortable night there!

As some packhorses were going out our way next day, we sent our swags with them, paying half-a-crown for carriage. We walked out 10 miles ourselves, and slept under a bridge over the Aberfeldie River, where they had left our swags for us. The next day we walked 22 miles, carrying our swags and water, as we knew we would not find any on the way. At dusk that night we reached the banks of the Jordan River where we slept under the stars beside our campfire.

The following morning, Friday, we crossed the Jordan and reached Jerico four miles further on. We were alarmed by this time to see how our provisions were disappearing!

I forgot to say that when we left Walhalla after restocking provisions and staying at the hotel, we only had two shillings and three pence between us, and we were nearly 100 miles from home!

After arriving at Jerico, we found that by cutting through the bush, we could cut off five miles. This we did, and after 12 miles walk through the bush – and frightfully rough it was – we reached the coach road 44 miles from home.

That night we built a 'humpy' of gum saplings, as it looked rather like rain, and a cold wind was blowing. As we lay on our rugs that night, by the roaring fire with a simmering billy, under the stars overhead and the dark bush all round, drinking cup after cup of steaming hot cocoa (of which thank heaven, we had plenty) we agreed that although the walking was fun and the country beautiful, camping in the evenings was the cream of the tour.

That night we went over our stores and found that we had just enough food for five more meals. That left us three meals for the next day and breakfast and lunch the day after. We then knew that at all cost we must reach Sunnydale in time for tea on Sunday.

Well we did it! We walked 22 miles two days running, thus completing the 44 miles which remained in two days, and reached Sunnydale at 4.45 last evening (Sunday) having a dessertspoon full of tea and a penny ha'penny between us! Thus ended our tour.

We walked 152 miles in exactly 10 days, carrying our food and bedding on our backs. We were a bit tired last night, I admit, and after a hot bath and a big tea we went to bed. We were never the least bit footsore and our feet today are as good as the day we started.

We weighed ourselves the day we started and again today on the same scales both times, and noted that George had lost four-and-a-half pounds, while I have gained one-and-a-half pounds! What you think of that?

I am as well as I ever was in my life, and not even stiff today.

My assets are one penny and I owe George two shillings and nine pence on the tour. The extra expense was owing to our change of plans, staying at Walhalla and buying camping requisites there. Originally you know we expected to spend all our nights in government shelter houses containing all cooking and eating utensils.

I must have money to go home with, and to buy a toothbrush as I lost mine on the tour – and to pay George with, and hundreds of other things!

Please send up about 10 shillings at once Mum, like a dear, and ask Jack if he would mind sending me a box of 'Imperial Special Rapid plates' for my camera as soon as he possibly can.

I shall probably be coming home next Sunday, but I will write again before that.

In the meantime, I am in want of money! I used your fifteen shillings, and also about seven and sixpence of my own private funds on the tour. I have now one penny, and no toothbrush. I owe the storekeeper at Warburton one shilling, and George two shillings and nine pence!

From Claude

CHAPTER 4

Second year Medicine saw the brothers spending long hours poring over their books and memorising bones of the skeleton. They both passed the year's examination, and during the long summer vacation, Claude went as a jackaroo to 'Thule', a Station owned by the Dockers, in southern New South Wales. He travelled to Albury by train, and then to Hay, and on to Cobar by horse and coach. He wrote to Mother:

'Thule'
Cobar
11 January 1909

Dearest old Mum
I was pleased and excited yesterday to find a very large mail for me. If you had seen the way I devoured your letters! I got two letters from you, one dated 31 December and one 7 January, also one from Lucile and one from Jack. I fully take back my complaints about small mails, and add 'long may it last'. The postal arrangements here seem positively disgraceful, I never feel sure that I have got everything that was sent to me. I got the felt hat last week, and the letter that went with it yesterday!

The revolver and bullets have not yet turned up. The coachman says that they have not arrived at Cobar. I don't know whether he is telling the truth or whether he has not called at the station for them.

So much for the mail!

What a broken-up Christmas the family has had this year. The first time on record! Lucile seems to have had a jolly time at St Leonard's. Thanks awfully Lucile, for the long letter, and the promise of another tie. I am very curious to know what the colour will be.

Now I shall plunge into news.

Last week has been the coolest we have had up here – during the last eight days the temperature has never been over 95 degrees. Last Thursday, seeing the tracks of two dingoes on the run, Fred took a gun and sat up all night at a tank waiting for them to come in to drink – but alas they came not.

At the same time Phil and I set out after tea to ' Paradise' about five miles away and took up our positions sitting on a horse rug beside the tank. Unfortunately, although the moon was nearly full, there were such a lot of clouds that most of the night was pitch-dark. We heard numbers of kangaroos hop up and could distinctly hear them lapping the water, but could not see a thing. Once or twice we fired at the sound in forlorn hope, but never successfully.

Phil quickly fell asleep, but I never slept a wink, I was too excited! I sat gripping my gun and peering at the sounds all night. At a quarter to five, it was daybreak and I woke Phil.

We rode home, arriving about 6 o'clock in time for the milking. Phil managed to sleep most of the day but I'm blowed if I could go to sleep – too many flies! However I went to bed early next night.

In all my 20 years, I have never struck anything to approach the mosquitoes that devoured us as we sat up that night. I smoked desperately but at the end of my fourth pipe (I had already had two during the day) I began to feel giddy and had to knock off! While I smoked they buzzed continually around my ears but would not actually bite my face. But fully made up for it on my hands! My wrists were swollen for couple of days afterwards! The continual drone and buzz all night was enough to drive you mad!

After lunch we set out for Yalcapo, a paddock 17 miles away, getting there about 4 o'clock, when we will start driving 500 sheep to another paddock. We will drive until dark and then tie up our horses and burrow a hole in the ground for our hips and go to sleep. At daybreak we will start way again and reach our destination about 11 o'clock.

The reason for this evening and early morning driving is that the sheep are fat and it would not do to drive them during the heat of the day. We shall be home for lunch tomorrow, so will just take some dry brownie and a water bag to allay our cravings at daybreak tomorrow. I shall add a line to this tomorrow before the mail goes to let you know how I got on. Fred is not going with us.

Tuesday 10 a.m.

Everything finally turned out all right last night. I say 'finally', because at times it seemed as though everything would go wrong! Phil and I had to go out yesterday afternoon to Yalcapo, a big paddock 10 miles by 5, or, 50 square miles. The tank in this paddock was practically dry, about two inches of slush in it. There were 500 sheep in the paddock, which had to be driven up the whole 10-mile length from the tank, and put into the second paddock from the Yalcapo. This meant about 15 miles of driving, which had to be done in the morning and evening, without the chance of striking any water.

We started after lunch yesterday and got to the tank about 4:30 p.m. We had a loaf of brownie and each had a water bag. After about two miles of driving, one of the water bags (Phil's) burst! You have no idea how dry one gets driving sheep in a cloud of red dust, knowing you only have one small water bag to provide liquid for two of you for two meals, and about seven hours driving. Anyhow we drove until 8.15 last night when darkness fell, then had some brownie and a sip of water after tying up our horses.

Making a pillow out of our saddles we laid down, and in one act, Phil was 'snoring like Miss Jane!' I did envy him.

We had only our shirt sleeves and no rugs, and after tossing about and raising dust over myself for a couple of hours I generated a raging thirst and nearly died of cold! So I got up, threw caution to the wind and had a good drink, then lit a fire and my pipe. Having finished the pipe and got warm, Phil still sleeping, I went to look at the horses, and made the comforting discovery that Phil's horse had broken away, and was probably home by now!

Being sick of my own company, I woke Phil and told him. He grunted and went back to sleep again. I sat by the fire and listened to a fox barking quite close, and a mopoke still closer. At last I fell asleep. I woke at 3.15. In an hour it would be dawn, and as we had to carry Phil's saddle unless we found his horse, I woke Phil and we had breakfast.

We both lost out penknives while sleeping on the sandy ground, and broke the brownie in half and each munched a great hunk and sipped water. Then we waited for daybreak and I dozed again.

At 4 o'clock I saddled my horse, and had the luck of finding Phil's grazing peacefully a couple of hundred yards away. About six we came on a fence, which told us we only had about five more miles to go. This was refreshing for we did not think we had come nearly so far the night before. At 7.45 am we had finished with the sheep and rode cheerfully for home, chasing a pair of kangaroos in front of us.

Suddenly my horse went dead lame, and we did the last three-quarters of an hour of our journey on foot, arriving about 8.30. To my great joy, Fred said the lameness was nothing serious! I had been in a terrible state ever since it happened, thinking that I had disabled one of the Thule horses. And precious little help I am here to make up for it! Phil does everything – he understands how. I go with him and watch and help him when I can – which is seldom.

Well, I have had a bath and a cup of tea and feel as fresh as a daisy, and had just noticed that my 'line or two' has developed into several sheets!

Goodbye Mum dear and good luck to you all.

From Claude

Claude went on with the story in his next letter.

23 January

On Wednesday, Fred and I drove around part of the run, having lunch out. We drove about 37 miles altogether without seeing anything worthy of note. In the meantime, Phil had done some boundary riding, and found distinct traces of two dingoes. He always does do something really useful when left by himself. He is a grand chap, and we get on splendidly, though it is much as I feared it would be – he makes me often feel so awfully small and foolish, by the common sense and coolness he shows in contrast to my innate stupidity. However, it is only natural, and it never does a chap any harm to have the last spark of pride knocked out of him – for it is only temporary!

To continue – on Thursday, we set dog traps for the dingoes and on Friday, mustered and drafted 1200 sheep. On Saturday, caught a small fox in one of the traps and skinned it. That brings me up to yesterday. Mail day, which I spent reading, smoking, perspiring and swearing by turns until mail arrived. With the mail came the revolver and bullets, which I began to fear had gone astray. Thanks awfully Mum dear for sending them. Will you write down what it cost you so that I can return it when I get back? Last night a very strange thing happened.

Reading in your letter your sympathy over my toothache, I inwardly thanked heaven that it had never returned after the tragic night which I spent moaning and putting fresh relays of carbolic in the hole. Finishing your letter, I had tea. Tea was nearly over, when apropos of nothing, Phil remarked what a comfort it was that my toothache had not returned. Immediately afterwards I began to notice a slight ache in a new tooth on the other side of my mouth! Within 10 minutes I was stamping and groaning round the barracks, my mouth bleeding from vicious attacks with a needle. After infinite pain I discovered a very deep hole in one of my upper molars.

I had a wretched night, putting in dose after dose of carbolic. Being a very sultry night each operation caused streams of perspiration and bad language to pour forth. At 2 o'clock I fell asleep on a sandy bed, and when I woke this morning, I could hardly tell you which tooth it was!

I think that carbolic of Fred's, which is exceedingly strong, must simply kill nerves, for after a night of agony, it has stopped all the ache! Of course it may be too soon to talk in this latter case, but I don't think so somehow.

This morning Phil and I found a fox in a dog trap, which we had set about half a mile from the house. I stood off and shot him first shot with the revolver right between the eyes! I must be improving, or else it was a fluke!

Fred and Phil went for a drive to look at the dog traps, starting about 8.30, while I stayed at home and skinned and pegged out the skin of the fox. Fred and Phil returned for lunch, and it is now 1:30

Now for a chat.

How absolutely ripping about your duck shooting Jack! I'm awfully glad, and you will have a marvellous time.

About your Peterborough invitation Mum, it certainly would be ripping, and as you say, it would make it nicer for you. I don't like refusing such a good offer. All the same, I am selfish by nature and really would rather stay here to the end. The climate doesn't disagree with me in the least, and I glory in the wildness of everything. So, though it sounds jolly nice, I'm going to refuse your offer. Besides, there will be Jack's expenses to pay – and I expect they will not be light, 1st class in the train and an expensive hotel no doubt, besides cartridges, etc. And I don't think we can have come out too well on our income last year, so its best to economise when possible isn't it? This however is not the reason I refuse.

We have grand games of tennis now, and I always play Fred and Phil. We're very even that way. I never play any other time than after tea at night.

The meals here are very wholesome and plain – since you ask Mum – the only thing is that there is no butter or green vegetables to be had. In every other way, we could not do better. Owing to the lack of vegetables, I have often to seek the services of Beecham's pills [laxatives], but I am in perfect health. There is a splendid library here and I do a lot reading. I sometimes miss the piano, but these occasions are rare.

The grapes are getting ripe and we have great feeds already. It is jolly hot in here at present, so I'll postpone the finishing of this letter for a while.

6 p.m. I'm not feeling too well today, owing to the consumption last night of six Beecham's pills. I have been left to myself all day, Fred and Phil having gone out together. It reached 102° this afternoon, and I felt rather uncomfortable, reading and sitting around by myself. It is thundering, but that means nothing as it has done that for three days, and no rain. We badly need rain now and I'm hoping it comes soon, or much damage will be done!

Well goodbye Mum dearest, with love to you all.
From Claude

P.S. Don't forget to get Jack to pay our Varsity fees before he goes away, and please write a letter enclosing a cheque from me – I have no time now. – C

The saga went on!

Claude as a jackaroo

Claude in the Botanical Gardens, 1909

26 January 1909

Last Thursday, Phil and I took 32 cattle to West Warbreckam, 10 miles away, and camped. There is a hut there with rice, tea and flour, sugar, salt and treacle, knives forks plates, etc. We took out some bread and meat, and a rifle. Before we started, Fred had remarked that one of the cows was very tame, so on the way out, the devil got into me, and I suggested to Phil we should try to milk her, and have milk for tea and breakfast. Accordingly, when we arrived, we fixed her head in the gate with fence wire and leg-roped her with my stock whip. Ass that I was, I sat down with a bucket and started to milk her. I got about a cup full of milk when the brute gave a bellow; pulled her head loose; broke the stock whip; kicked over the milk bucket and departed! Pender, the rouse-about, had lent the whip to me, and I was awfully cut up about it as they cost a good deal!

During the evening, Phil shot away all the bullets we had brought and only got four pigeons. We finished these at breakfast, and making an early start, set out to find 12 horses in a 25 square mile paddock. The nearest fence of this paddock is 10 miles from the homestead. In the centre, or close to it, is a tank. We went to the tank together, and then separated, arranging to meet at 12.30 at the tank for lunch.

At 12 o'clock I was close to the tank but early, so I thought I would ride out the towards the centre of the paddock to see if I could pick up the tracks of horses. I quickly found some tracks, and they took me into some scrub where after some very difficult tracking I utterly lost them, and coming out of the scrub, I made for the tank again.

Twenty minutes riding should have seen me at the tank, but after 40 minutes, and no sign of the tank, I knew I must be wrong. Still, in the direction I was going, or thought I was going, I should have struck the fence in less than an hour, but after more than at an hour's hard riding, I knew I was not going in the direction I thought I was. The sun was overhead. It was after one o'clock.

You can't know the helpless-hopeless feeling, when one has no idea where one is, or which direction to take, and there was absolutely nothing to guide one as to which was north, south, east or west. I was utterly bushed, and very thirsty. I knew that if I could only keep riding in any one direction, I should strike a fence, but the chance of keeping one direction when there's nothing to guide you, and you have to keep making detours to avoid scrub, are small.

Besides, when I reached a fence, I would not know which fence it was, and the paddock was 20 miles around, and at the nearest point, 10 miles from home. All very comforting!

Still my only hope was to try and keep this one direction and I rode hopelessly on till about 2 o'clock, when by the kindness of Providence – it could be nothing else! – I struck wheel tracks! Then I remembered that Fred had driven Phil through here last week, starting from the tank, so following the buggy track backwards, I arrived at the dear old tank at 2.30! I felt awfully ashamed of myself, as there was Phil, still waiting. But what was my relief when I reached him to hear that he too – the infallible Phil – had been bushed and had just arrived!

We then set out together and got the horses about four. Going all the way home that night was out of the question, so we drove them in to a yard near the hut and camped. We had no more food, so I boiled rice and baked bread. The latter had a very hard crust, but it was not too bad. We ate these with treacle, and came home early next morning (Saturday). We cut chaff all the morning when we got home, then young Davidson came over from Bedooba about lunchtime, and we played tennis all afternoon.

Yesterday we were up at daylight, and mustered and drafted some sheep to be sent to Sydney for sale. Bob Pender and Adam McIntosh are driving them to Cobar, which will take them 10 days, where they will be trucked to Sydney.

Phil leaves next Wednesday, and as Fred wants to see the sheep safely on the train, he is going to drive Phil to Cobar. So I expect I shall be by myself from Wednesday till Sunday, when Fred returns.

I figure I shall enjoy the month after Phil leaves even more than for last six weeks. I shall have to do things myself, and use my own head. I shall be able to notice things and report things to Fred on my own responsibility, and I hope, make myself useful.

Phil is a great chap and it has been awfully nice for me to have had him to show me things, and teach me for the last six weeks, but I have never had an opportunity of doing things for myself and comparatively, I have not had much to do with Fred, as Phil and I have always been sent out together, whilst Fred did something else.

George Cole, who is in Queensland, suggests my meeting him at Albury, and our going down to Melbourne together. We could not do that, as I come in the mail train and he is in the Express, but I might stay the night at Springhurst and come on in the Express with him next day.

I hope you will like Peterborough Mum, and have a really good change there.

Thanks so much for the tie Lucile. I think it will go awfully well with my grey suit, as the other does with my green one.

Thanks so very much for your letter Jack. Have a good time at the Lakes.

Goodbye, with love to all.

Claude.

PS. Bob Pender won't let me give him a new whip! C.

Claude's final letter from the station concludes his adventures.

16 February 1909

This will be my last letter to you before I am back in the South Yarra again. I'm sorry I only wrote so little last week, and I shall make up for it now.

You may remember that last Tuesday as soon as we had tea, Bob, my droving companion, and I went down to a tank about a mile from here, intending to watch all night for the dingo. So much I told you last week.

We took a billy of cold tea and some brownie and arrived about sunset, when we were both absolutely struck helpless with amazement to see, wallowing in the water, a great savage looking creamy yellow dog – none other than the dingo! He had never been seen before and his presence only known by his great footprints, and the dead and crippled sheep!

While we were still stupidly fumbling in our pockets for cartridges, he looked up and saw us. With an ugly snarl he dashed off into the scrub and left Bob and me kicking ourselves, and gnashing our teeth. A couple of hundred yards away in the scrub he stopped and bayed defiance – a deep fierce bay he had; very unpleasant to the ear! We sat tight however, on the off chance of his coming back, or his mate coming. Foxes innumerable came in unsuspectingly and lapped the water. We could almost have caught them they were so close – and foxes are supposed to be cunning!

It was about 2.30 am when I was getting pretty sleepy, and was sitting dreamily staring at a bare patch of ground about 20 yards off – when suddenly in that very patch, something, dimly seen in the moonlight, leapt out of the scrub and came to an abrupt halt as if listening. I dared not raise my gun, as it was looking straight at me, though I was in the shadow, and it could not have made me out. Slowly, I put my arm out and pinched Bob with all my might. He raised his head sharply – instantly saw the dog and in a flash raised his gun and fired! A cloud of dust arose, and we heard scampering feet die away. He was too quick and fired low! We could have wept! We cursed until daylight and then came home, determined to try again next night.

Accordingly next night found us in the same place. Bob instantly went to sleep, so I dared not allow myself to even close my eyes and sat keenly listening and watching. Bob woke at intervals with a start and consistently swore he had never been asleep!

By 2 o'clock we had not heard a sound. We came to the conclusion that they were too frightened to come in again. We got up, drank our tea and put on our hats, and were just going to start for home when we both fell flat! For my part, fairly shaking with excitement! As we were about to start, a most horrible sound arose about a quarter of a mile off in the scrub. An awful gruesome wail – the most weird and mournful thing I have ever heard! When Jack was going to camp by himself at Yalthong, someone told him that if he heard a dingo howl, he would probably turn and run for his life back to the homestead! After three or four horrible howls, the next thing we heard was the thundering of a mob of sheep galloping madly – and then after half-an-hour without a sound, a loud 'lap-lap-lap-lap'! We had not heard a sound of his coming in, and after every couple of 'laps' he paused, as if listening intently. He was, we found in the morning, 18 yards from us, and strain our eyes as we would, not a thing could we see! After a whispered conference, I covered the place where the sound came from, ready to fire if I caught sight of him, whilst Bob took off his boots (he seemed to me to make an awful noise with his boots), then carefully stood up, and still could not see it!

He then began creeping towards the sound. The 'lap, lap' still continued, and I was frantic with excitement and afraid that the dog would hear my heart beating! I have never been in such an awful state of suspense in my life, and the perspiration streamed off me! Suddenly, after standing with his gun raised for what seemed to me an age, 'bang!' went Bob's gun! Instantly followed by a scampering of feet and he was gone!

I got up and mopped myself, and listened to Bob cursing gently. We argued over how much of the charge he got, and how far he would get before he died. We lit the fire, and heated our tea, after which we lit our pipes and yarned until daybreak when we started to track the dingo.

The track was punctuated with splashes of blood but after a mile of tracking, the track became so faint, and the sun became so hot, and we became so bad tempered, that we chucked it in and came home for breakfast. After breakfast I went to sleep, as I had scarcely slept for two days and two nights. I spent the day resting and reading, and the next day, Fred drove around part of the run and saw a lot of dead and crippled sheep. The dingo's work!

On Saturday, I put on my green trousers and waistcoat and one of my white coats and my new good felt hat, and rode over to Bedooba, the Davidson's place. Mr, a very nice man, and a dead image of King Edward – Mrs, a common old thing with a perpetual ailment of some sort. Miss, a conscientious silly sort of girl in many ways, with a mincing walk, but I think, a good heart and a kind nature. Bessie, a little girl of 12 or 14, very pretty, and as old fashioned and responsible as you please – always clears the table, folds the cloth, helps make the beds, feeds the fowls – a regular little housekeeper.

Besides all these, there is Will Davidson, a boy of my own age, and a very nice fellow. He and I had some great games of tennis. He just beats me nearly every time!

I rode home on Sunday in time for the mail by which I got two letters from you Mum and one from Lucile. Also, a telegram from George Cole. The telegram was to say that he would get out of the Sydney Express at Albury, on his way down, and wait there about six hours for the arrival of the mail train in which I will be, so we can go down together. This will mean I will not stop at Springhurst.

Well goodbye Lucile and Mum, this letter will keep you going with something to read for a while since Peterborough is so quiet.

I shall be home on Friday night, 26 February.
From Claude

PS. For the last fortnight I have been getting to know Fred better and better, and we get on famously now. I'm only sorry I have got to leave so soon, things being thus, but it is better to be friends in the end, rather than take a violent liking to a fellow at first and then getting sick of him, isn't it? CM
PPS. I have not won back my shilling yet. After last night's shooting we were dead equal. CM

CHAPTER 5

And so, Claude returned to The Grange, likewise Jack, from his duck shooting adventure, and they both settled in to their studies.

Lucile married Stanley Elder, a Melbourne lawyer, in December 1910, and no further record of Claude appears until 1912 when he and Jack commenced their final year of medicine. Jack had gone to live in Trinity College, whilst Claude stayed in his old 'digs'. Term had begun, and Claude had just returned from a visit to Trinity College. He wrote to mother, who was staying in the country with the Langmore relatives, at 'Wattle Park,' Woodbrook, via Castlemaine.

'Tweedle Dum and Tweedle Dee', Claude (left) and Jack as young medical students

April 1912
(Saturday night)

Dearest old Mum
You'll begin to think I am wasting stamps writing to you so often, but I prefer to spend my money this way to any other.

Thanks so much Mum darling for the cheque. It was very thoughtful of you. But you know I have some money in the bank which I may use when I like – so please don't give me cheques until it is quite convenient, as I am in no hurry whatever.

Mum dear, you must not worry about little things like my socks – I have lately bought two new pairs, and none of them have any holes.

I'm so glad you're having such a quiet restful time – a change always does one good – and I'm glad for you to have a complete change of environment and companions, as the old ladies at Melrose, though excellent old bodies in their way, must become wearisome after a time. They are all too old to be companions to you.

I am feeling a bit lonesome tonight. This afternoon I was up at Trinity with Jack, where he had invited Lucile and Letta Yencksen for afternoon tea. Lucile left early to feed the baby, and I came home in the train with Letta. She is quite young you know – we used to play tennis with her and Nora Cunningham and co. when we were quite small. The child was prattling cheerily of dances and tennis parties with these other little girls whom we grew up amongst, and whom we never see now – somehow it made me feel old and slow and uninteresting, and 'out of things'.

I have just left Jack in his pleasant study among all of the other jolly boys up there, and crawled back to The Grange and had tea with the old girls and children. I can't quite describe the sort of lonesome depressed mood that is on me tonight – but I feel 'out of things' and on the shelf.

I don't want to growl, but I know I shall be all right soon when I start work, but I miss old Jack terribly tonight. Jack and I always were such companions together, and I do wish the jolly old boy was here – you see, there's no one at all to talk to – and I want to talk to someone. That is why I am writing to you, my dearest old Mum. What a comfort you are dear Mum. You're the greatest blessing of all the great benefits that God has given me – and may He spare me you for many years. I don't know what I would do without you.

Well, I think it's time I was a little more cheerful – in fact I feel so already. Writing this to you has done me a lot of good. I had a talk to Dr Maudesley the other day about Father. He said he could not exactly say why he remembered him, but he says he has a very good memory for his cases, and it came back to him when he is started on the train of thought. He described to me a good deal about Father's illness. He asked where Jack and I were living, and was awfully nice.

Well Mum dear, I will do some work now.
With much love.
Claude

PS. Later.
I feel much cheered now. Max rang up and had a long yarn with me. He asked me first to lunch tomorrow, but I am going to Lucile's, and then to supper, which I accepted. Somehow

the Butlers always give me the impression that they really like to have me there, and it's a very nice feeling to have. Goodnight dear old Mum.

His next letter to mother was more optimistic and cheerful, as work had started in earnest.

Just a line, as I am very late starting tonight. Well dear old Mum, I wonder how are you are getting along. I sincerely hope you're not getting bored up there all this time – but I don't think you will. I think Woodbrook is a sweet little quiet place, especially Wattle Park. I wonder if Kathleen and baby have gone up there yet. I hope they have, for otherwise you'll be getting lonely. By Jove I do envy you Mum dear – how I would love to be able to take things easy in a quiet little nook in the country – and read Dickens and Thackeray and Shelley – and forget the bustle and strain of this life down here.

I have had a pretty solid day. This morning we had to inspect the Blind Asylum. That was interesting, and it is perfectly amazing what those poor blind people can do.

About 11.30 I sneaked away from there and ducked over to the Alfred Hospital, where I worked until 1 o'clock – then lunch, and back to the Alfred until 3 o'clock. I then had to rush up to the Women's hospital (where I was really due at 3 o'clock) and stayed there from 3.30 until 5.30. It is now 8 o'clock, and I don't feel a bit inclined to work!

Of course the reason I feel slack is because last night I went to *Kismet* with George Cole's theatre party. Really Mother, it was perfectly glorious! The most realistic and brilliant thing I have ever seen! It is simply the kind of life described in the Old Testament placed so vividly before your eyes that you forget where you are and positively live with the people on the stage!

It simply makes you shiver in parts, and the sensual abandoned life of the old Egyptians, with their harems and eunuchs and utter squalor and cruelty are almost too vividly reproduced! I sat between Miss Greig and Enid Russell Brown. I dreamt of Egypt and the wonderful costumes and the strange Mohammadan customs all night.

Work seems to be a perpetual scramble – I seem always to be struggling to keep up with the doings at the hospital, and always to be a little behind, no matter how I struggle. However one can only do one's best, and leave the rest in Stronger Hands. Anyhow I must start work now, as it is nearly half past eight.

I am going up to Trinity tomorrow afternoon, and to see Lucile for lunch on Sunday.

Your loving Claude

Final year medicine was then, as it remains to this day, a hard slog. Long days are spent in the wards, and at lectures, and every spare minute is spent studying, usually into the small hours of the morning. At that time the final exam was held at the beginning of the next academic year, with the Christmas break being utilised as 'swatting time'. Just before the Finals, Claude wrote a despondent letter to his mother, who was again staying in the country with her relatives.

Sunday February 1913

My dearest Mum

I am writing this on the top balcony with a lamp, there's not a breath of wind. Jack has gone up to Lucile's for tea, and I have been in at the Melbourne Hospital doing instruments all afternoon. It is very obvious to me Mum dear, why I never do any good at my work. I'm simply not bright. So it is scarcely my own fault is it?

We are shown, you know, scores of different instruments in quick succession, told the names of each, the name of the inventor, and its use. It is the easiest and least important part of our work, and the other chaps have no difficulty over it, but I am a perfect ass at the game. I invariably ascribe each instrument to the wrong inventor, and muddle them all up – of course I shall force myself to know them before the exams, and don't anticipate much trouble, but it strikes me forcibly what a difference there is between me and the other chaps.

So you see Mum, I'm working uphill. I cannot ever expect to do much good. It remains for me to turn what ability I have to the very best account. I am not going to be downcast over it, but it is disappointing, after working all the year and keeping my goal in front of me, to feel so utterly unprepared now that the end has come. I do not need rest in the least Mum. I am perfectly strong and well, happy and fit and inclined for work, but cannot help feeling conscious of my abysmal ignorance, and dreadful memory.

It is a great comfort Mum dear, to know that you are thinking of us in our work, and I know, praying for strength for us. Mum darling, I'm a miserable insincere wretch. I pray for hope and courage, but do not and cannot bring myself to trust. I have to simply struggle to feel the great presence and strength of God within me – and often cannot realise all His mercies to me.

I went to Church before breakfast last Sunday, but not today. I shall go again next Sunday. The one following this is the day before the exams. I have written to the Quins to know if we may go up there on Saturday and come back on Sunday afternoon, but I have not yet got an answer. At any rate I will have the last Sunday evening with you.

Make the most of the change and enjoy the fresh air. Keep moving the fingers and eating a lot.

Come back a healthy fat and sweet old Mum.

Your loving Claude

Finally with 'swat vac' over, the dreaded month of examinations commenced. After the last exam, Claude took the train to Hamilton in the Western District, and stayed with George Cole in a boarding house. It was here that he received the good news.

'Myrniong'
Hamilton
Sunday April 1913

My dearest old Mum,

So I got it!! I now have no wish unfulfilled! No ambition unrealised!

Oh Mum, I should be thankful! When I look back over all those miserable days – the long nights of study – the monotonous days, and lonely walks to and from the hospital – always hoping, longing doubting and fearing – and then that unhappy time of exams, when I was perfectly certain that it was all over, and that all the hopes and ambitions and work had collapsed in utter failure – when I tried to say, 'Thy will be done' – and couldn't.

When I remember all this, which was so lately – and try to realise that I have now got everything that I have so longed for – Oh Mum, I can't feel thankful enough! I simply am not capable of it! I hope it will be a lesson to me for the rest of my life, if I can only remember it.

The night before the first exam I found in my evening reading, a Psalm – a very well known one – I forget the number – the last verse was 'none of them that trust in Him shall be desolate'. I tried to trust, and failed miserably. Yet I am not desolate – I have had every wish granted!

Oh Mum, I want to realise how great is God's mercy to a weak thing like me – but I can't.

Mum, I write all this to you because you are the only one in the world to whom I can speak all this, and speaking of it helps me to realise it all to some slight degree – though I can't do so fully – it's impossible …

It's simply lovely up here. Living like a prince – hot baths – early to bed – ripping food – tons of meals – tons of motoring. Mr Jenner and George are such ideal companions. Mrs Jenner and Miss Greig are both just sweet. As Jack said, this is a beautiful place and quite the finest about here. The weather is perfectly glorious.

This morning we went to Church in the car. It was the Scotch church. I don't like the Service a bit, but the parson, a huge heavy man called Barber – a schoolmate of Mr Jenner – is a splendid fellow and preached one of the finest and most inspiring sermons I have ever heard.

This afternoon we motored out about four miles and had afternoon tea with some people, and came home by 6. It's now 8:30 p.m. and Mrs Jenner is singing, while we are all reading and writing.

On Tuesday there is to be a dance here – for George and me as far as I can make out – there are no other young people and the house.

On Wednesday we are going to motor to Mount Gambier (110 miles). It's awfully pretty I believe, with caves and things. Then we will motor back on Friday.

Mrs Jenner is singing 'Husheen' – she has a sweet voice.

Goodnight, my darling Mother. Take care of your precious self, and be in the pink of health and happiness when your happy and thankful boy comes home.

Thank God for you Mum – the greatest of all His mercies.

Claude

Sunday

My dearest old Mum,

I got your letter last night when I got home, for last night we returned from the tour. Words fail me to describe that trip! In all my experiences of other people's kindness – and it is pretty big – I never struck anything to equal the joy of the last week!

Last Tuesday, Mrs Jenner gave a dance – and your poor little son was made out to be something mighty like a lion. I was 'the doctor' – but I couldn't get rid of the feeling that it was a joke, calling me that! Anyhow, I was introduced to 20 or so girls (George already knew most of them) and had the time of my life! We had a 'sit down' supper, and Mr Jenner got up and demanded a speech from 'the doctor'!

I was really thankful for my previous experience in that line – for I felt more confidence in myself. I just got up and said a few words, and then proposed the toast of the host and hostess, which entailed Mr J replying, so I had my revenge!

I met some awfully pretty girls!

Next day we started for this tour. There were Mr and Mrs J, Miss Greig, George and myself – also Mrs Andrews, Laura Andrews (rather pretty, aged 21, buxom, good-natured and painfully matter-of-fact where scenery is concerned) and Noel Dixon, aged about 24 – very nice – nephew of Mrs Andrews, and driver of their car which is another huge 'Hotchkiss', very like ours.

George and I took it in turns to drive the Andrews car, there being thus four in each car. We drove through Coleraine, where I went to the Haynes two years ago, and thence to Casterton, where I went to the races and the ball at that time. Then we motored 60 miles to Mount Gambier in South Australia, completing over 100 miles for the first day!

We began to feel a long way from home, and had to put our watches back half-an-hour, owing to alteration of the time from Victorian to South Australian reckoning.

We spent two days in Mount Gambier motoring around seeing all the sites. It is a most beautiful place! I had no idea that such scenery existed in Australia! It is different to anything I have ever seen. Old volcanoes and craters and beautiful blue lakes, so deep that they have never been have fathomed, one in particular on which swans were swimming. There were the most beautiful reflections I have ever seen. You literally could not distinguish where the water line commenced.

We simply sat and looked and looked. We talked of nothing but scenery till dinner-time at the hotel that night, and after dinner, got into the cars and drove up to see the lakes again by moonlight. It was a glorious night, with a large moon and a few fleecy clouds. The air was absolutely still and cool. I shall remember that night to my dying day.

The lake we went to is deep down in an old crater, and you have a beautiful winding road to motor up to get there. Then you climb down the crater to the shores of the lake. All around is big forest of huge pine trees, extraordinarily close together. Must be just like the Canadian forests. The ground is covered with a thick coat of pine needles and you don't make a sound as you walk.

The lakes were perfectly still with the moon path and stars and clouds reflected. There was not a sound except the occasional cry of a swan. The latter swam slowly about, silhouetted against the moon and causing a silver gleam in the water in their tracks. It was so mystic – knowing that the water was such a terrific depth – it's hopeless to try and describe it to you. Some day when I get my car I shall take you there!

On Friday we left our comfortable hotel in Mount Gambier and drove to Naracoorte. This is a rotten little town, with streets white with lime. Every house is built of limestone – pure white. The water is frightfully hard from lime. All for miles around is like chalk – the whole place looked bleached!

On the trip to Naracoorte we passed large vineyards, where lots of people – men women and children – were picking grapes. They called out to us, and waved bunches of grapes, all along the road! Mr J said it reminded him exactly of motoring in France. We stopped at a quiet place and helped ourselves from the loaded vines.

Seven miles out of Naracoorte we came to some wonderful caves. You're in a barren looking paddock, when suddenly you come to a hole with steps leading down. This leads one into a maze of underground passages opening out every few yards into big roomy vaults. The walls are of glistening crystalline rock, and the roof and floor are a mass of the most beautiful stalactites and stalagmites. They are almost transparent when the torch is held behind one (we each carried a torch) and the colours and shadows are simply beyond description. It was simply like fairyland!

We stayed overnight at Naracoorte and did a big stage of around 150 miles next day, which brought us home about 6 o'clock.

Each day we had a picnic lunch by the roadside, cooking chops or bacon or something and boiling our billies. It was so glorious! There being the two cars, we raced whenever the roads allowed and had all kinds of fun! The route we came home took us through Harrow and over the roads along which I used to drive little Jane Haines in a buggy and pair two years ago. It was full of pleasant recollections.

Tomorrow we're going for a 50-mile drive out to a mountain near here in both cars again. We're going to have lunch there, and after that, the Andrews are going on to Camperdown, taking George with them. They spend the night there and go on to Melbourne next day.

I come back with the Jenner's to Myrniong, and will stay here another week. I'm coming home on Monday 28 April just in time for work on 1 May. I feel it would be a sin to leave this heaven any sooner than necessary! Of course I shall miss dear old George, but Mrs Jenner is perfectly sweet, and said tonight how sorry she was that I could only stay one more week – and that she would crowd as much as possible into it.

I sleep like a log – about 10 hours – and eat like a horse – glorious food! I'm taking a tonic, as I think when all conditions are favourable to picking up, that is the time when a tonic does most good.

Went to Church again today, and heard a Mr Flynn, who is one of the Inland Mission in the Northern Territory. He spoke of the Territory in a most interesting way, telling stories all the time. We are going to a lantern lecture by him tomorrow – 100 views of the Territory!

Must stop.

Much love from your joyous and lucky old
Claude

Unfortunately, Jack did not graduate at that time, but had a 'supplementary examination', which put him six months behind Claude. It would seem that George Cole did not graduate either, as Claude was the only one lauded as 'the doctor' on their vacation in Hamilton.

Claude's next task was to obtain a position as a Resident Medical Officer, and if possible, in his old hospital 'the Alfred', which was considered the plum appointment. He had appeared on the Honours List in the examination results, so his chances were good. His old mentor, Mr Hamilton Russell, a renowned surgeon wrote him a good reference:

Telephone Central 7184

85 Spring Street, Melbourne.
Claude Morlet has been an industrious and excellent student of the 'Alfred Hospital' Clinical School. He has taken high Honours in both medicine and surgery at the recent examinations for the Melbourne Degree, and I think he has fairly established his claim to be appointed one of our Resident Medical Officers.

[signed] R. Hamilton Russell FRCS Eng.
Senior Surgeon to the Alfred Hospital.

April 1st 1913

He had similar references from four other of his teachers, and accordingly, he was appointed to the staff of his old hospital. He maintained a close relationship with Mr Hamilton Russell, who was an old bachelor. He would invite Claude to his apartment to spend the evening sitting by the fire. Claude said they would sit for hours without speaking, and ultimately, the old surgeon would stand up and shake Claude's hand, and thank him for his company as he showed him out.

Claude remained at the Alfred for the remainder of the year, then gained a position at the Children's Hospital, and then at the Victorian Eye and Ear Hospital, where he was working when war broke out in August 1914. This was to shape his destiny. Claude volunteered for service the day that war was declared but was not called up until the end of the year.

Meanwhile, Jack graduated in August, and after a period as a locum in the Alfred hospital, he was appointed to the Children's Hospital in Brisbane.

Claude took a month's vacation and took Mother by train to Brisbane to visit Jack, where they had a most happy time. The travelled to Toowoomba, and stayed with the Langmore relatives who now lived in the town. Walter Langmore drove them out to 'Prairie' where Mary proudly showed the boys the home that their father had taken such pleasure in building, and where both Lucile and Claude were born. They returned to Melbourne before Christmas, when Claude was called up, and commissioned as a Captain in the Australian Army Medical Corps.

On 5 December 1914, Claude boarded the troop ship *Kyarra* at Port Melbourne, bound for the war, although he didn't know where.

Mother and a friend came to see them off, but the time dragged on with no sign of the ship sailing, and so, with a final wave from the dock, she went home. At six o'clock that evening Claude wrote to mother, saying that she did well not to wait, and that by the time this letter reached her, he would be far away at sea, and '*very happy*'.

— Diary — 1914

Dec. 6th Sunday –

Very rough – boat pitching & heaving all over the place – Rose about 8 a.m. & had shave & bath – Upon deck, a handfull of officers, looking particularly healthy walked when possible & staggered when not. Had a good breakfast with about a dozen others.

About 11 a.m. some dozen or so very sick-looking nurses came on deck, settled themselves on chairs & never moved all day:

Very rough all day – Spent time reading "Drill Instruction" and eating – felt very well all day! Towards evening a few more officers turned up.

CHAPTER 6

Off to War!

Claude Morlet's diary and letters from the First World War

Claude's first letter to his Mother, dated 5 December 1914, was written on board the troop ship.

SS *Kyarra*
Port Melbourne

My dearest Mum
It's five to six and we haven't gone yet. Am so thankful you didn't wait any longer. You poor dear. I knew how you and Em must have been aching all over! They have not even sent the people on to the wharf yet. There are still many of the poor tired things there watching us.

Goodbye my darling Mum. I shall be at sea and very happy when you get this.
Claude.

Claude commenced his loose-leaf diary.

6 December **[1914]**
Sunday
Very rough. Boat pitching and heaving all over the place! Rose about 8 a.m. and had shave and bath. Up on deck, a handful of officers looking particularly healthy. Walked when possible and staggered when not. Had a good breakfast, with about a dozen others.

About 11 a.m. some dozen or so very sick looking nurses came on deck, settled themselves on chairs, and never moved all day.

Very rough all day – spent time reading 'Drill Instruction' and eating. Felt very well all day. Towards evening a few more officers turned up.

7 December
Had a good night – much calmer today. Scores of nurses came on deck and choked up all the available walking room with their chairs: spent the day reading and waiting for meals: and studying the art of drilling men. Since I have a commission in the army thrust upon me I am determined to justify my position by having a knowledge of military matters.

8 December

A beautiful calm day. Half of the deck cleared for cricket and the other half choked with convalescent nurses; had half an hour cricket and then retired to a quiet nook on the boat deck and read 'typhoid'.

After lunch, walked until 4 p.m., and then tea, after which I retired again and read a French novel. *Tres moutard!* Had a long talk with Le Messurier, a pal of Stan Elders. A bonzer chap.

Found Falconer (my batman) convalescing, and instructed him on his duties. After dinner, a grand concert on the deck given by the 'other ranks'. Some jolly good voices!

Start reading French tomorrow with Kay. Had a yarn with Follit, a bonzer chap.

11 p.m. going to bed – a pleasant and interesting day!

9 December

A calm sunny day – had to wear drill uniform, the other was too hot: read French with Kay for about an hour in the morning. He has read a lot, and has a very good vocabulary, but no idea of the pronunciation!

Read 'enteric fever' until lunchtime, then strolled aimlessly about and basked in the sun until mess.

I had forgotten to speak of mess arrangements; Kay had to arrange the seats, I was a little anxious as it is not much fun to be seated amongst chaps you don't care about for every meal, for 7 weeks or so.

To my delight however, I found myself in a high position on Kay's right. On my left, is Plant, and opposite to me are Follit, Foxton, and Alcorn. Lower down the table are Tate and Watson on my side and Sabine and Sutherland on the other side. On the whole ship I could not have a have picked out nicer and jollier fellows than those all around me.

After Mess many of the nurses and captains danced. I had a long talk to Major Jackson in the smoke room instead.

I'm satisfied that the nurses should have had a ship to themselves! They really are a perfect nuisance! They occupy every comfortable and sunny corner with their chairs, cackle and chatter incessantly, at the top of their voices. Show off and 'cheek' such of the fellows whom they knew as residents, call them by their nicknames and generally disgust me in every way!

The 'Alfred girls' are among the few who know how to behave themselves. Of course the 'old birds' are all right – but many of the younger ones are really frightful females!

10 December

Today it is delightfully milder and the sea is calm and slightly misty.

At 7:30 a.m. physical drill on deck in pyjamas. This is to be an institution and consists of deep breathing and various exercises gone through. About half-a-dozen officers of No 1 General Hospital attend, under the supervision of one of our NCOs.

At 10 a.m. the parade of all ranks for a lodgement of places to boats in case of disaster was a farce! We just stood aimlessly about for about 1½ hours.

From then till lunch listened to the gramophone belonging to the Adelaide Stationary Hospital of which Le Messurier and Verco are the captains. Both, especially the former, are bonzer chaps. At Mess, No. 2 General Hospital challenged us to a hockey match. They are a heavy athletic lot of chaps from Sydney and there is the keenest rivalry between No. 1 and No. 2.

We accepted their challenge knowing that we would have a very poor chance. The teams were five a side; ours consisted of Kay, Sutherland, Follit, Sumers and myself.

In the 1st quarter they scored 4 goals to nil. Then we set our teeth and bucked in again with all we knew. We beat them 7-6! It was wildly exciting! The barracking was furious and we were simply exhausted and dripping, but glowing with delight over the victory. They were greatly surprised and forthwith challenged us again for today, with two different teams to play.

After a seawater bath and dinner, I joined the party on the top deck, smoking and listening to the gramophone – no nurses present! – while below us a dance (officers and nurses) was going on.

Then bed as usual at 9.30, after a supper with Le Messurier.

The hockey match took place, and amongst tumultuous applause, No. 1 General Hospital again won the match 4–2.

That evening at Mess, after they had solemnly toasted the Mess, the Colonel stood, and in an impressive silence, gave the loyal toast 'The King!' to which all stood and responded.

After this, No. 2 General Hospital sent over a steward with a tray of drinks in acknowledgement of our having won the match.

Claude's table stood and turned to face 'No 2', then raised their glasses and toasted them.

A courtesy that they then returned by toasting us. It was the most exciting mess that we have had.

Daily life went on, and Claude's disdain for the nurses (except those from the Alfred) remained unchanged!

They reached the Swan River Estuary and anchored just off Fremantle, but were not allowed ashore. A pilot boat brought newspapers, which told of 'glorious news of a naval victory!' The diary records:

Christmas Eve

At sea.

After lunch, we had a game of hockey. One of the ship's officers was playing. He was fuddled and excited with whisky, and managed to give me a bang on the mouth with his stick. My teeth protruded through my lower lip – very painful!

Colonel Syme sewed my lip up. There was no catgut to be found, so he could not stitch the inside, which was left gaping. There goes Christmas dinner! I shall not be able to eat tomorrow!

Claude ready to leave for war, 1914

The SS *Kyarra* in Colombo

'Crossing the line' on board the *Kyarra*

Christmas Day

Lip swelled up like a cucumber. Frightfully sore! Communion and was out of the question! I could hardly speak all day – have spent a miserable Christmas moping and reading a magazine. Christmas dinner was a hopeless failure. I could scarcely eat anything, and each toast stung my mouth.

Went to bed early and disgusted with Christmas 1914!

Claude wrote a plaintive letter to his mother telling of the event, and how he missed his Christmas dinner! He posted it at Colombo.

His next letter tells of the Officers on the ship, and his thoughts about those around him.

6 January 1915

My dearest Mum,

We are again approaching a port, THE port where we hope to get instructions at least concerning our destination! The sea is dead calm and has been so ever since we left Fremantle, weeks ago! I did not think that the ocean could be so calm for such a long time. The old boat has been chugging slowly along on an even keel for a month! We're all very bored with the ship and each other with few exceptions. Follit and I continue to see a lot of each other, and my opinion of him is as yet unchanged. He is a most charming companion and an excellent fellow. I wish Mum that I could adequately describe the scenes that take place on this boat. I'm sure that 'Table Talk" would give a large sum for sketches of Col. Syme and Col. Maudesley chasing one another about the deck in pyjamas at 6 a.m.

Colonel Springthorpe, lying on his back and solemnly raising one leg in the air all while taking deep breaths, going purple in the face and looking as if to bust his boiler!

Miss Dalrymple and Miss Butler are most interesting ladies, having travelled so much, and I spend a lot of time enjoying anecdotes of Russia and other interesting countries.

I have never really told you who are on board Mum and I think perhaps it would interest you.

I shall begin with our unit.

The Colonels you know are, Ramsey-Smith, Syme, and Maudesley. The former, who is in command, is a most unsociable and ill-mannered old man. No one likes him, and he sits by himself or with 1 or 2 nurses each day, and develops and prints photographs. He makes no attempt to get to know any of his own officers, never returns a salute, answers with a barely civil grunt any attempt at politeness on anybody's part.

Maudesley is a most benevolent and well-liked old chap – everyone likes him and he has a courteous word and a smile for everyone.

Syme is, I think, the most popular colonel on the boat he is a real little brick – enters into all the sports, fancy-dress ball, etc. We think no end of the little man, and no one could be more unprepossessing in appearance.

I must tell you about his bit at a fancy-dress ball. He was dressed as an old woman with grey hair, spectacles, and a bonnet. He was simply splendid! Everyone roared with laughter at him the whole night. Next day he went to the trouble of putting on the whole rig-out again so that we might photograph him. Scores of pictures were taken of the little chap; he stood patiently by until the last enthusiast was satisfied.

Majors Dunhill, Summons, Argyle and Barrett are all well known to you.

From Queensland are Major Jackson, McDonell, and MacLean – the last two are bricks, both of them jolly old chaps, full of fun and most good-natured men.

Of the Captains, Alcorn, Plant, and Kay are well known to you. Follit I hope you will know someday, Tate and Watts are Melbourne Hospital residents, very nice but very quiet. Sutherland is a practitioner of the northern suburbs of Melbourne, fat, good-natured and jolly. Hume and Turnbull you know of, and Johnson is rather bumptious person but means well, Mum – these are the men, with whom I am to work.

As regards men from the other States, those from New South Wales consisting of No. 2 General Hospital are about the purist crowd of unmitigated bounders imaginable! If they do, as I suppose they do, form a specimen of the profession in Sydney, I thank my lucky stars that I had been educated in Melbourne among gentlemen. Their colonels are old Colonel Martin, OC troops (OC = 'Officer Commanding') and that signifies that he is in absolute command of us all. He is a nice old chap and a thorough soldier, though he is an old 'lodge doctor' from Sydney, and practically unknown in the medical world. He is a popular OC however, and a capable and experienced officer.

Colonel Nash from Sydney and Colonel Springthorpe from Melbourne are their other colonels.

Their Majors are Stewart, Reid, Carter and Campbell. The last two are nice fellows, particularly the last who is a most able physician from Sydney.

Their captains are in my opinion a lot of spoilt, ill-bred young cubs.

The South Australians (No. 1 Stationary Hospital) are a fine lot of chaps. Colonel Bryant from Toorak in command, Major's Corbin, Newland, Wilson and Powell are a splendid lot of men, and Captains Le Messurier and Verco are bonzer chaps. Le Messurier knows Stan Elder quite well.

The Tasmanians (No. 1 Clearing Hospital) are also a fine lot of men, commanded by Colonel Giblin, who is every inch a soldier and a splendid fellow. Major Richards, a dear old chap, and Major Gordon (from Carlton, Melbourne).

Captains Jack O'Brien, Tommy Atkins (who was at College with Jack) and Lieutenants Crock, Carlisle, and Boddam.

They are a very exclusive crowd, always sitting together in a group on the deck, and do not have much to say to any of the other officers – but Miss Butler assures us that they are delightful lot of chaps – trust a pretty girl to find that out!

The West Australians I will not bother to enumerate, as you'll never have heard of them before. No one seems to have! Some of them are only harmless, but others are absolutely objectionable! They come in the same category as the New South Wales crowd.

This may all be censored, in which case I will have wasted a lot of energy!

I haven't mentioned Foxton, our Adjutant, who is as fine a chap as I ever wish to meet. He comes from Ipswich Queensland, and his quiet, determined, strong and as tactful and as good-natured as a man could be.

That is an outline of the men on board: I have been very moderate in my criticism, as I don't know who might read this before it gets to your hands.

I wonder what has been happening all this time in old Melbourne? It seems ages since I saw any of you Mum, and yet it is only just a month. I would give a lot Mum dear, to have half an hour with you and the Elders this morning. Though I would be utterly miserable if we were turned back now and went home!

I am longing to get to work on these wounded men, and am sick of doing nothing. I intended to read quite a lot on the trip, but it is quite impossible. The boat is so teeming with people there is not a quiet spot anywhere.

I wonder has it been very hot in Melbourne? I do hope you're taking a change at the seaside or in the mountains, and not staying in dusty old Melbourne all the summer.

We have just come in sight of land of Mum, at last. It is Aden, where I shall have this posted, and we should arrive in about an hour. We are not to be allowed on shore, and we're only supposed to stay for a couple of hours to fix up about papers and get orders. I'm sending back my diary up-to-date. I hope you can read it.

Ever so much love, my darling Mum.

From Claude

CHAPTER 7

12 January 1915

I haven't written my diary for several days, as I finished the book, and the refills were packed into the hold of the ship. I have now got them out and shall try to remember what has happened.

After posting a letter at Suez, we started up the canal about midday. My impression of the canal was somewhat marred by the wretched carbuncle on my left side. Still it was really most fascinating gliding up the still water, with desert stretching away either side. Just a lake of sand until in the dim distance, a huge rugged mountain, absolutely barren and precipitous, rose up and obscured the horizon.

On either side of the canal are thousands of Indian troops, some British regiments and a few Australians. They are expecting a Turkish attack, and are strongly entrenched on either side of the canal – splendid looking men. They cheered and shouted at us, as we slowly steamed past, signalled at us with their flags and waved us forward encouragingly. Their officers would step forward and shout, 'Where are you going?' To which we always had to answer, 'We don't know!'.

About 3 o'clock the pain in my side was intense and Follit offered to open it for me. There was no local anaesthetic to be found, so he made 2 incisions without. By Jove it did hurt!

Then after that I sat and sulked and pitied myself on the boat deck, while we passed through mile after mile of this fascinating canal. In the distance we saw an occasional oasis, with its grove of the palm trees and water well.

A most glorious sunset finished the day. It was quite beyond description. I had never conceived or anything so wonderful as these eastern sunsets. I do not wonder that the Arabs fall down and worship at every sunset!

There was no moon, and it was bitterly cold and pitch-dark. My side was still very painful, and I went to bed in a bad temper. I had a disturbed night owing to pain from my side, and noise of yelling niggers.

I crawled out about 7.30 to find us moored at Port Said, where we had arrived at 1 a.m. Close alongside us was a French cruiser, and the other side was the *Kaiser E. Hind*, a P&O liner.

About 10 a.m., in a party of 6 officers I went ashore to see the sights.

I forgot to say that at breakfast Keith Barrett and young Plant, Gum's brother, came on board and breakfasted with us. They had come down from Cairo to see us. They gave us all the latest news of our friends in the 1st Division, and seemed very well and happy.

They did not seem to think there is much chance of a Turkish invasion, as the Turks would have to march right across the Sinai Desert, carrying their water.

As soon as we landed, we were surrounded by swarms of niggers of every colour, size and shape, trying to make us buy things! We wandered about the streets, watched a conjurer (with which the place abounds) and looked at postcards. We then went out to the eastern Exchange Hotel, and got our hair cut.

Outside the shops, on the pavement, groups of chairs and tables every few yards where one sits down, orders a drink, and is besieged by vendors of everything under the sun!

We all met at the eastern Exchange for lunch, and had a real good feed. After that, Follit and I went around and bought a whole lot of cakes and sweets, as our two girls had been entertaining us for afternoon tea, supper, etc. ever since we left Colombo. We gave the parcels to Follit's batman to take on board, and then got a carriage and drove slowly around the town, all through the native quarters and in all the odd corners. It is a filthy place!

We stopped at the Casino Hotel where we had afternoon tea, and found our girls doing the same thing! All four of us then went on board, just as the sun set, which as usual, was just perfect.

We slowly steamed out of Port Said, which soon became a smoky mass of dark chimneys and spires against a deep red glow, slowly fading into blackness.

Claude wrote to his mother from Port Said, telling her of their further adventures, and how he could 'dimly remember sitting behind Lucile on a donkey at Port Said and howling lustily at the sight of the nigger donkey boy'.

He sent the loose-leaf diary pages cobbled together with cotton by post, but later, to avoid censorship, he sent segments of the diary with people who were returning to Australia. Today, the diary remains in its original fragmented state. The entries continue:

14 January

At about 8 a.m. we were in sight of Alexandria. Here we expected that some of us would land and the rest of us proceed to Malta and Europe.

At Suez, the OC, Colonel Martin had landed and gone up to Cairo by train in order to see what was to happen to us. We hoped he would be waiting on the wharf for us when we arrived at Alexandria, and that we would learn our fate at once. To our disgust however, we remained anchored in the harbour, and heard that the OC would not come aboard until the next day.

We were not allowed ashore, but just sat around, and spent all day watching the boats in the harbour.

Just before dinner, about 6:30 p.m., a telegram arrived from the OC at Cairo, saying that majors and colonels might have 48 hours leave, but captains had to sleep on board, but have leave during a day.

We instantly sprang into boats and went ashore for the evening. We had dinner, a party of 6 of us, at the Windsor Hotel. Not up to much! Then went to a 'Cafe Chantant'. It was a huge hall with a stage at one end and tables and chairs covering the floor. The place was crowded with every description of man and nigger, all speaking French. There were some boxes around the sides, which were filled with women. The show started at 9:30 p.m. No charge for admission, but we were expected to have a drink! The show consisted of cinematographic pictures, dancers and songs. All in French.

We stayed till after midnight, and the programme was not nearly finished. We then went to a shooting gallery where we fired unsuccessfully at moving targets.

Follit and I got separated from the others, and took a carriage down to the wharf. We directed the cabbie in English. He seemed to understand and drove off. After about 15 minutes' driving he stopped and made some unintelligible remark. It then dawned on us that he didn't understand a word of English. We then tried him in French and German, without success. After aimlessly driving about the streets for some time we found an Egyptian who understood our French, and he directed the cabbie.

We had an exciting trip across the harbour in an open boat to the *Kyarra*, the sea being rough, and got aboard at 3 a.m.

15 January 1915
Savoy Palace Hotel
Alexandria
Egypt

My darling Mother
Here I am in Egypt – whether for a few days, a few months or even a few years, I have no idea in the world! I wonder if you have received any of the letters that I have sent back to you from every port?

I hear on every side that the Censors are stopping our letters, and the empty envelopes delivered. I do hope this has not been my fate! I'm quite well Mum, and very happy. I'm revelling in every moment ashore, and feel now that I'm really in a strange land under unique and fascinating circumstances.

To walk or drive about the streets with one or more brother officers, being saluted on all sides by soldiers of every variety of colour and dress, from Sudanese, Sikhs, Egyptians, British regiments and our own Australians – all belonging to the same old Empire, makes one begin to realise the immensity of Great Britain.

The streets and people of course are breathlessly interesting to me. I take such an intense interest in everything I see but I can absorb only a fraction of it all!

We arrived yesterday morning, but we were not allowed to land until 7 p.m. We then came off and had dinner at the Windsor Hotel there, for which we were afterwards sorry as this place is much the best. We went on to a Cafe Chantant – where the singing and dancing entertainment was exceedingly bad, but we revelled in the novelty of it all.

There were 6 of us together last night. Majors Wilson and Powell from South Australia, Captains Le Messurier and Verco, also from South Australia; Follit from Maryborough Queensland, and myself. We got back on board about 1:30 a.m.

This morning just Follit and I are going about together. We had been through the museum, and have done a lot of shopping. We're now going to have lunch and then drive out to the Catacombs.

I shall not try to describe Alexandra just now. The weather is glorious, and I'm awfully well. The carbuncle on my side was very sore and bad but it is now slowly getting better.

I shall not post any more of my diary home, as it is too uncertain in delivery. We had a whole day in Port Said, and had a most interesting ramble about the place.

The sunsets and sunrises are just glorious now, with warm days but cold nights.

Love darling Mother.
From Claude

15 January

Follit, Kay and myself decided to stay here and explore Alexandria. The others, or many of them have caught an early train to Cairo for the day.

We went first to the museum, then went to the Savoy Plaza Hotel, which is quite the best, and had morning chocolate. We then went down town and did quite a lot of shopping. My wristwatch was rusty and had stopped and my field glasses case was broken – these I got fixed up, and had some Colombo photographs developed. We returned to the Savoy for lunch, which was jolly nice, then took a carriage and went to see the Catacombs. These are caves approached by a winding stair, and hewn out of solid rock in the middle of the town. There are very many chambers all opening in to one another, the walls containing alcoves in which are placed the bodies of those who died in hiding. Many of the skeletons still remained but a lot had been removed to the Museum.

We drove to Pompey's Column – a fine granite erection 80 feet high with two sphinxes in front of it. Some deep excavations leading under the column we went through, but our guide couldn't speak any Christian language, so we could not find out much about them.

We returned to the Savoy and a jolly good dinner, after which we went to three 'Cafés Chantants' until about 1.30.

Everyone is short of money. We have not been paid a penny since we left Australia, and at every port and at the bar while at sea, we have been spending hard. I lent Follit 30 shillings some time ago but he cannot repay me. Myself, I have only a few shillings left.

Tomorrow we must all be on board at 6 p.m. as we are about to be finally told of our fate. I hope we go on to Europe – I want to see action!

16 January

I was very tired this morning and slept in until about 8.30. My side is still painful and it is difficult and painful for me to get dressed. It was raining hard when I did get up, and I was depressed and worried over the scarcity of money. So I shaved and got dressed slowly, and missed breakfast.

I then borrowed 30 shillings from Alcorn, and sallied forth to cable for money. Follit asked me to cable for him too, and also Kay. The latter gave me a pound for his cable, but Follit was broke. I went ashore with Le Messurier and when it came to the point, I hadn't enough money to send the cables! I had to borrow it from him.

I sent off the cables and did some shopping with the change, and then Le Messurier and I had very good and very cheap lunch at an Italian restaurant.

After lunch we took a tram to a suburb called Ramleh, where there is an Indian military hospital, established in a huge hotel. It is exactly like us except that the nurses are all male niggers. The officers who showed us over, are all IMS men, and most jovial and cordial. We got back to the city of at 4:30 p.m. went up to the Savoy and had chocolate, and then took a carriage back to the wharf.

We arrived on board about 6:15 p.m. We were about the last on board, and the orders were all read by the time we turned up. All of us are to disembark here! 'No. 1 General Hospital' is to be established at Heliopolis in a gigantic and beautiful hotel, and the officers and men to be under canvas in the desert.

'No. 2 General Hospital' is to take over Mena House Hotel at Gizeh.

The 'Clearing' is to be close by us at Heliopolis 'No. 1 Stationary' at Maardi, with the

Light Horse, and 'No. 2 Stationary' is to be a Venereal Hospital at Cairo! Damned glad, as they are a rotten lot of bounders, except Billy Sawyers.

Our girls turned up tonight, they have been at Cairo and had a great time.

Follit has been on duty all day.

17 January
Sunday

I have been on duty all day. Follit and Kay went off together this morning I gave Follit the remainder of the money I had borrowed from Le Messurier, as I could not get away. Have had very quiet day and enjoyed the rest.

I watched a lovely sunset from he deck. I have written a whole lot of letters and postcards for the mail this evening, but I doubt if many of them will get through the censor.

My side is now rapidly healing up.

18 January

Still no money!

After calling at Cook's to find this out, we went down to 'Davis and Bryan' a big general store here, to see if they would open an account with us. The proprietor, Mr Bryan was very nice to us, and took us into his room, and gave us coffee. He made no trouble about the credit!

We asked him if there were any duck shooting to be had here and he gave us a letter to the manager of the Eastern Telegraph Company. This chap was discouraging. Evidently he didn't want his shooting interfered with, so we went up to 'Reading and Bonnett' the gunsmiths.

They agreed to lease us guns for 2 shillings a day each, and wired the station master at Dammanbur where there is good snipe shooting, and put us up to getting shooting licences.

The 'Bibarshee' of police who gave us the permits was a typical young English Varsity man, tall, fair with a soft little fair moustache and very pronounced, courteous English 'Dontcha know eh what?' manner.

Finally we lunched at an Italian restaurant, and longed for the money to arrive! We did some shopping, and flirted with a charming French girl at the Savoy, where we had afternoon tea.

I returned to dinner while Follit dined with an old schoolmate.

Still no news of money!

19 January

Up at 5.30 a.m. Follit, Turnbull and I had an exciting rush for the Dammanbour train and just missed it. We caught another at 7:15 a.m., a terribly slow train. Just charming views from the train window. The country is all absolutely low-lying and flat, all cultivated and irrigated. White mist was lying on the flats, with just the top of the palm trees projecting above the sea of mist, with the sun shining on it.

We took an orderly with us to carry the guns and ammunition. Arrived at Damon at about 9:30 am, and had some breakfast. Hot chocolate, and rolls with butter and strawberry jam. We then got into a carriage with our guns, etc. We drove several miles across these irrigated flats where men and women toiled, and children drove heavily laden donkeys about.

Scores of camels carrying enormous loads, and tiny little donkeys on which were seated big men, so big that they had to hold their feet up to prevent them from dragging on the ground.

Finally we reached the snipe country. Page and the orderly mounted guard over the carriage and our coats, and a nigger, or rather an Egyptian, accompanied each of us to carry the game, and off we went. There were lots of birds, but they were very shy, and snipe are very hard to hit. We shot badly!

Turnbull never hit a thing; Follit and I each got 7 or 8 snipe, and he got a duck too. We got back to the town at 1.30, had lunch, and caught a train home about 2:30 p.m. Went straight to Cook's. Follit's money had come, and we were saved!

Came on board, got the 2 girls and took them out to dinner. Afterwards, we sent them back to the boat and went to the Savoy, where we smoked and yarned till 10:30 p.m.

At 6 p.m., I received a cable from London 'no money here' – cabled to Australia for some.

20 January

Slept in this morning – had breakfast in bed, and rose at 10:30 a.m. When I got up, I found out that No. 2 had all gone to Cairo by an early train with their baggage and all completely disappeared from the *Kyarra*! Felt very guilty not having said goodbye.

Went ashore with Kay and rambled about the streets. Went up to the Khedivial Club, of which we are honorary members, and had lunch at his expense at the Star of Italy Restaurant.

22 January

Went ashore with Follit about 10:30 a.m. – had a drink and read in the Union Club, and then paddled about the city. Then had a peep at the bourse, and a drink and a read at the Khedivial. Had lunch there and then Follit and I both went sound asleep in the Reading Room – very strong liqueurs!

Had supper in the hospital – quite safe in that direction, – the pretty one says 'nothink and anythink'. That's settled me! Bed at midnight.

I forgot to say that No. 2 Stationary Hospital went away today. Was terribly sorry to lose Le Messurier and Verco!

23 January
Saturday

The most beautiful morning! I rose late and went ashore with Major Dunhill and Captain Johnson just before lunch. Had lunch with them at the Union Club, where I met Follit, Turnbull and some others.

After lunch they started to play billiards. Well it was a lovely afternoon, so I strolled out in the sun. Instead of cabs, there are dear little carriages here for hire at 2 shillings per hour. Some have poor old horses but some are just ripping, with dashing pairs and glittering harnesses. In to one of the latter I jumped, and drove up to the Savoy. I picked up Fran, and took her for a drive out to Ramleh where we had tea and got home about 5:30 p.m.

Left, a military funeral, March 1915; (right) tents for the orderlies, photo taken from Claude's window at the hospital

Went back to the boat for dinner. Felt restive after dinner, so went ashore again. Ran up to the Savoy and said goodbye to Fran, for this is our last day here. We entrain for Heliopolis tomorrow morning. Rather a tearful farewell.

24 January

Reveille at 5:30 a.m. – Breakfast at 7 a.m. All on the train at 9 a.m. Started at 9:15 a.m. Heartily glad to see the last of the old *Kyarra*!

A jolly trip in the train. One wagon was reserved for officers. We have a merry lot in our carriage and thoroughly enjoyed the trip! Arrived at some station with an impossible name about 1:00 p.m. All de-trained, and were assigned various duties. I was told to convoy 30 nurses by tram straight on to the hospital, where I duly arrived with my charge. Nothing was ready for us at all. No body was here to receive us. I made the girls put down to their baggage in some rooms on the 1st floor and await orders.

Now for my first impression of this place, which I have never seen anything to compare! As the tram drew near to Heliopolis there was on each side of us nothing to be seen but desert stretching away, while in our immediate vicinity, scattered houses, square and white, lined the tramway. Straight ahead of us appeared a belt of trees, to the left was the shining white city, whose towers and domes gleamed in the brilliant sun as we approached.

The tram ran down a fine and broad street at the edge of the town, separated from the desert by a row of tall sandstone buildings. Presently these buildings came to an end and were replaced by one colossal edifice of creamy sandstone, set back from the road from which it was approached by huge iron gates, leading into a stretch of garden. A huge dome surmounted the building, which was neither ornate nor beautiful to look at, but impressively big – massive and imposing!

A broad flight of marble steps leads up to a spacious tiled piazza on to which opened the front door. The interior of this palace actually baffles description! The enormous flag floored hall with a flight of marble stairs on either side led into the most beautiful …

(The diary entry peters out, but Claude's letter to Mother tells of the wonderful 'Palace' he now lives in.)

1st Australian General Hospital, Heliopolis

Claude with nurses

1st Australian General Hospital
Heliopolis
15 January 1915

My darling Mum
I won't write too much tonight as I am pretty tired, having had a worrying day.

We're at last settled in our hospital in Egypt – oh I wish I could, by describing our home, give you just a vague idea of this wonderful place!

We are quartered in the Palace Hotel – the most magnificent hotel in the world – and the most gigantic and beautiful building I have ever dreamt of! It's quite beyond description – the massive sandstone exterior with marble steps, and marble pillars – the magnificent hall of marble flags and marble pillars on either side – the walls of carved and fretted sandstone inlaid with polished marble of different colours and the ceiling rising up into an immense dome of solid stone with windows of stained glass in beautiful designs.

The actual building without any fittings cost one million pounds to build, and the Foundation Stone was only laid in 1910!

The Palace was built by a wealthy Belgian syndicate, with money derived from Congo plunder and was to be an enormous casino, like Monte Carlo, but when it was built the British Government refused to give them a licence to run it! Now however, it has been commandeered for us. It seems so absurd and so wicked see about 50 men marching in quickstep with their heavy boots through this beautiful place. Their 'tramp-tramp-tramp' ringing on the marble flags.

The Medical Ward is in a most glorious circular apartment with parquetry floor and a beautiful ceiling rising up to a dome. The patients, of which there are not many yet, lie and gaze at the ceiling. The weather is just perfect – beautiful sunny days and crisp cold evenings.

We only arrived yesterday, and have not got settled at all yet. I shall not post any more diary home as it might get censored and never arrive.

The little camera Lucile gave me is a great success! I hope to have some quite decent photographs to bring home.

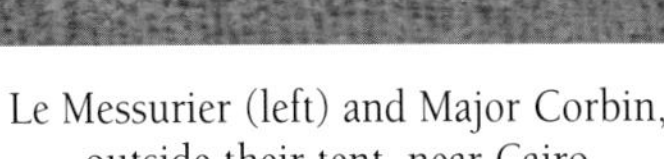

Le Messurier (left) and Major Corbin, outside their tent, near Cairo

Sightseeing in Cairo

Our quarters are very comfortable – I have a fine spacious bedroom, with a large bed, sheets, pillowslips, etc. and of course the excellent Faulkner, who is a great success!
God Bless you Mum darling.
From Claude

The diary continues:

1 February
On Saturday 30 January life in Egypt began for me in earnest.

In the morning I was ordered to see two nurses off to Alexandria in the train. I went off with my charges in an ambulance motor wagon and returned for lunch. After lunch I asked permission to go out for the afternoon and evening, and to my surprise, I got it!

Went by tram straight to Mena House. About 1-3/4 hours on the tram, and I had my first glimpse of the pyramids!

No. 2 Gen. Hospital is at Mena House They all look tired and depressed, and have worried looks. There are about 600 patients there, some of them desperately bad pneumonias. We had afternoon tea there, and then went on to the camp.

Went up to the 2nd Field Ambulance, but they were all out. Back to Cairo where I did some shopping and then to the Continental for dinner. After dinner, the Major and I went to the Casino de Paris and then took in the Palmarium …

(The next section of the diary has been all crossed out, and appears to have described the women at the Casino and the Palmarium.)

Major MacLean went home about 1 a.m. with some others, I however met Sutherland and we stayed till about 2.30. We met Gum, and then all returned in a taxi about 3 a.m.

This was my first day out in Cairo – I made the most of it!

2 February
Sunday
Stayed in bed for breakfast. I was waited on by the indefatigable Falconer, and then had a few holes of golf before lunch. In the afternoon went for a stroll with Ethel Butler. It was a lovely afternoon and I enjoyed the quiet peace of her company after the riotous revelry of the night before. My head was not aching a bit since I got up!

Falconer has just looked in to bring me some fruit. He has heard from home. A letter from his wife – he is just beaming!

He is a most excellent fellow, Faulkner; and I am very much envied, and quite proud of my batman. He has been promoted to Lance Corporal, and is the only batman who has received promotion. Nothing is too much trouble for him, and he looks after me as though I were a child, but always in the most respectful and deferential manner.

At 5:30 p.m., our little Frenchman came. Follit and I have arranged with a Frenchman to come and talk French to us for an hour every day until further notice.

3 February

Today our work started, the Hospital really being used for the first time! I am to be house surgeon to Majors Jackson and MacLean, and also assistant to Barrett in eye, nose, etc.

I did my wards with the majors in the morning, and then did some refractions, etc. with Barrett.

In the afternoon Bert Sutherland and I did some shopping, and then went up to the City and explored two beautiful Mosques. I have bought a lot of new clothes. I found that the uniforms I have, while they are excellent for rough service work, are hardly suitable for keeping up the prestige of Australia amongst British Officers when one walks the streets of Cairo and dines at Shepherd's Hotel.

Had just time to run home in time for our daily French lesson.

5 February

Work in the morning. Our cases very uninteresting, merely trivial ills, dislocations, sprains, etc. from amongst the men camped around us.

In the afternoon, Follit, Sutherland and I went off intending to tour through the Muski, but instead, we visited the Caliph's tombs.

One leaves the city abruptly at the foot of a group of hills composed of loose earth and stones – not a blade of herbage of any kind. Then after 10 minutes' walk through these hills and valleys, one suddenly comes upon another city with hundreds of houses grouped in tidy streets – domes, minarets, etc. – all the windows upon close inspection, are nailed up. The streets are absolutely empty – the backyards of all houses are full of graves – truly a city of the dead!

We walked through the streets, (it is quite a big city) – not a sound! The silence was most striking, compared to the huge roaring city only a mile away over those hills!

We went up to the Citadel – an enormous powerful structure perched on an eminence above the city – it is a gigantic castle, surrounded by a huge wall, inside which it is like a town itself. We only had a walk through a small portion of it and went through the alabaster Mosque of Mohammed Ali, which is on top of the highest point.

These mosques are the most wonderful mysterious things! I can't describe them really, except to say that they are like little cathedrals with high, domed ceilings, which are usually of marble mosaic or beautiful china mosaic, and walls covered with mysterious hieroglyphics and carvings.

We got back late for the French lesson, and spent the evening yarning until about 11:30 p.m. in Follit's room.

Heliopolis
10 February 1915

My own darling Mum

I have just received a long letter from you dated 3 January. It is a ripping to get letters from home!

My darling Mum I feel as though I were back in Melrose, sitting beside you in the big armchair – which you always insist on my having – as I read your letter. I can almost hear your voice. Thanks so much for sending Jack's letters on. I enjoy reading them tremendously.

Egypt is a kind of fairyland – and a most expensive place to live! I get every afternoon and evening off, and with few exceptions, tour about seeing the sights and sparing no expense. Our life here is easy and pleasant. I have about 40 surgical beds, and about 20 eye and ear beds, which keeps me going, besides which, I assist in the ophthalmic surgery. Soldiers and officers stream in from the regiments camped around us with a variety of ills.

You'll have seen in the papers of the attack on the Suez Canal, and of the defeat of the Turks. They attacked the Canal between Kantara and Ismailia, and were thoroughly routed by the Indians' machine guns, and also by the warships in the Canal, laying down a barrage of fire from their guns. They say thousands of Turks were killed!

It was very hard to realise that this was all taking place so close to us, whilst life here in the City was just the same as ever, the streets thronged with Arabs and Egyptians, French and Italians, but mainly with khaki-clad Australian and British Territorial soldiers and officers. The whole atmosphere just teems with 'the Military'.

Regiments and convoys, ambulances and supply columns stream past our gates all day long going to and fro. Thousands are camped in the desert all around Cairo within a radius of a few miles; the streets are just one mass of khaki!

Everyone has burning to get to Europe, and the one topic of conversation is about the prospects of getting across in the spring.

We have not got any of the wounded here yet – there are so many military hospitals about, and they rapidly absorb the wounded. The only wounded man and I have seen was an officer whose revolver went off as he was cleaning it, and shot away two of his fingers!

The medical wards are filled with men with pneumonia, influenza, and bronchitis. The isolation tents are about a mile away in the desert, with measles and other nasty diseases, and the surgical wards are full of dislocated joints, sprains, appendicitis and other commonplace events.

Many of our captains are detailed off to assist in other hospitals, which are understaffed, and they just come back here to sleep, going away in the morning. One of these is Follit, but he only works in the mornings, so he and I go to see the sights in the afternoons and evenings together.

It's cold here Mum dear, and getting late. I shall continue this at another time, and just do my night round and go to bed now.

Good night my dearest Mum.

The letter continues:

11 February

The day before yesterday Mum was your birthday. I was wondering all day what you were doing, and how you were. I wonder if you felt me wishing you 'many happy returns of the day'?

We have golf links in the desert just behind the hospital. In fact the course goes past the gates. One becomes a member for 3 months for 10 shillings. Needless to say, I am a member but have only played twice as yet. There are tennis courts on hospital premises, as well as the Club opposite, so we have any amount of recreation.

Faulkner is going to shift my things into the room occupied by Sutherland tomorrow. He, poor fellow as you will have heard by now, has been sent back to Australia with a batch of sick and undesirable Australians. He occupied a beautiful suite of rooms – bedroom, bathroom and sitting room opening off one another, so I shall live in luxury now!

Poor little Sister Lempriere is one of those also going back to Australia with them, and about 8 other nurses, to look after the sick soldiers. I have given Sister Lempriere some photographs and a letter which she has promised to give you when she arrives.

I simply cannot describe to you what a beautiful place Egypt is, and what a glorious climate! A each day is warm and sunny and still, and I often lie on a cane lounge on one of the many terraces and piazzas and bask in the sun with a cigarette and *Art in Egypt*, which is a splendid little work by Maspero, for which I paid 6 shillings.

I told you I think, that Follit and I have a Frenchman who comes every day and talks French with us for an hour and a half. I really don't think we improve at all, as we never practise or read French except when he is here – there is so much else to do! He is a dear little chap, and takes tremendous pains to teach us.

It is whispered amongst us Mum that we may go to Europe in a few weeks! This is probably not true at all, but who knows? We may even be packing up when you get this. I shall be sorry to leave this beautiful place, as I don't suppose I shall ever see Egypt again – but it will be grand to at last get to the actual war, and do something for the poor soldiers!

I wish you could trip across here and see it all with me – Egypt is such a wonderful mystic and romantic place. I often feel inclined to pinch myself to see if I could really be asleep and dreaming all these beautiful scenes and sights! I haven't been up the pyramid yet. I should like to have a pair of rubber shoes when I do climb it, for I don't fancy slipping on those stones and falling from its stupendous height!

I was delighted to get a postcard from old Sam the other day, from Shah in France. It was good to see his old handwriting again. Both he and George are well, and apparently not in action at present. The postcard was dated 23 January 1915 and was less than a fortnight old when I got it.

Well Mother dearest I'm going to bed now. Goodnight my own darling Mum, and God bless you.

From Claude

The diary continues:

Saturday 13 February

I have omitted to fill up my diary all this time! We have all been having a quiet life here, working in our wards and either playing tennis or shopping in Cairo in the afternoons. One day Follit and I went to the pyramids where we arrived just at sunset. It was very thrilling, and the picture of that sunset, I shall I hope, never forget, as we stood in the desert with the pyramids glowing in the rose light with a background of the verdant Nile country half veiled in rising mist.

The huge Mena Camp of 18,000 men was on our left – from which 'retreat' was sounding from the scores of bugles, and the great red sun was sinking into the burning sand behind us.

All same I am disappointed with the pyramids, there is no use denying it! I feel it's because they're just the same colour as the sand, and the fact that they slope so, instead of being perpendicular makes them seem much smaller when one is close to them, than when viewed from a distance.

On Sunday I was on duty all day and had a pretty strenuous time. Follit and Turnbull went to the races and then the Club and lost a lot more money! In the evening I got Kay to do my work for a short time then went for a little stroll with Ethel Butler. I had taken her to dinner at Shepherds the previous night. She is a dear girl – as sweet natured and affectionate a person as ever I saw – but what a child! And after travelling twice around the world too! And having such a varied and wide experience of men and their wicked ways –

(The next part is heavily crossed out!)

My work during the last fortnight has been most distasteful! Poor Major Jackson has been put in charge of our isolation tents, about a mile away in the desert, and he goes off there every day, where they have about 300 beds of measles and venereal diseases. I don't know how I have the face to growl about my work when I think of his! For a man of his calibre – a surgeon of his capacity, a man of his prestige, to be passed off on 300 good-for-nothings to treat their foul diseases all day and every day! It's terrible!

I, of course, was to have been his house surgeon, however, his beds were divided up amongst the other three. My only senior then was MacLean. He, poor old chap, after one operating day, got bronchitis and asthma and he has been in bed ever since. That's settled him for now.

Syme has taken over his beds and I, who was to have been primarily 'house surgeon' and secondarily 'assistant in the eye ear and nose and throat work', have become exclusively the latter. That means that I am at the beck and call of Barrett, whom I despise and dislike.

I do lots of dirty work such as testing hearing, and doing refraction – taking histories, and doing what I'm told. He is the most irritating and impossible man to work under that one could imagine! I am getting peevish and impatient with the nurses and short and curt to the patients under the strain.

Alcorn doesn't seem to have much to do, so I am trying to get him interested in the work. I shall coach him up in it as much as I can – and perhaps some day he may relieve me altogether – who knows?

14 February
Sunday

Well! Barrett was operating this morning, and showed off disgracefully to Dunhill whom he invited to come and watch. After cauterising a couple of tonsils, he thought he'd be clever and cut one out without an anaesthetic! The blooming thing haemorrhaged and we had a frightful picnic!

Barrett completely lost his head, and finally had to get Syme in to sew the pillars of the tonsil bed together. The poor man plunged and lunged about, crying out all the time, and when Syme finally, after much difficulty, stopped the bleeding, Barrett was covered from head to foot with blood and vomit!

I did not finish my work until 3 p.m., and then Plant, Major Macdonald, Follit and I went to town and visited the Muslei. We got a guide and strolled about in those tiny closed in lanes, so narrow that hessian and other material is stretched across from the upper windows of one side to the other, forming a broken, ragged looking roof to the street, effectually shutting out light and air from these squalid rookeries, where not one strong beam of sunlight can ever penetrate.

The weirdest, most extraordinary sight, is this native bazaar – these absurdly narrow lanes of asphalt or more commonly cobblestones are lined on either side by an endless succession of stalls where Arabs, old and young, large and small, male and female, sit tailor fashion and a display their wares. The latter are really well worth seeing! Tons and tons of cloth – every possible shade and texture, oriental in pattern and brilliance – brass work, jewellery, carpets – tin ware, spices and cigarettes – such a promiscuous and extravagant jumble I have never dreamed of!

We visited a mosque, then took a carriage back to the City, and had afternoon tea at Gault's, a fairly decent restaurant, the biggest here, and then returned for our French lesson. We were a quarter of an hour late and our teacher had cleared out, thinking that we were not coming!

Poor little beggar, he has had so many disappointments waiting frequently half-an-hour for us and then we don't turn up at all, that it's no wonder that he gave us up tonight!

15 February

I finished my unpleasant and irritating duties at 2:30 p.m. (It's not the work I mind – I want to work, and the more I get, the better I am pleased – it's Barrett. He irritates me to distraction!)

Follit and I set off to the pyramids. We drove in one of our motor ambulances – there are 14 altogether – to Cairo and hired a motorcar from there to Mena. As usual, it was a most perfect afternoon, and the car was a beauty – I simply hugged myself, as in company of my dear old friend, I raced through the fresh keen air with the warm sun shining from a cloudless sky.

The road to Mena is just magnificent, being perfectly smooth and level, and lined on either side with a beautiful avenue of acacias of some sort, for about 6 to 7 miles. Stretching away on either side are the beautiful brilliant and green cultivations of the Nile Valley.

I have never conceived of anything so gorgeous as this green cultivation. No wheat or barley field in Australia comes within streets of it. The greenness and luxuriance of it is startling – absolutely vivid.

About 4 p.m., we arrived and had tea at the Tea Gardens there. When we came out, we found that a mist had risen from the Nile, and threatened to completely ruin our view of

Left, the Sphinx, which affected Claude profoundly, and right, the City of the Dead

the pyramids! We mounted camels, and rode around to the Sphinx. It's face was in deep shadow but even so we looked at the wonderful still, strong face gazing steadily out over the desert – gazing, gazing, as it has done for four or five thousand years – and did not speak for some 5 minutes.

Personally it took me a few minutes to realize the wonder of it, and how that millions of people had looked at it and wondered just as I was doing – and had died and been forgotten – yet still it remained and gazed across the limitless desert. Thousands of storms and hurricanes – thousands of cold nights and hot days – and still it gazed steadily motionless, and strong. It baffled time!

We saw it in the worst possible circumstances as regards light and time of day, and yet as I looked at that wonderful stern strong face, the shadow giving to the features an unmistakable expression of lonely sadness, yet with such strength and dignity – I felt creepy and shivery, and about 2 inches high.

We explored a temple close by, 'the Temple of the Sphinx', buried in the sand. How those enormous monoliths of granite were brought from Aswan and shaped as though they had been putty, fitted together; the joints and angles just the perfection of architecture, the gigantic things fitting in to one another as though moulded. It's absolutely inconceivable!

We climbed up the pyramid of Cheops! I know that my head does not stand heights, and it was not without some of misgiving that I tackled it. Follit did it quite without help. I am thankful to say I managed without the usual 3 Arabs, – 1 holding each hand and 1 shoving behind. I just had one old man who kept a step above me all the time and reached his hand down to me occasionally when I asked him.

I felt I was in the sky somewhere, with nothing but a worn sloping narrow step on which I stood, between me and that frightful fall, when my old friend informed me that we were nearly halfway! There was comparatively little view from the top on account of the mist.

Surely the Pyramids will never again look upon an encampment of 18,000 troops, with thousands of horses; bands playing, and convoy wagons rumbling about. Over all this, old Cheops towers – the soldiers and their wagons and horses; the Arabs with their donkeys and camels – all looking like tiny crawling insects at his feet.

It certainly was a bit more than sensational, going down! One walks to the edge of the terrific height and steps over! The desert stretches away far below, and the ants of human beings are beneath one's very feet. My head swam a couple of times I had to grip the stone with both hands and wrench my mind off the frightful eeriness of it.

We motored home and had dinner at the Club, returning about 11 a.m.

16 February

Finished work about 3 p.m.

Went with Follit and Argyle across to the lines of the Light Horse and borrowed 3 beautiful horses. The weather was as usual just perfect. We had a ripping ride over the desert, and got home in time for our French lesson! Follit and I have been sitting over the fire, yarning and reading ever since dinner.

I have changed my room for Sutherlands, and have now got a luxurious suite with a bathroom on one side and a sitting room on the other, and a beautiful big bedroom in between.

17 February

I was on duty all day. A glorious day as usual, and when I was not admitting or attending to patients, inspecting meals, etc., I was sitting on one of the terraces in the sun, with the big felt hat on.

At 5:30 p.m. I had the French lesson. I really don't think I improve in the least, and am getting thoroughly dissatisfied.

About 8 o'clock I got Follit to do my duty for me whilst I went for a short walk with Ethel Butler, whose birthday it was. I got back to find a violently drunk and struggling man vomiting all over the marble flags of the hall, whilst about 10 men sat on him to keep him quiet. We tied him firmly into bed and gave him 1/3 of morphia. He was soon asleep.

20 February

Finished work about 1:30 p.m. and set out for a ramble with Follit. I do love going out with him. He is a most interesting and entertaining companion. He has travelled widely; is desperately interested in everything he sees; is fond of eating and drinking and doing things comfortably, and damn the expense! I have a very strong affection for him, and thoroughly enjoy being with him.

We took a carriage from Cairo to the Zoo, where we strolled about laughing at the monkeys and marvelling at the giraffes. The latter are the most extraordinary creatures I've ever seen!

We got back to Cairo at about 4:30 p.m. and went to an orchestral concert at the Kursaal. It was simply glorious, and we sat and basked in the beautiful music until 6 p.m., when the orchestra (about 70 performers) withdrew in spite of the resounding applause.

We had our hair cut and shampooed, and our boots cleaned at 'the Expert's' shop where people come in and sit down as at a barber's, whilst they polish your boots till you can see your face in them!

We then dined, the two of us, sumptuously at Shepherd's, and afterwards strolled around to the Continental and watched the usual Saturday-night dance in progress.

Tommy Dunhill introduced us to his wife and stepdaughter – a vividly pretty girl, Una McKellar, who seemed to have scores of majors and colonels tailing after her!

We got restive, and longed to dance ourselves, so we went to the Palmarium (in spite of my resolutions) and had a waltz each with Lydie. Confound it! I'm sorry we did now. But we didn't know any of those ripping girls at the Continental and it gives one the pip to watch and not join in.

We got home about 2.30. I did not sleep well, and felt very rotten and cheap.

21 February
Sunday
Woke with a rotten headache and dry tongue. After doing of my wards I began to rapidly feel better. Skimped my work and was finished about 11 a.m. Follit also finished early and returned from Abassia.

We went across and had a round of golf – as usual a perfect day. Lunch at 12:30 p.m., and then in our best uniforms, we set out for Cairo with Tommy Dunhill. There we met his wife and the beautiful Una, looking as fresh as a bird after the previous night's dance.

We all caught the train for Baragle, which is about three-quarters of an hour's train journey through the marvellously fertile Nile country, the fields vividly green on either side of us with lucerne, rye and Lord knows what – with hundreds of natives working, assisted by camels, donkeys, buffaloes, goats and children, all of which patiently laboured, and got frequently and soundly beaten!

We took a trolley pushed by natives to some beautiful gardens with glorious green lawns, and showers of bougainvillea, which frequently festoon real big old gum trees and groves of poinsettias in bloom.

Una is a sweet girl, and most awfully pretty!

We got home about 5 o'clock and all had afternoon tea at 'the Groppi', where one wanders about and spears one's cakes from a vast and varied selection displayed for the purpose – sits down with one's plate-load, and is bought tea or coffee in due course by the French or Arab waiter.

26 February
At work till 4 p.m., then went into town and strolled around until 6.30 by myself. I wandered in and out of Shepherds and the Continental. I must confess with the secret longing to see the sweet face of Una McKellar in the street, or on one of the terraces, but failed!

After dinner, wandered about with Follit buying biscuits, and then met Ethel. The 3 of us repaired to the roof where we sat in the moonlight till 10:00 p.m.

27 February
Saturday most of the chaps, Follit, Corbyn and Turnbull included, went to the races this afternoon. I did not feel justified in chucking money about in that fashion, so I decided not to go with them.

I was working until 4 p.m. and then went to an orchestral concert by the same orchestra as last Saturday, by myself. I thoroughly enjoyed the music, which was really very fine indeed. Concert was over at 6 p.m.

I bought a couple of cold drinks, and then unable to resist any longer, rang up Una, to see if she was going to the weekly ball at the Continental. As served me right, Mrs Dunhill answered, and said that they were only going to the ball if they could not arrange to go to Saqqara the next day (Sunday).

That put an idea into my head. Follit and I had thought of going to Saqqara this day also! I instantly rang up the Major to see what his plans were. He said he wanted to go but did not know how to arrange it. I told him Follit and my idea of going also, and offered to arrange for a party of we two, himself, and charming daughter! He agreed!!

So I stayed at Shepherd's for dinner, where I met Balcombe-Quick, also by himself and dined with him. After dinner I went around to Cook's and arrange for a guide for the next day.

Spent the night in pleasing anticipation of the morrow, with those blue eyes, misty and bewitching, dancing before my eager imagination in rapturous dreams! *(The last was deleted, but just legible!)*

28 February
Sunday

This day will surely rest in my mind as a most a most delightful spent in Egypt. I rose at 6:30 a.m. and saw all my cases before breakfast.

At 8.45, Follit, Dunhill and myself were ready to start. We were joined at the last moment, I was annoyed to discover, by Kay, who butted into our party, bringing his own lunch.

Besides this, there was a high wind blowing and we thought the desert would be a perfect sand storm. With such a gloomy forebodings we reached the station in Cairo at 9.15 a.m. precisely. Here matters took on a rosy complexion for me at once, at the sight of Mrs Dunhill and her daughter, who looked perfectly charming, albeit, I soon found out, having been up till all hours the previous night at the dance!

Well, the ladies met us, and also my guide with the lunch basket and our tickets and we were soon comfortably settled on the train. Especially me, with Miss McKellar beside me! An hour on the train brought us to our unpronounceable destination where we mounted donkeys, which Hassan directed us to.

Although I have now been 6 weeks in Egypt, this is the first time I have been on a donkey! I absolutely refused to allow any donkey boy to whip the poor little devil, though all day he was dying to do so. I have never seen anywhere such cruel brutes as these donkey boys!

Una looked perfectly sweet on her white donkey, though how she did it on a hideous beast like that, I'll never understand! We started off amid a cloud of dust, and a babble of shouting Tommies, braying donkeys and jabbering Arabs. Such a din of shouts and cries, braying, laughing and jabbering I never heard in all my life. The first spot of interest was the wonderful Colossi of Rameses the 2nd.

Instead of the majestic calm, which should have reigned about these marvellous statues, the scene was a hideous brawl!

Carved out of one enormous mass of solid granite, with the astounding accuracy and clearness, the exquisite detail and softness of outline, which characterise the wonderful works of these Egyptian artists of 6000 years ago. Old Rameses lay there silent and still in the spot where he has been for nearly 6000 years – 6000 years!! It just bewilders and paralyses the imagination!

For 6000 years there alone in the desert, with that steady gentle and slightly sarcastic expression – deaf to the jabbering Arabs and braying donkeys – heedless of the unspeakable Tommies who climbed on to him with their hobnail boots – sat on him, dozens at a time – and lit their pipes, spitting and swearing and shouting and guffawing. And there the wonderful statue lay and will live for years and years, long after those pigs are all in their little graves – utterly forgotten.

Una on a donkey

It was just too much for us altogether! We drew aside and waited patiently in the shade of a palm tree until the brawling braying rabble had passed on, and their cloud of dust had vanished in the distance. We then remounted our little donkeys and ambled off across the desert.

What a fortunate thing it was that two donkeys, Miss McKellar's and my own, seemed to have such an affection for each other as to wish to travel close side by side, away from the party. Consequently I thoroughly enjoyed the hour and-a-half ride over the desert!

Ultimately we arrived at Mariette's house. Mariette, the great Egyptologist and investigator to whom the world owes the great Necropolis of Saqqara.

We had lunch at the house, which has a lovely building set in the midst of the desert. Swarms of Tommies lunched there at the same time, but our guide produced a fine spread from our hamper and laid a table in a corner for us and then waited on us as we ate.

After lunch we set off to see the tombs of these nobles of the 5th Dynasty, some 5000 years ago – the massive granite halls, pillars and doors – the lofty apartments and above all the marvellous pictures painted in relief on the walls – absolutely baffled description! Everything was in the most perfect condition, and looking at those wonderful designs so beautifully executed, those colours so bright and fresh looking, it seemed quite impossible to realise that these were really done 5000 years ago.

The ride home, though good fun, was scarcely as enjoyable as going out. Partly because the dust was worse, and also because my donkey seemed to have lost his companionable vein as regards Miss McKellar's animal, and displayed a most regrettably unsociable propensity in that direction.

We were all very tired in the train coming home, but I'm sure that this was the happiest day I have had in Egypt.

1 March 1915
Monday

I found this morning that great things had been happening whilst we were away at Saqqara yesterday! The 2nd AGH had orders to pack up, and behold they send all their convalescents out to us – about 200 of them. All day yesterday they had streamed in, and there seems to have been perfect chaos the whole day. My own wards were filled up with deaf people and I had a furiously busy time trying to catch up with them.

Fortunately Barrett was terribly busy interviewing generals, etc., so I was left pretty much to myself. I was working hard until about 4 p.m., when Dunhill and his family turned up for afternoon tea.

I showed him around a bit, and took Miss McKellar up on to the beautiful roof where the warm afternoon sun glowed on her pretty face and gave me thrills of pleasure – she really is a lovely girl – – – *[crossed-out section]*

Later dragged old Follit out for a drive. It was just ripping, trolling along the bank of the Nile by moonlight, and we got home about 11 p.m. I was soothed and sleepy.

23 February 1915

My darling Mum
Here we are still in this Arcadia. Working pretty hard, but loving every minute of it.

I posted my last letter to you last Monday, a beautiful sunny afternoon, as Follit and I were on our way over to the pyramids. This was only the second time I have been out to them, and the first time was on a grey dull day when we arrived before dark only just in time to see them at all. So on this occasion, Follit and I took a motor. We had a glorious run out – it was about 11 miles from Cairo and almost the whole way the road – which is absolutely level and smooth and straight, and lined on each side by a magnificent avenue of green acacia trees of some sort with big pods about six inches long – runs through the wonderful cultivated fields of the Nile Valley.

Thus on either side of us, as we sped along, stretched one continuous sheet of the most brilliant and luxurious green that I have ever dreamt of. There are in Egypt no fences between the different rural properties, the country being divided up only by little irrigation canals, which form the most marvellous network everywhere through the country of the Nile Valley. Thus each little farm and property, some of them less than an acre in size, was really a separate little island, rectangular or square of the richest green surrounded by its little irrigation canal, like a small drain.

I am writing before breakfast as the mail goes out at midday and I shall be working very soon. Hence Mum I shall not attempt to describe the pyramids and the Sphinx with the huge Australian camp with 18 to 20,000 troops at their feet. I enclose a couple of photographs, which I took that afternoon.

We had a ripping day, climbed to the top of the pyramid of Cheops and from that vantage point watched the sun set as it dipped slowly, a vivid fiery ball, beneath the vast glowing sheet of desert.

Twice during the last week I have a borrowed a horse and been for ride to the different places to see around Heliopolis. I can get a horse whenever I want one, as the Light Horse is camped quite close to us in the desert. I hope to have another ride this afternoon.

Yesterday evening, Monday, I made Jim Elder come over to see me. He is camped with the 14th in the desert about a quarter of an hour's walk from here. I have been over to see him there, but it is not very comfortable, owing to the annoying discrepancy in our ranks. I sent a corporal to look for him, the corporal and Jim stood before me at attention. The corporal salutes and says 'Private Elder sir' and I dismiss him. Jim and I talk, but Jim feels awkward and unhappy all the time with his mates watching us.

So I made him come and see me over here. He arrived about 7 p.m. I made the poor old beggar have a hot bath and a good stiff whisky, the former of which was an unheard-of luxury for him! I then took him in to Cairo and gave him a real good dinner!

We waded through a many-coursed spread and bottle with good effect, with some excellent music by a large string band, which kept things lively. We ate till it was time to go, and Jim said he had not had such a dinner since he left Melbourne! He looks fit and strong and well, but has got thin and has a bushy moustache.

Major J.W. Barrett is very busy administrating, as he is 'Adjutant and Registrar', so I do nearly all the work in the Eye and Ear Department. There's an awful lot, as the sand of the desert plays the deuce with the men. I am also doing a good bit of operating, as Major

MacLean very kindly hands many of his operations over to me.

By the time you get this you'll probably have received another cable for money, as I shall soon be getting low again, unless I get another remittance. Egypt is fully worth spending money on, and it would be impossible for anyone to see Egypt as cheaply or in circumstances so unique as I am at present.

The Bank of New South Wales, London, tell me that they have as yet received no remittances. We don't know when we may move to Europe, so next month it would be wise to have the remittances sent to London in case we move suddenly.
From Claude

5 March 1915
My own darling Mum,

I wish I could have a peep at you in peaceful old Melrose, in your garden room tonight. I wonder if it is very hot, and are you sitting out on the lawn in front of your room? You dear beloved Mum, I hope and pray that you are well and happy.

For myself, I have had about the hardest week's work I have ever had, and I'm not tired tonight though it is just 10:30 p.m. and I have just finished having been going hard, scarcely stopping a moment since 7.30 this morning.

As you know I am Major Barrett's assistant in the eye, ear and throat ward. Also, I was house surgeon to Major MacLean. However, it was soon apparent that the eye and ear work was assuming such formidable proportions that I'd have to devote myself solely to it. I therefore, most reluctantly, had to give up my surgery and am now solely the assistant to Major Barrett.

I wish I could make you realise in even a slight degree what this position of mine entails.

Let me begin by saying that knowing Major J.W.B. as you do, you will not, I am sure, be the least surprised to hear that he is absolutely running the show here! Everyone is utterly disgusted, bitterly disappointed, and depressed under this egotistical unmethodical, un-military man. But no more of that until I return, and then you will read my diary!!!

Suffice it to say that Major Barrett, for the first week or two, did a good deal of work in the Eye and Ear Department, presumably until he might find out how much I knew about the game. But being a tremendously busy man, spending his whole time and substance in interviewing generals and dashing about in motorcars with colonels and gentlemen with about 40 initials after their names, he now has practically left his work in my hands!

I rise at 6 o'clock in the morning and with a staff of five nurses and two orderlies, I work like a nigger the whole day long. You have no idea of the colossal job it is – biggest thing I have ever been up against!

I have 60 beds, all full up, and all day long a steady stream of men comes from all the encampments in Egypt with letters from their regimental medical officers asking for examination and a report on condition of the men. Major Barrett and myself are the only eye and ear men in the Australian Army in Egypt – and as I said, Major Barrett has his hands full with his position in this unit – (his title is 'Adjutant and Registrar') – without doing any professional work!

When you remember that all these thousands of troops are camped in the desert, in sand up to their ankles, where even on the calmest day the atmosphere is dim and misty with dust, you will realise in some slight degree what an enormous amount of throat disease, nose disease, and above all, eye disease there is here. The men breathe an atmosphere that is loaded with germ-infested dust. Pneumonia and other lung diseases are naturally the rule, but the first organs to feel the strain are the eyes, ears nose and throat. So you can see how I am occupied.

7 March –

I stopped writing on Friday night, mum to have supper in Follit's room and then to bed. And was too tired to describe to you what was happening. I will try now –

You know our rooms have been changed, and we're now up on the 3rd storey. This is part of the scheme to expand the hospital as regards its accommodating capacity. Patients are now pouring in, and we were pushed for room as things were arranged before. My new room overlooks Heliopolis, which is to say that my window does not face the desert. It is a jolly nice room, and has another small room off it, which I use as a little private sitting room.

Well, as I sat here writing to you the other night, the whole 2nd Australian Division – that is, the whole 2nd and 3rd Contingents and the New Zealanders – marched past my window on their way out into the desert where they bivouacked in the early hours of the morning.

I have an uninterrupted view of about half a mile of street from my window, as I am just opposite the corner and can see therefore in both directions. About 18,000 men marched past in the moonlight. It took over two hours for them to go by!

All day and every day, troops stream past the hospital, regiments of horse and foot, guns and ammunition columns, ambulances, etc. – we are all quite used to that – but I have never seen so huge a body of men in full fighting equipment in motion before!

They came in streams – hundreds and hundreds. It was a still, moonlit night, and the monotonous tramp, tramp, of the infantry as they steadily came and went in an interminable line, echoed from the asphalt street below, until one really ceased to hear it from the absolute monotony of the sound.

Next came the Light Horse, coming into view and vanishing into the gloom by the scores and hundreds – beautiful horses in the peak of condition, and splendid men that make one proud of being an Australian!

Then came the artillery – the incessant rumble of the guns, streaming past in that mighty procession – I wish I had counted them! There were numbers and numbers – any one could have blown us up as we stood at our windows in the moonlight

As I sat writing to you in my window, I had my Father's binoculars beside me and I kept looking away down the moonlit column for familiar faces, but the moonlight was not bright enough for this.

At length, as I wrote, the sound ceased and I went on writing, thinking that they had all gone. The silence was so complete after the long monotonous tramp, tramp – it was as though one were miles away in the Australian bush.

After a time I looked out the window to see how the stretch of road looked without the gigantic column, but to my astonishment, just at my feet, stood a whole regiment of Light Horse! A thousand horses and men, troop after troop, standing absolutely motionless and silent in the moonlight! They had not passed after all. This was just a halt – and there they stood for 15 minutes, motionless, without a sound – not a horse neighed – not a man spoke – not a stirrup clanked. It was the most impressive sight I remember!

And now Mum, I shall look up my diary, and see what has happened worthy of note since I last wrote.

After the Banage trip with Major Dunhill and his charming wife, beautiful step-daughter, and old Follit, which happened last Sunday week and which I have described in my last letter I must confess that I spent the rest of that week in pleasing anticipation of my next meeting with this most delightful family. Miss Una McKellar has made a very marked impression – for she really is awfully pretty, and with a charming girlish manner, and living in Wallace Avenue, Toorak, talking to her made home feel quite near.

The week following this jolly little trip was most uninteresting, and passed slowly with plenty of work, and a couple of trips to Saqqara in evening, just going to Shepherd's, you know, where you are sure to meet everyone that you ever have seen and known in Australia!

Last Sunday was the most beautiful and most delightful day I have ever spent in Egypt. Oh I wish you could have been with us Mum dear – it takes so long and looks so uninteresting to write it down.

Major Dunhill, Mrs Dunhill, Miss McKellar, Follit, Kay and myself started off at 9 o'clock for Saqqara …

[Claude described in detail the desert trip.]

About 3 o'clock we rode home – one-and-a-half hours exciting donkey ride across the desert. We galloped and raced the poor little devils about, but they really seemed it to enjoy it! The hour's railway trip home was rather an anti-climax, but we all dozed. I have never enjoyed a day so much I am quite sure!

Ever since then Mum, I have been working mighty hard. I bucked in last week for all I was worth, as felt I was due for some hard work after such a ripping day!

Mum I cabled to you yesterday for money. I hope you did not get a shock, but I am spending a lot. I don't think it is squandering, or waste, for I shall never see Egypt again and I am being educated and seeing things which I could not see without money, and which I shall remember to my dying day.

God bless you and Lucile and her children, and Jack and Stan, Mother darling. I can almost hear the Melbourne Grammar School clock striking half past 11 as I say good night.
From Claude

6 March
Saturday

I have not written this up for nearly a week and what a week! I had been working like a nigger – not putting my face outside the gate since Monday!

Turnbull and Follit have gone to the races this afternoon. Being pretty hard up, I was not keen on accompanying them. I finished my work at 3:30 p.m. and started off to town, glorying in the warm sunshine and fresh air, and feeling like a liberated jailbird!

I went to the Cable Office and cabled for money – I am jolly short of cash. I was then about to go to another orchestral concerts – they are held every Saturday – when I met Major and Mrs Dunhill who persuaded me to go and have tea with them.

Mrs Dunhill is the dearest little bright-eyed woman – motherly and girlish at the same time. After tea at the Groppi, we all got into a carriage and drove down to the native bazaar. The Major is, of course, a genuine artist and a connoisseur of carpets and such things.

He and Mrs Dunhill simply revelled in Persian and Turkish carpets and brassware, whilst I looked on and tried to pick up a few scraps of knowledge and to appreciate merit, which I never dreamt existed, in the smallest details.

About 7 o'clock we took ourselves from the bazaar and the Major and his wife dropped me at Shepherd's, and went home. I dined alone in the Grill Room at Shepherd's.

Mrs Dunhill had told me that she would take Una to the weekly Saturday night —— *(Crossed-out section).*

After roaming in and out of that brilliant assembly of officers in flaming Mess uniform I ran straight into the lovely girl herself looking perfectly ravishing! She was, of course, booked full to the brim, and I had expected this, however, I booked some dances for next Saturday!

I then came home, well pleased with myself. *[The last section difficult to read, and heavily deleted![*

Heliopolis
17 March

My own darling Mum

I had just been reading and re reading your letter dated 15 February. Oh the delight of a home letter!

Private Noall, who is rather a thick-headed fellow, with a mighty poor idea of military discipline, spoke to me the other day, saying that he had heard from his mother, who was playing with you in the croquet tournament – I'm so sorry you got licked – but I suppose it was Mrs Noall's fault!

Well mum dear, as to news!

Since last I wrote, I have been hard at work looking after the sore eyes and deaf ears of the Australian army in Egypt. I have had poor old Frank Lind in with otitis media, but under my able treatment – ehem! – he is rapidly getting better!

I have two ripping wards with about 30 beds each – with marble pillars and gorgeous ceilings – and besides these I have a suite of four rooms on the ground floor where I see the out patients, who come up daily from the sick parades of their different regiments. I have now got a fourth-year medical student has an orderly in the Eye and Ear Department, and am teaching him a lot. I will soon have him efficient enough to help me quite a lot.

Barrett looks in occasionally, and is off again.

Since writing last week, nothing much has happened to me, but a few things have happened which are worthy of note. First of all, poor major Dunhill, who I respect and admire more and more, has got seriously ill with quinsy and septic throat, caused of course, by the desert! Luckily, the day before he got ill, he had safely installed his wife and daughter in a 'Pension' (i.e. a boarding house) just opposite the Palace, and so they are with him all day long. The poor old beggar has been miserably ill, and having a rotten painful time.

I can get a horse whenever I like from the Light Horse lines, just near us, and I have been for a couple of rides and walks with his stepdaughter Miss Una McKellar, who is a sweetly pretty girl, awfully like Lucile, but with rather less character.

I love being with her, not only because I can't resist a pretty face, but also because it is so like home. We talk about Toorak, and compare the people and houses with Melbourne. Then of course, she comes from a Station near Stawell, and knows the Grampians well. So you see, she is a charming companion. Unfortunately for me, I am not the only one in this opinion!

There was a tremendous fuss yesterday, when the whole staff, officers, nurses and men, had their photographs taken. It was, we all consider, a most scandalous and disgusting thing! The photos are to be sent to the King, the Minister of Defence, Lady Munro-Fergusson, etc. and of course, will be in every Illustrated Paper in Australia. They took the thing in the middle of the day, and the whole work of the hospital was at a standstill for one hour! If they consider they are doing their duty to their country by leaving 700 soldiers, some of them desperately ill, to look after themselves, while the whole staff, in whose care they are, go and get photographed for the sake of a selfish advertisement – well, it's not my idea of serving my country!

I had a whole room for sick men to examine and treat, and refused to leave them, and am therefore not in the great photograph! Seven others of us also absented themselves and of course, poor major Dunhill was in bed – so it can hardly be called a representative gathering!

I cabled to you the other day for money, which promptly arrived – just like you! At the time, it seemed that we might move quite soon, so I asked you to remit to London. Now however, the time seems to be as far-off as ever again! Nevertheless, I hope you'll ask Stan to send me £20 regularly each month to London.

I have little hope of saving much money, and I think that it would be false economy. I shall never be in these countries again, and I am laying a store of memories on which I can brood for the rest of my life, and as I am earning the money, it would be foolish not to make the most of it and see everything I can afford to see.

God bless you my own dear Mother. Give Lucile and the dear children, and old John and Stan my love most heartily.
From Claude

20 March
Saturday

Work until 2 p.m. Was determined to go to the weekly concert at the Britannia Theatre and then to dinner at the Continental and dance afterwards.

At 1 p.m., orders were posted by which I was Orderly Officer. Was consequently going like blazes, attending to the discipline of the place – meting out punishment when necessary, admitting cases and seeing and treating others; rushing from one end of the hospital to the other to meet crises, etc., until 11:30 p.m. Turned in very tired.

21 March

Barrett meddled and interfered, and blocked me most of the morning. Had hoped to get out into the sun and air this afternoon, but was working until 4 p.m.

Was about to start out for walk with Colonel Maudesley, when Whitford and a friend of his arrived to see me. Had to stay in the hospital with them until 6 p.m. Then went across to Heliopolis House and had ice-cream and watched the cinema with Miss McKellar and

Miss McCullough until 7 p.m. Refused an invitation to go back with them to dinner, and came home to find that Barrett had fallen on the steps at Shepherd's, and cut his elbow! I put a stitch in it – without comment.

24 March

Worked until 5:30 p.m. Today I excised an enormous pair of tonsils, and had a good brisk haemorrhage after it! Everything was covered with blood. But eventually it stopped, and Barrett who had been out, came in at the right moment to find the chap comfortably in bed again!

About 5:30 p.m. went into a town and had a haircut. Got back at 8 p.m., and rang up Miss McKellar and went over to the Pension for dinner. Had a delightful evening talking to the pretty child and her mother.

Returned about 10:30 p.m. to find – hoorah! – an Australian mail! Got into bed to read it. First of course, Mother's letter, and there I read of the birth of a little son to Stan and Lucile! I hopped out of bed and seized my whisky bottle and rushed off to find someone with whom to drink the baby's health. Found Turnbull and toasted the little blighter most heartily!

25 March

I rose at 6 a.m. and dashed into town to send a cable to congratulate Stan on his little son. Had breakfast in Cairo and got back about 9:15 a.m. Worked until 4 p.m., then had afternoon tea on the terrace of the Heliopolis House with Miss McKellar.

At mess, I shouted beer and got them all to drink Master Elder's health! Perhaps it is a unique experience for a baby to be toasted by an Officers' Mess on active service, many miles away.

Jim Elder came in that evening to see if I had heard the good news. He had been marching all day and was very tired, poor beggar.

29 March

Fine weather today.

I worked until 3:30 p.m. when there was a review of the troops at the aerodrome by Sir Ian Hamilton. I went over to watch it by myself, but really one could see nothing but a huge cloud of dust, which enveloped the whole scene like a curtain!

I strolled over to the isolation camp and had a long yarn to Major Jackson. In the course of it, he gave me the use of his horse in the mornings before breakfast and also Colonel Maudesley's horse for a companion! I was terribly pleased and instantly hatched a scheme whereby Miss McKellar and I should go for an early morning gallop before breakfast!

I took his horse out for a preliminary canter on the spot, and seeing Miss McKellar ahead of me about to go in to her gate, I dashed forward. The horse slipped and fell flat on its nose and on my right leg! Beyond a scratch or two and a badly bruised knee, I was not hurt, and the horse did not even have a scratch, to my intense relief.

Had a hot bath and went early to bed.

1 April

Up early both yesterday and today, and had a ripping gallop before breakfast – which was a day so delightful, that I did not get in until after 9 a.m. Breakfast was then long past, and I went without. Of course Falconer had bought me a cup of tea and a couple biscuits with my shaving water, as he always does, so I was not so badly off. I worked hard all day and felt very fit.

There is a glorious big moon just now, – and I have been promising myself a trip out to the pyramids and the Sphinx by moonlight ever since we got here.

Tonight, Follit invited me to dinner at the Turf Club at 8 p.m. and after a sumptuous repast, we hired a motor and dashed out to Mena in the glorious moonlight. Before we arrived however there were quite a lot of fleecy clouds in the sky, which kept veiling the moon. The old pyramids gleamed at us in the silver light long before we had reached them, looking more immense and mystic than ever before, in the dim shadowy light.

We arrived at Mena House and took donkeys up the causeway to the foot of Cheops, and around him to the Sphinx. The soft patter of little beasts feet as they bravely ambled up the hill in the lovely cool atmosphere, with that enormous wonderful moon hanging over us in the dim the silent desert – I could hardly believe it was not all a dream, that it was actually my own self that was taking part in this impressive scene. We left at the donkeys before arriving at the Sphinx and strolled around it in the sand.

Fleecy clouds were blowing frequently across the face of the moon, casting fleeting shadows over the whole scene and producing such a changing, altering picture of light and shade, far more effective than would have been the still steady stare of the clear full moon.

The expression of that marvellous face changed every moment. Now it was clean and brightly lit up, gazing at the horizon with a peculiar steady, wise understanding smile – yes, it was watching the world – that little restless world, now writhing in some new war – men fighting and struggling and dying – as they have done, generation after generation. Yes, it had watched them do so for 6000 years. Yes, it quite understood – it was used to their little struggles, joys and sorrows. It had watched them come and go for 6000 years.

I felt infinitely petty – infinitely futile and small. Merely one, and an utterly unimportant one, of those poor, struggling, short-lived men.

A cloud is passing over the moon. How the expression changed! The smile has gone. The forehead wrinkled. The lines of the whole face had become drawn into a pained and solemn expression. The shadows about the mouth, which had produced that wonderful smile, have faded into a uniform grey, sombre shade. The face looks old. Unspeakably old, careworn, sorrowful.

'Oh poor weak unhappy men – why must you struggle and tear each other to pieces whilst your wives and loved ones thousands of miles away wait for you, and long for you in vain.

'Oh cruel relentless time! Must I live on here forever and gaze on this misery and distress? 6000 years have I watched, and their sorrow and pain, their hatred and cruelty are now no less than in the days of the Israelites.

' Poor sad unhappy things – so small – so temporary.'

And now the cloud passes, the sorrow fades – the expression softens to contentment, and infinite patience.

'Fight on little men, you will soon all die – and your children will take your place, and for a time, a few generations, will live happily together. It will pass, this misery and turmoil. It will pass, and come again – I know – I know.'

As I gazed at the wonderful monster, those gleaming shadowy pyramids rising majestically up from the sandy waste, I felt overcome with admiration for those ancient Egyptians – those mighty kings, those magnificent artists and sculptors, 6000 years ago, and here is their handicraft actually before me.

Yes O wonderful thing, well may you pity us stupid little men, so modern and conceited.

But what of your makers? What of the mighty man who moulded that marvellous face and gave you those 6000 years of life? Dead – gone – ages and ages ago – and you, his handiwork, live on to tell of his might …

We got home about 1 a.m.

Meanwhile, back in Australia, Jack had enlisted, and in April 1915 sailed for England where he joined the Royal Army Medical Corps. He spent the next three months in camp at Eastbourne and Aldershot where he had a happy time and made a lot of friends. He was then posted to the 67th Field Ambulance in France, close to the front line at Amiens where he remained for a few months.

He was then sent as Medical Officer of a transport ship to Salonika where he was to remain for 3–4 months, attached to an Advanced Dressing Station in the mountains. One morning while exercising the horses and running with them in the snow, one became excited and reared then kicked Jack, breaking his right arm. He was sent to Cairo to convalesce.

1st Australian General Hospital
28 March

My own darling Mother

I was delighted to get your letter telling me of the birth of my little nephew. I was terribly excited and pleased to have it, and Jim Elder and I congratulated each other most heartily. I have really only time for a short note this week, and as I have written several others, I have left it a bit late.

The weather is steadily warming up here and will soon be terribly hot. We had an experience yesterday, which was not encouraging. An Egyptian dust storm!

The whole desert rose up into the sky, and the sun became invisible. The light faded until there was left nothing but a pale yellow glow. The wind howled around us, and talk about dust! Eyes, teeth, ears, etc. were full of it, the moment when put one's head out of the door!

Our poor men camped in the desert! We wondered how they would live through it. The Arabs laid down flat on the sand and covered their heads with their robes.

About lunch time the wind dropped. It was then still and sultry – the air heavy with dust – when suddenly, hordes of locusts descended on us!

I have seen these locust plagues before here, but yesterday's was the worst I have ever seen. It is beyond description! Do you remember the grasshopper plagues we saw, you and I, in the northeast of Victoria some years ago? Well that was absolutely nothing compared with this! The air was thick with these huge heavy insects and the whole atmosphere was just a moving mass of them away up for several hundred feet high. They shut out what little yellow light there was, and it became almost dark. They stripped every leaf, every green thing in sight was shredded and bare. They only stayed about an hour, and left scarcely a green thing behind them!

I have been working very hard and am going to ask for a few days' leave of absence. I hope to take a trip up the Nile to Luxor. I read about it in a guidebook Mum, it is one of the sights of the world. It will be pretty expensive, but money well spent.

Since I left home I have saved a bit over £50, and have been quite extravagant, but am now only spending money on things that are worthwhile.

I have decided to have all my money paid to me here in Egypt, as it seems it will be many, many months before we move from here. If we ever do it all!

If I have it all here, in the Anglo Egyptian bank, I can remit some to London regularly, until I have a little pile there, and then remit back to Melbourne. It is unsatisfactory never knowing when you may get money again, when you are in a strange land, and at the whims of chance.

Nothing of note has happened during the last week. Major Dunhill is much better now, and last Wednesday I dined with Mrs Dunhill and her charming daughter Miss Una McKellar, and last night (Saturday) I dined with Mrs Summons and Florrie Sproule in Cairo. After dinner we went to the usual Saturday-night ball at the Continental Hotel – the most brilliant function always – with flashing Mess uniforms and beautiful girls – almost entirely military, the girls being wives and daughters of generals, colonels, brigadiers, etc.

I am well Mum darling, but going a bit stale on Eye and Ear work – it's so monotonous!
With tons of love
Claude

3 April
Good Friday

Up early for a gallop, this time with Miss McKellar. Home at 9 a.m.

All day we had heard rumours of the army moving – it seems as though it is true this time but there have been so many false alarms.

Had a hard day's work and went to bed early.

4 April
Saturday

Did not get out till after dinner in the evening, then went into town with Follit who was bent on going to a Service in the Coptic Church out of curiosity. I went and had a shave instead, and met him and later at the Continental. Miss McKellar had promised me some dances!

Cairo presented a most extraordinary appearance! As a rule, on Saturday night especially, the place is simply choked with troops and one has to elbow one's way along the street through them. Tonight there was not a uniform to be seen! The streets were quiet and deserted, except for a few natives. I could hardly believe my eyes.

Presently I met a whole battalion marching in column down the street. They were absolutely quiet, and marched straight to the railway station. Then I understood. The army is moving at last!

The Continental and Shepherd's presented a most sombre and deserted appearance. A handful of officers – fat colonels and medical men – were the sole representatives of the glittering throng of shining gold braid and brilliant Mess uniforms one usually sees there. A dazzling throng of handsome men and pretty girls!

The dance went off quietly. There was no crowd, no bustle or noise.

About 11:30 p.m. everyone quietly got into carriages and motors and slipped down to the station. Follit and I had a carriage together – then at the station everything was a bustle of excitement!

A long train was at the platform crammed with troops. Hundreds of horses were being led into trucks in a continuous stream. A band was crashing out popular tunes on the platform. Pretty girls were leaning in the windows bidding tearful farewells.

How I longed to go with them! I would give my soul to be on that train! I feel a miserable worm, staying here in luxury while those brave chaps go out and get shot.

We got back into our carriage and went back to the dance. I had several with Miss McKellar, who dances very well, but there was an air of depression. A cloud of gloom has settled over the whole city.

We had supper at 12.30, and at 1.30 everyone left hurriedly to see another trainload of troops off. Follit and I could not stand it, and as the trams had stopped for the night, we motored home and arrive shortly after 2 a.m.

7 April

Nothing worthy of mention has happened during last few days. Each morning I had have been for a gallop with Miss McKellar and worked the rest of the day. One evening I went for ride with Follit.

I am getting more and more excited over my leave which dates from Friday night 9 April until Monday night 12 April. I applied for 72 hours leave, which is our right every few months on Active Service. It was granted at once, and then Follit applied, and his was granted too. We have now been here for three months, and I have worked very hard indeed nearly all the time.

Follit and I are going to take a trip to Luxor – ancient Thebes – the wonderful royal city, capital of Egypt from the 18th to the 20th dynasty, about 1500 BC to 1100 BC. This is of course the great winter tourist resort of Egypt where all the millionaires and wealthy dukes, duchesses, earls, etc. of the old-world, and the Americans, gather. It is 400 miles from Cairo, on the banks of the Nile, and entails a 12 hour train journey.

Tonight I heard from a private soldier from the 14th that Jim Elder is sick. I went straight over to the camp and found the poor old beggar groaning with pain with colic and dysentery. I sat with him for a while but there was nothing I could do.

9 April

Rode over the early this morning to see how Jim was feeling. Found him much better.

The infantry regiments at the aerodrome camp, one quarter of a mile from us in the desert, are absolutely on tenterhooks, expecting hourly to receive orders to move to Europe. I expect they will be gone when we return.

I was terribly busy all day, finishing up my work at 5 p.m. All was ready. Falconer had packed my bag and he and Thomson, Follit's batman, went off to Cairo with the luggage.

Follit and I left about 6.30 p.m. in our uniforms, helmets and putties. We went to

Shepherd's, a deserted looking place nowadays, and sat on the terrace and had light refreshments. At 7.30 we quietly strolled down to the station where we met the batmen and our luggage. There is no sleeper or dining car on Friday nights, so we had a hamper dinner, and proposed to sleep in our carriage.

An awful crowd of Tommies and Light Horse officers are also going in the train, which to our disgust was crowded. The Mounted regiments were left in Cairo, only the infantry having gone to the front, and hence these fellows were able to get leave. To our intense relief we got a carriage to ourselves. A real bit of luck!

At 8 p.m. we started. It had been a warm day and it was still close. About 8.30 we got out our hamper and dined. We had got the hamper from Shepherd's, costing 12 shillings and sixpence, and by Jove, we did polish off the good things therein!

About 9:30 p.m. we rolled ourselves in our rugs and slept soundly, having a whole seat each to lie on.

10 April
Saturday

Woke at 6 a.m., train drawn up at a station and everything covered in dust. The Tommies were having a great time swaggering about the station and ragging each other.

As the train rushed along in the cool morning air this scene on either side was just that of a typical rural district. Rich tracts of cultivated land under wheat, maize or lucerne, where men, women and children laboured, together with donkeys, camels, buffaloes, cows and goats in a beautiful jumble. Women carrying pitchers of water about on their heads, each one robed in black with the black 'yashmak' up to her eyes.

It soon began to get very hot, and the dust was disgusting. On each side of the line, a couple of miles away, a long range of barren and rugged hills hid the horizon. Quite suddenly and unexpectedly at 10 a.m., the train drew in to Luxor.

We handed our luggage to a hotel porter, who put us in a carriage, which took us to the Luxor Hotel. In this dreadful season, this is the only hotel open. The popular tourist one, the Winter Palace on the banks of the Nile, was closed because there are no tourists. We drove through the streets, typical dirty run-down squalid streets of Egyptian towns, and reached the hotel in a few minutes. It is quite a nice little hotel, with a luxuriant oriental garden in front, with deck chairs and tables in the deep shadows of those beautiful luscious green trees.

We got two very nice rooms, each with a balcony overlooking the garden, and having got rid of the army of Arabs, who followed us up the stairs each carrying some item of the effects, we each had a jolly good hot bath and a shave.

I had been recommended a dragoman by Colonel Nye before we left, so I sent an Arab out in the street to look for him.

At 11 a.m., Follit and I met in the garden where we indulged in iced drinks, having had no breakfast. But as lunch was at 12.30, it was not worthwhile eating anything.

As we sat there, cool and happy, the dragoman – Georges Michael by name – came and interviewed us. He is an elderly Arab – a most respectable old chap – a Christian strange to say, and hence his civilised name. We arranged with him that he should manage everything for us, make out a timetable, provide conveyances, donkeys, etc., and do all the tipping, and that at the end of the day, we should give him £2.10.

The timetable he made out for us started at once – we were to see the Temple of Luxor before lunch!

We walked out of the gate, Follit, Georges and myself. The sun was very hot and we were thankful to have our helmets – and were hot even so! Strolling quietly down the street we had not gone 50 yards when we found ourselves on the bank of the Nile. The river here is exceedingly broad; a most imposing sheet of water. On the opposite bank the desert stretched away, barely above the level of the water for about three miles, where a range of a ragged barren hills obscured the horizon. To our left the river was bordered by a road, while on the right, reaching almost to the actual bank of the river, were the wonderful imposing ruins of the Temple of Luxor.

If one could only have a have a peep at the scene 3,500 years ago, what a spectacle it must have been! That broad stretch of water which now contained a few boats and barges and one or two yachts, must have been covered with swarms of small craft of all sorts, while moored at its extensive quays would have been numbers of war galleys with the slaves leaning on their oars.

Over the whole scene, the great temple – glittering with silver, gold and bronze, the great columns and pillars, brilliant with their enormous pictures carved in deep relief, and vividly coloured – must have towered majestically. The enormous statues of the kings and gods stood silently watching the busy scene.

CHAPTER 8

6 May 1915

And now I take up my diary again having neglected it for a whole month – and that, the most eventful and interesting month, and by far the busiest, since our arrival here.

I will try to give a brief sketch of what has been happening, so as to be in a position to continue from now onwards.

For a week after our return from Luxor, things were quite eventful. My wards were in an awful mess! Barrett had bungled everything! The books were chaotic, the patients were ill, neglected and miserable, and the nurses worried and exasperated. I have never yet had such a welcome home after an absence than I did from that brief three days' holiday by all the nurses, patients, and orderlies! It was really very nice! But I realised it was not on account of my own virtue, but the un-methodical ways of Barrett.

For a week or 10 days then, I went for early morning rides with other fellows or with Miss McKellar – ran the Eye and Ear Department here until about 5:30 p.m. – went for strolls before dinner and printed photographs after dinner with Follit.

One morning we were told to discharge every available patient and make room for a trainload of sick from somewhere. There was a hum of excitement through the great building all day – preparations were made and all leave stopped. Mess was at 6 p.m. instead of 7 p.m. and about 7:30 p.m. a long white ambulance train drew in.

It is really very fine, this great hospital of ours. The railway line comes to our very back

Hospital train, Heliopolis, 1915

door. The train draws up not more than 10 paces from the hospital garden, having come direct from the coast at Alexandria. There were 15 or so motor ambulances waiting to convey the bed cases straight up to the door – and a vast crowd of Arabs and Egyptians pushing around the guard, full of curiosity to see the wounded!

The train stopped and the patients got out and carried their swags into the hospital on their backs! The ambulances returned to the garage empty!

These cases were 200 men who had been laid up in the 1st Stationary hospital for about four or five weeks with measles, colds, pneumonia, etc. and were now all sent to us for convalescence, so as to make room for wounded if necessary, over there.

The story the men have told us was this.

They belonged to the 3rd Brigade. This brigade (9th,10th, 11th, 12th battalions) had left here six weeks ago and proceeded to the island of Lemnos where they had remained ever since in their transport ships, taking an occasional route march on shore and then returning on board.

The harbour in which they were at anchor was large and deep, and filled with warships of the Allies, and about 100,000 troops on transports – English, French and Australians.

The 1st Stationary hospital was on the island in tents. (Le Messurier, Powell, etc.) and the horses were camped along the shore – also some Turcoes and Zouaves. The weather was bitterly cold, and the food on the transport was bad and the troop deck life monotonous and unhealthy.

For four long weeks they had remained thus, scores of them falling sick each day, and more and more transports arriving, with warships coming and going. All while the thundering of guns could be heard in the narrows where the Allied Navy was bombarding the forts. Lemnos is two hours' sail from the narrows.

Suddenly a Hospital Ship arrived, and took off the whole contents of the Stationary hospital. The ship steamed straight across the Mediterranean and its contents were entrained at Alexandria to Heliopolis where they arrived at our very door after three days' travelling from Lemnos.

The excitement subsided and we settled down again. Things were absolutely quiet for a week, and we had very little to do, although my ward of 55 beds was full of chronic discharging ears.

I then, foolishly, decided to improve the shining hour by taking up French again. I paid five guineas down at the Berlitz School, which gave me 30 lessons of one hour. I intended to have a lesson each day for a month.

I'd just had three lessons when things began to happen! Troop trainloads of sick arrived, in quick succession from Lemnos. The men brought with them the news that the troops were about to commence the landing at Gallipoli the day they left, so that by now (three days later) they must be in the thick of it!

The very next day, the first actual trainload of wounded arrived from the front! They were all quite slightly wounded, and told us that hundreds of the severely wounded had been kept at Alexandria – in a huge military hospital there, only the less severe cases being sent on to us. There were about 200 sent to us, so there must have been very heavy fighting!

Later the same night came another trainload – many of them with serious wounds! We were all working until 2 a.m. or later making them comfortable and dressing their wounds.

This was Saturday. The next day, Sunday, came the inundation! Trains started to arrive about midday, and wounded were pouring into the hospital all afternoon.

My whole ward together with all the medical and surgical cases that could be moved were sent down to Luna Park skating rink, about half a mile away, and I was ordered to go with them. I went down there and found absolute chaos! In a building which at 2 p.m. should have been absolutely empty except for a stack of Arab beds (made of light basketwork), there were, at 4 o'clock, 400 patients, medical, surgical, eye and ear, and about 80 wounded men. Our staff consisted of four nurses and two officers, Flecker (a poor simple fellow, who had been transferred to us from a Light Horse Regiment), and myself.

Flecker was an absolute blank! He went around asking men their names in a hopeless way, and finally about 7 p.m., gave up and went up to the palace for dinner.

I dashed about and wrote out requisitions for food, medicines and dressings, and rushed to and fro to the palace and got them. Imagine trying to keep peace single-handed among 400 men, convalescent and slightly wounded, when only 300 eggs were obtainable for their tea! It was with the utmost difficulty I could get anything for the poor devils at all!

There they were, all herded together in this huge hall, sick and wounded of every description – 400 of them! It was an awful task. The nurses worked like bricks, and later in the evening they all got into beds and, poor exhausted creatures, slept soundly.

At this juncture Ramsey-Smith turned up, the arch swine! He had the effrontery! – the colossal cheek! – *the damned insolence* to look around at the sleeping mass of men and remark, 'What a great thing it is to be ready. So well prepared was I for this crisis, so well made were my arrangements, that I have been able to sit quietly all afternoon and enjoy my afternoon tea'.

Oh the *pig*! The unfeeling, unmitigated *scoundrel*!

Here it was utter chaos! The most hopeless pandemonium! The rankest and most outrageous mismanagement with nothing ready, nothing prepared. Everything messed up, and in utter confusion. The preparations having been commenced while the patients were actually arriving, and that is how the swine speaks!

I had no dinner and got to bed at 2 a.m.

I got up at 5:30 a.m., and went down at Luna Park shortly after six. I supervised the men's breakfast, and they were all fed, and something like order obtained by 9:30 a.m., when Flecker arrived again and I got orders to return to the Palace, where I was criticised by Barrett for having taken matters into my own hand whilst Flecker was in command!

I suppose that was right, but I know that if I had not done so, those men would have starved for 24 hours, and not one of them would have received any medical or surgical treatment.

About nightfall of this day (Monday) trains began to arrive again! The surgical staff, with Syme away on a hospital ship, where he had gone about three weeks before, and Dunhill away on sick leave (he and family sailed for England on the *Malena* in the middle of the rush), was hopelessly inadequate to deal with the rush!

Major Maclean is senior surgeon, Bert Sutherland and Jack Tait being the other two. So utterly mismanaged was the thing that, at 7 p.m. on this Monday, Jack Tait found himself responsible, solely, for 250 wounded men – some of them desperately ill! The thing was absurd and impossible! I offered to do anything I could, and he handed 57 beds over to me.

They all filled up before 1 a.m., many of them with terrible wounds! I worked all night with them, and at 7 a.m. had a shave and a bath and went off to Luna Park. Here I fixed up my 50-odd 'eye and ear' cases, and then came back and ploughed through the outpatients. This kept me going until lunchtime. During the morning I had to discharge all but seriously wounded cases to Luna Park. This left me with about 30 empty beds. I worked amongst the wounded the whole afternoon, and about 9 p.m., another train arrived. My 30 beds were again filled, and I worked at them until about 3 a.m., and then went to bed exhausted.

Next morning (Wednesday) I was up at 6.30. Had breakfast at 7 and went around my Luna Park cases from 8 until 9.30 a.m. I came back and did some dressings before outpatients arrived. I saw out-patients then until lunchtime, and did dressings and extracted bullets until dinner at 7 p.m. At 8 I started operating, which I continued until 11 p.m.

One case had a bullet in his skull above the ear, pressing on his labyrinth causing vertigo. I had shown the case to Barrett who absolutely funked it, and ordered me to report it to Maclean as Chief of Surgical Staff. This I did, and Maclean told me to operate at once!

Next morning, Barrett happened to notice this man in the ward and asked the Sister when had Maclean operated on him. Sister said that I had done it the previous night and removed the bullet. Barrett sent for me in a rage and asked me how dared I operate on 'his case' without permission! I reminded him that he had ordered me to hand the case over to Maclean, so that it then became his case, and stated that I received orders from him to operate, which I had done. He told me I had absolutely no right to have done so, and that this was nothing short of impertinence! What could I say?

He went off to the Colonel (the swine, I mean), who sent for Maclean and told him to appoint a man to take over my ward. Maclean said he appointed me and had every confidence in me. Smith said that he would not allow the appointment, as I am Major Barrett's assistant, and shall hold no other position at present.

Thus on Thursday morning at 10:30 a.m. I found myself no longer a surgeon, merely assistant to the Eye and Ear Department, with about 50 cases at Luna Park and a few outpatients.

I nearly wept! I swore till I was hoarse. *If only that hound Barrett and his fellow fiend would die and I could jump on their dirty corpses!*

After lunch I found myself with nothing to do, although the whole hospital was standing on its head with work, and as short-handed as it could be!

I met Flecker in a corridor. He had been recalled from Luna Park, and Brown sent there in his place. He was another derelict, without a job, and we started to yarn. I told him how I longed to be transferred to a regiment, but where was I likely to find a man who would change places? To my amazement he instantly gave me two names of medical officers of Light Horse regiments whom he thought would like to change into a base hospital!

I almost embraced him, took down the names and rushed off for my belt and helmet. On the way I met poor old Follit, whose troubles I shall speak of in a moment. I told him the great news, and he and I shook hands and we sallied forth to interview these men.

The first was Campbell of the 8th Light Horse. Oh no! It was quite a mistake – he did not wish to change!

Our hearts fell into our boots. With a hopeless feeling, we sought out the other man, Betts, of the 9th Light Horse. To our joy, he hopped at it, and was as keen as mustard. We fed the fire with judicious and tactful eulogies of the manifold advantages of base hospital. Yes, he would exchange!

And now my heart sank into my boots. Here was dear old Follit, my best friend, in a far

Claude's best friend, Follit, at the hospital

Major Argyle

worse plight than myself. Wretched as I am, how can I take the thing and leave him in that dreadful predicament? No! He would not hear of it! It was absolutely my own affair, I had discovered the nugget and he would not dream of taking it from me. I insisted, and said I would not apply anyhow, so he had better take the opportunity. Finally he agreed.

Endless interviews and negotiations followed, and finally at midday today – Sunday – he was transferred from the 1st Australian General Hospital to the 9th Light Horse Regiment.

They leave for the front in about a week, so he is just in time. I am glad – delighted to have got him out of the hole he was in – but I must say, it was a sacrifice! For I long and yearn to get out into a regiment – out of the clutches of this arch pig Barrett! I'm going to shift into Follit's room when he goes – it has a bathroom attached. I shall miss the old boy most terribly. He has been a true and splendid friend to me – my only real friend here. He is a fine young man of strong character. A gentleman to the core.

And now I am left with scarcely anything to do. I am getting rid of the Luna Park patients day-by-day. There are only about 15 left now, and they are all chronic.

Barrett has about a dozen beds here at the palace for wounded eyes; they are mostly beyond saving. He has done six extractions in the last two days, without offering to let me do one! And I have done the whole of his work for three solid months!

I have felt pretty knocked out the last two days, and have had a good deal of diarrhoea – but am better now. Today, Sunday, I got through my absurdly small amount of work by 11 a.m. and have loafed ever since. I took a run out to the infectious hospital at Abbassa after lunch in an ambulance car to see poor old Kay, who has had scarlet fever for the past six weeks. He is all right again now and will be back quite soon.

Argyle has been away for about three weeks. The lucky beggar was sent to Lemnos to fix up an X-ray plant in the Stationary hospital.

A train arrived last night and another is expected tonight. Poor Major Maclean is laid up with a septic finger, making our surgical staff weaker than ever – so that fellows are coming in from the field ambulances and lending a hand.

Spent the evening on the terrace with Sutherland and a few Light Horse officers listening to the music and watching the cinema. About 11 p.m., the train arrived. I did not even go downstairs, so disgusted was I at not being allowed to participate.

Major Argyle accompanied the wounded back from the front – he is brimful of interesting experiences.

10 May
Monday

I was given a little surgical job, 'assistant to Furber', who has 35 beds. Furber is quite a boy, a perhaps a year my senior in medicine, but he is a very decent chap, so I pocket my pride and make the best of things. Nothing occurred worthy of mention. Another train arrived this afternoon, and Furber and I only got four cases – all slight wounds.

Vincent Riddell is here, shot in the shoulder. He is doing all right. Jim Borrowman was a patient of mine with a bullet in the shoulder, which I took out. He is all right. Colin Johnson is here with a bullet in the thigh – he is improving.

There is too much desperately interesting material all round me to be able to write it down, but I shall try to jot down briefly some of the more striking stories when they occur to me.

Heliopolis
16 May 1915

My own darling Mum

I'm so sorry I must only write a short note tonight, for I am dreadfully tired. If I were to try to write a decent letter, I should fall asleep in the middle. It has been a very, very hard week – but a splendid one – and most enjoyable.

Each hospital train that arrives brings a load of these heroes, whom I shall never cease to admire and respect. The bravest, finest fellows in the world; all as cheerful and happy as though they had just returned from a football match, when in fact, they've come from the most awful massacre you can imagine.

The two remarks one is continually hearing on all sides as we tend these ghastly wounds are 'Oh but I'm all right,' and, 'How long will it be before I can get back to the trenches?'

The stories they tell of the charges in the face of a hailstorm of bullets and that fearful shrapnel – the rescues of each other – the bravery of their mates – (never themselves do they mention) – the suffering and pain and misery – all told with bright, eager faces and cheery smiles. Oh Mother, I am proud to be an Australian!

These stories are too many, and I am too deadbeat to write them tonight. If I only had time, I should write them up in my diary – but I never have a spare moment for that nowadays.

One tale I will just briefly tell. My patient was shot through the thigh. A nasty gaping wound. He and his mate were the sharpshooters of the regiment, and had crept forward in the low scrub in front of the trench to try to get a clear view of the Turks. After crawling about 50 yards, they came to a stretch of open country, which had to be crossed.

They waited for a little lull in the incessant fire, which was being poured into the trench behind them, and then both rose together, put their heads down and made a dash across the open stretch.

Immediately there was a roar of fire, and my patient's mate fell with his arm shattered. He shouted that he was hit! My patient stopped, turned back and ran towards him. When about 10 feet from him, he too fell, shot through the thigh!

The two of them lay there in that open patch in front of the trench which was about 80 yards away, in a storm of bullets, which cut up the grass, and ploughed up the ground all around them. My patient urged his mate to keep still, but he could not help rolling about, for the agony of his smashed arm.

They lay there, waiting second by second for another wound, in the centre of a hail of bullets; shrapnel bursting all round them, and in full view of their mates in the trench! Presently, a young sergeant came along the trench, looking for these two men. The soldiers in the trench pointed them out to him, lying out in the open. The Sergeant calmly took a rope, stepped out of the trench, and dashed across to the two men, in the face of the withering fire, which the Turks kept up on the trench!

He reached them without being hit, seized the man with a shattered arm, and dragged him towards the trench. He then tied the rope around his waist and flung the end into the trench, into which his mates hauled him. The sergeant then dashed again to where my patient lay alone in the clearing, put him on his shoulders, and staggered back into the trench with him, where he arrived in safety without a scratch!

My patient says that as the sergeant carried him to the trench, the bullets whistled around them, over their shoulders; between their legs; spurted up the sand in front of and behind them, and how it was that they were not both killed by a dozen or more bullets each, he cannot understand!

He says that he will never forget how that young sergeant saved their lives, and that he was a true hero! The men in the trench cheered wildly as he stepped into the trench with his burden, and his Colonel who had watched the incident, sent for him and told him that the deed would not be forgotten!

The sergeant's name is Jack Duffy, from Victoria, and he is slight and dark – that is all the information I can get about him, but he sounds very like my brother Jack's room mate in Trinity, although I do not even know if he has come to the war.

This is only one of the many such stories of bravery and heroism among our splendid men!

I have a ward of 63 beds, crammed full of wounded. I am all day long doing dressings, setting fractures, extracting bullets and doing operations. I do all of Barrett's work, as he is always out – calling on the Generals and the Sultan, etc. – interviewing Brigadiers, and taking business trips to various parts of Egypt … This entails rushing to various parts of the hospital to have consultations with the other officers when their patients' wounds involve the eyes or ears, and also attending to a small ward of 15 beds, containing nothing but wounded eyes.

So you see, I am going hard all day long, and when a train arrives – which nearly always happens at night – I get mighty little sleep. However I'm perfectly well, and proud to be able to help these poor beggars.

My dear old friend Follit went off at 2 a.m. this morning to the trenches with the 9th Light Horse who are going as infantry. He is a splendid fellow and a true and genuine friend. I shall miss him dreadfully. He is a brave fellow, and will be invaluable to the regiment. By this time he will be almost in earshot of the guns! I am anxious about him – he does not know fear, and will never think of himself!

I tried to get Jack and Max to run up to Cairo from Suez, and catch the boat again at

Port Said, but they could not manage it, and have gone on to England, without my seeing them. I was terribly disappointed, but got long letters from them. They both seemed very happy, have had a ripping trip.

Thank you so much Mum darling for the handkerchiefs. They were most awfully nice, and just what I was wanting.

I am going to bed now, so good night my darling old Mum.

With love to the Elder family.

From Claude

26 May

Another long period since I last wrote up this diary. I am getting lazier day by day over writing.

I am writing now in the little eye surgery on the ground floor. The coolest spot in a whole building. I have left the rest of the diary upstairs in my room on the 3rd floor, and so I cannot see where it was exactly that I left off. However, I remember that the weather was reasonably cool, and that I was without a surgical ward of my own, doing nothing but eye work and watching the Barrett swine doing extractions while I gave the anaesthetic – besides assisting Furber.

For several days I had a very little to do, and everyone else was frightfully busy. I got more and more restless and disgusted, and finally, after pestering Barrett and Maclean continually, I had my old ward returned to me.

I found 20 empty beds – the convalescent and slightly wounded cases having been sent off to Luna Park the day before. The ward was handed over to me at 7 p.m. At 8 p.m. a train came in and I had all my empty beds filled at once, some of them being desperate cases!

These men were all Territorials, mainly Lancashire Fusiliers. The poor beggars had a dreadful time at the hands of the Australian AMC! Most of them had been wounded eight days before, had been dressed by the regimental medical officer in the field; had lain on the beach for 48 hours waiting for a hospital ship; had then been moved to the ship, which lay off at anchor waiting for more wounded, and finally crossed the Mediterranean to Alexandria and entrained for Heliopolis.

While on the ship, they lay crowded together on the iron deck, with a life belt for a pillow –1700 of them, with only two medical officers to look after them! Naturally only a picked few of them were even looked at on the boat.

When I took down their dressings that night, I found the wounds foul, stinking and neglected, and in a filthy condition, and the men exhausted and worn-out. I worked hard at them, but their troubles were not over yet!

After they had been in bed about one hour, orders came that another train had arrived, and room must be made for the bad cases! All the less severely wounded of the new arrivals, who had at last been made comfortable, and who, quite exhausted, had mostly fallen into a deep sleep, were again hauled out of bed, placed in a motor ambulances and packed off in the night air to Luna Park where they would get scant attention, poor food, and be crowded like sardines. By the time I had been through the lot, it was 4 a.m.

Next day, I was up at 6.30, and went through my Luna Park cases before breakfast, after which I did my wards up here at the Palace, and saw eye out-patients until 11 a.m. Then I went into my wards were I spent the rest of the day trying to clean those fearful stinking wounds, and operated like mad, extracting bullets, opening abscesses and amputating fingers, etc.

At 10 p.m. I had just finished at the ward, when more cases arrived from the front! I had then six empty beds, and all were at once filled with very bad cases. I got to bed at 2 a.m.

Up again in early, and saw Luna Park Clinic before breakfast. I worked hard all day as before, and sent to Luna Park all those who were, after dressing and attention, such as extraction of bullets, able to walk and look after themselves.

By 9 p.m. I had finished, and then was told that another train was expected at midnight!

I was very tired, but was afraid to lie down for fear of sleeping. At 1 a.m. the train arrived. I had three empty beds, and stood about and watched the patients streaming into other people's wards, expecting each one to go to mine.

The process was endless. I was aching all over. I thought, 'Well I would sit down for a while in the eye surgery, and visit my ward every few minutes so as to receive the cases when they arrived'. It was dark and quiet in the eye surgery and the chair was comfortable.

Next thing I knew, it was striking 4 a.m.! I listened. All was quiet; the patients in bed, the staff retired hours ago! I crawled round to my ward feeling like a worm! Yes my beds had been filled – no one could find me, so they had got Furber, who had been working like a nigger himself, to fix them up for me!

From that day until this, there have been no more trains, and no more wounded admitted! The fighting has been bad; the casualties heavy, and other hospitals, such as Alexandria, etc. have been crammed – but we have been left severely alone!

Day by day the weather has got hotter and hotter and is getting nearly unbearable, with scorching sun and blasting winds howling over the desert.

The wounded are slowly improving – the stench has somewhat abated. I still have to operate almost daily to keep them all draining. They're nearly all fractures of some bone or other, sometimes several, and are all filthy and septic and foul, owing to the initial neglect. All are healing badly and improving far too slowly, whilst the general health of the patients is getting weaker and more feeble, owing to the awful heat.

Two men in particular, one with a bullet wound in the buttock which penetrated the ileum and has given rise to an abscess inside the pelvis, near the rectum, and one with a fearful comminuted fracture of the femur near the trochanter. Both are dying of sepsis and exhaustion, and all through the long scorching days, with a perfect storm of flies around them, these fellows lie gasping for breath in a bath of sweat.

Since, owing surely to selfish motives of fame and kudos, the authorities insist upon our remaining in this awful climate, and these disgracefully unsuitable conditions for a hospital – albeit in a palace, with every convenience (on paper) and fitted out in such a splendid and lavish scale. Since this must be so, thank God they have just enough respect for the lives of Australian soldiers not to send us more wounded, for they will die, without a shadow of a doubt, any that are bad when they get here will die from the exhausting effects of this fearful climate.

6 June

I take up the thread of this narrative sitting alone in my little eye surgery in my shirtsleeves this hot Sunday afternoon.

Last time I was writing I remember was just before the reinforcements arrived. The *Kyarra* came in, bringing us scores of nurses and three officers – Major Ramsay-Webb, Captain O'May and Captain Frank Wheatland. My surgical ward was forthwith handed over to Major Webb, and I became once more, the assistant oculist.

Barrett went away for two days to inspect the *Kyarra*, and two medical officers and six nurses had to be found to take the *Kyarra* home full of wounded. The officers were to be Pigeon and Storey – the latter from No. 2, who was anxious not to go if he could find a substitute.

Being heartily sick of Barrett, eye work, Egypt and the 1st AGH, and all belonging to it, and having no good friend since Follit left, and apparently nothing to look forward to but eye work to end of the war, I sent an application to the DMS Egypt, asking for the position.

I went over to No. 2 at Gazereh that evening to speak to Colonel Martin, who has considerable influence of with the DMS, to try and get his support – but he was out.

Next morning Barrett came home and sent for me at once.

'I hear Morlet, that you have applied for a ship home – is that so?'

'It is sir, and I intend asking for your support in the matter'.

'That's all very well, but I can't get on without you – who is going to do the eye work?'

'Why sir, I am not an eye specialist. Any of the officers here can do as well as I can.'

'They have not the experience. No, it's no good Morlet, you shall continue the eye work until I have no further need for you.'

'And when is this likely to be sir?'

'When I can procure a substitute for you from amongst the eye specialists in Melbourne – probably in about three months.'

'Well sir, I have been hard at it now for five months, with only two days' holiday and the work is heavy. May I have an assistant from amongst the reinforcements just arrived?'

'Yes, I will send you a man, and you can instruct him, but he won't be any good for some time yet.'

And thus my dream was quashed! Next day however, Frank Wheatland was sent around to the eye surgery, where I was at work, to report to me for duty. So now there are two of us, and I spend a lot of time teaching Frank. For I feel that if ever I am to be liberated from this loathsome job, it will be through the medium of this Assistant. It was just an inspiration, my asking for one!

16 June

I am free! I can hardly yet believe it!

This morning Barrett sent for me and told me to report myself at once to Colonel Maudesley. He seemed to be in a rage. I went at once, wondering what the blazes had happened!

Maudesley was in his room. He got me to sit down and proceeded to say that Turnbull was being sent to Alexandria to take command of a convalescent hospital which was being opened there, and that I was to take over his work here!

Me, to take over the work of an experienced physician who has been doing a major's work for months! With absolute command of 75 beds! It took my breath away!

The dear old chap proceeded to tell me with a smile how it was that he got me. He said, 'I went to see Barrett, and told him that it was necessary for you to be attached to the medical staff, as Turnbull was leaving.'

'Can't be done.' Says Barrett. 'I require Morlet in the Eye and Ear Department'

'But,' I said, 'You have already an officer there, Captain Wheatland – you cannot require two assistants'.

'You'll have to find someone else,' says Barrett. 'Morlet has got to instruct Wheatland in the work.'

I said, 'Morlet is not the Oculist of the hospital. It is the Chief's duty to instruct his assistant.'

This simply bowled Barrett out! The result is, I have this morning bidden farewell to the Eye Department *forever!*

Praised be the Lord!

Heliopolis
6 June 1915

My darling Mum
This will not reach you I know, for about six weeks, but I cannot let anyone go back to Australia without sending something home. Captain Pidgeon, who is taking the box for me, used to play tennis in Jack's Pennant team at University. He is a ripping chap!

I sent in an application to go back with him in the *Kyarra* in charge of wounded, but Barrett cannot do without me until he gets another oculist to take my place.

Do you know Mum that 1,000 wounded have been admitted within the past two days! To this place alone, and we are the far-back base of all, and only get wounded when all the other hospitals on the lines of communication are full.

So there must had been a fearful action within the last week! We get little or no news – the men can only tell us of incidents happening immediately around them, but know nothing of the actual situation of the forces. You hear far more than we do, away over there, for all sources of news are muzzled and gagged here, as Egypt teems with spies!

Now, about the contents of this box. The brass work is typically Egyptian work. I bought it all down in the native bazaar or 'Muski' in Cairo. It is brass, inlaid with silver and copper, and all absolutely handmade – one can watch them doing it here in the bazaar.

I want you and Lucile to have which you fancy of bowl and jug. The little ashtray is for Stanley, and the tiny Cleopatra's Needle (obelisk) – a mere trifle, but I saw it made – is for Miss Turner. Please tell her not to imagine I'm giving her a present, it is so absurdly small. It is merely a little idea, as it were, of the genuine Egyptian Muski.

I wish you could come with me Mum, as I rambled down that marvellous place. I cannot describe it, as I should be writing for a week, and then give you no idea of it.

The little necklace is for my dear little blue-eyed niece from her 'Uncoo Cord'.

The little sarcophagus I am sending to little brownie Katrine, it opens, and the tiny mummy is inside.

To my baby boy, whom I have never seen, I'm sending the tie pin, which is 'the Key of Life' – the emblem of eternity, which the king of gods, 'Ahmen Ra', is always depicted as holding. May the little man have a long and happy life and be a credit to his father – a chip off the old block.

I'm sending him, as well, what the Arab in the bazaar called 'Moses in the bulrushes'.

The tiny box opens and you will find Moses inside.

Well, Mum dear, I must stop and go around my ward before the heat gets too great.

Young Lieutenant Cook (you call lieutenants 'Mister' when addressing them) is taking some paintings for me. There are really splendid, and give you an excellent idea of the warm glowing tint which the sunlight on the desert throws up over everything.

The pyramids look exactly like this painting, soon after sunrise in the morning from the roof of the palace here, about 15 miles away. The blue of the Nile is very true too, showing the shadowy mists, which arise in the evening and obscure the banks in a bluish haze.

They will, all my life, bring back vividly to my mind the life in Egypt.

Love to all.
Claude

P.S. Mr Cook is a medical student. He is a nice fellow, and was given to me as an assistant in the eye work. He has been closely associated with me ever since we arrived, and has become invaluable to me, learning the work quickly and conscientiously. I shall miss him a lot.

Cook will be able to give you vivid stories of the eye department, should you be able to meet him. C.

17 June

My new ward is going to be a success I am sure. I like the nurses, and am revelling in treating sick men and watching them get well.

I had not taken over my new duties more than half an hour when I had a tragedy! Turnbull had intended to lumbar puncture a man of whom he suspected of some cerebral trouble, but had been too busy in the end to do it.

While I was in the ward, doing my first round, this chap became violent. Only having some vague information about him from Turnbull before he left and not really knowing anything about the case at all, except that Turnbull was going to puncture him, I did it on the spot to quieten him. To my horror, he dropped back dead! I artificially respired him for half-an-hour but it was no good!

I had a horrid feeling that the confidence of the patients and more especially, the nurses, in their new officer would be shaken by this, although I quite understood that this is a thing that happens on rare occasions and is absolutely unavoidable. The post mortem showed a huge abscess in the temporal lobe of his brain – so I was then quite relieved!

After having my ward for about 10 days, we were suddenly inundated with about 30 new officers from Australia – reinforcements!

A complete re-arrangement of the staff of the wards took place. I was quite sure I would be turned out of mine, or that someone would be put in charge and I made the assistant. This is done universally throughout the hospital.

My old surgical ward is now in the hands of Major Wells and three captains as assistants. The Eye department contains three captains beside the great *Lieutenant Colonel* (JWB). To my surprise and joy, I had been left undisturbed, in absolute command of my big ward. While assistants had been supplied all over the place, there are still lots of officers doing nothing.

I wonder how long it will last? They say still more reinforcements are expected later on ...

Heliopolis
20 June 1915

My darling Mum
News of Jim! He's all right; well, strong, and untouched.

Some wounded or have just come in this afternoon from the 14th. The regiment is resting in a valley out of the firing line. Jim has been promoted to sergeant and has been in the thick of it. He was, for 17 hours, left by accident with another man in a corner of the trenches, while his regiment retired and was there under the most fearful fire, in one of the hottest corners of the campaign! Jim came through unscathed, and is resting with his regiment.

They said the weather over there is jolly pleasant, with occasional showers. The men are well fed, better than they were while in camp here at the base, and they occasionally get vegetables and fresh milk in the trenches! There is little happening there, our men just holding their trenches and waiting, presumably until French and British come up from the Point of the Peninsula on our right.

Irregular and half-hearted fire is kept up by the Turks on our trenches, but except for the ever-present snipers, many of who are Germans, and really good shots, there are very few casualties amongst our men. Our artillery has got off very lightly, and is suffering very little at all.

There are said to be already too many medical officers over there, but if I do ever have the luck to go, I will cable you in good time before I leave.

My poor batsman, lance-corporal Falconer, is being invalided home! His health has broken down in this fearful climate, and he is looking thin and miserable. He has been laid up for about a month. He has cared for me very well and is a good fellow. I'm very sorry to lose him.

There really is no more news to tell you Mum dear. It is fearfully hot here, but tomorrow is the longest day, thank goodness! There are two more months of hot weather – but we never know what two months will bring forth in these days, do we?

The battalions of a third contingent have arrived in the desert. George Cole is Medical Officer of the 24th. He is just the same as ever only thinner. 22 new medical men arrived here last week as reinforcements to our hospital. They have absolutely inundated us, and have arrived when everything is quiet and there is nothing to do, whilst six weeks ago we had to bear the brunt of that awful rush unaided. We have done all the work, and now they have arrived and have been given all best billets, our patients taken from us, now that we have practically cured them, and handed over to these blighters who, all these long months, have been living in the bosom of their families!

For myself I cannot growl. I have been very lucky! Hume Turnbull you know, was one of the senior physicians, and when he was sent away to take over an 800-bed hospital at 'Ras el Tin' in Alexandria, his work was handed over to me. I knew that reinforcements were coming, and quite expected to be deposed from my exalted position when they arrived. But to my surprise and gratification, Colonel Maudesley has left me unchanged, as one of the three senior physicians – responsible to no one for my work!

My ward contains 60 patients, but is capable of holding 70 at a pinch. I'm awfully lucky, because many men, such as Bert Sutherland, who are years my senior have been now placed in junior positions as 'Assistants' to the new officers. Most of them have only just joined the Army, and are in no way worthy of their senior position. This, I suppose, is 'the fortunes of war' – or gross favouritism, which is the same thing!

Fortunately, although I feel it keenly, it has in no way affected me, owing to the fairness and goodwill of Maudesley, and I feel sure, to the recommendation and support accorded me by Turnbull before he left. To both of them, I feel very grateful.

I am horribly jealous of these new men and do not like any of them. I always hate newcomers. Eight of them use my bathroom!

Dear old Major Stanley Argyle has been transferred to the 2nd the General Hospital at Gazireh. We miss him a lot.

Love to the children and Stan. With a hug for your darling self mum dear.
From Claude

10 August

To take up the thread of this journal again …

I'm still here in Heliopolis. That is my chief grief, and yet perhaps it is as well that my natural impetuosity has been curbed so long.

Reinforcements had been crowding in to this place, which now resembles a huge boarding house. Almost the entire staff has been standing around looking at each other and doing nothing but getting in at the road of the few who have been working. I have been left unmolested, in charge of my ward – and jolly busy I have been!

The weather has been fiercely hot and thousands of troops had been arriving every few days from Australia and going into camp in the desert nearby. The result is that every day, crowds of them are sick and are sent to hospital.

Summons, McDonald, and I have charge of all the medical wards and we take it in turn to 'receive'. Hence each 3rd day, anything from 20 to 30 more patients flood into my ward, suffering from heat stroke, diarrhoea, dysentery, influenza, tonsilitis, and also a few typhoid and meningitis cases.

I have lost a good many cases now and have had several sleepless nights with the poor beggars, but it is very seldom one saves a man with a medical disease, once he gets on the downward path – at least such is my impression with limited experience.

So, since I last wrote, my life has been just a quiet but busy base hospital existence – each day exactly like the last, ward work all morning, usually a sleep after lunch for an hour or two, then afternoon tea and ward until six or 6.30.

We have dinner at 7 p.m., and some form of mild recreation in the evening, such as a picture show, or a moonlight drive with a girl, etc.

Night round, and then bed about 12.

11 August [Claude's 27th birthday]

And now the rush has come!

Ever since the glorious landing, fearful massacre that it was, our troops have been sitting in the trenches, harassed day and night by shrapnel, sniped mercilessly, and falling sick by the hundreds with typhoid and dysentery.

Two terrible and fateful attacks had been made on Achi Baba – both failed, and everyone has been waiting and waiting for the advance that must come – and the awful carnage that will come with it. And now it has come!

About 5:00 p.m. on Saturday evening 7 August, after 24 hours bombardment by the guns of the fleet, our men advanced and attacked.

The 3rd Light Horse Brigade was utterly smashed!

The 4th Infantry Brigade was torn to pieces!

Hospital trains have been pulling in all day. Heliopolis is crowded with wounded.

13 August

Train after train for the last three days – still arriving every few hours – the palace and four auxiliaries crammed full – wounded all over the place – no news of my friends …

Today the OC sent for me. Barrett, Manifold and Ramsay-Smith were there also.

Barrett addressed me,

'Morlet. Do you want to go to Australia tomorrow morning?'

'No Sir, I want to go to the Dardanelles'.

'No chance of that my boy, you may go back to Australia if you like, but you must decide now. Will you go?'

'No Sir'

'Very good Morlet.'

I went out.

Does he take me for a snivelling shirker? Want to go back at a time like this? With my friends being killed and the poor beggars crying out for help? Good God!

It is now nearly a month since I sent a written application to General Ford, asking that I'd be sent forward to the Dardanelles. It was ignored.

Only a week ago, 10 medical officers were sent from this hospital to Gallipoli! As soon as I heard they were going, I went to Colonel Ramsey-Smith and asked him as a personal favour to let me be one of their number. He said the list was full, but I should have 'the next chance'.

And then I'm told today, 'There is no chance of that, my boy'.

Well, that's the fortunes of war! I shall do my best wherever I am – but oh, it is terribly hard to have to stay here. Well, well, I must make the best of it and, since they won't let me go, why I'll make the best of my life in dear old Egypt.

Since Ramadan, I am more resigned to base life than ever before …

Chapter 9

Ramadan 1915

This is a 'fast' for 'one moon' (30 days) in the faith of Islam. For this period, no Muslim may eat or drink or smoke between sunrise and sunset.

This you can imagine is a terrible trial, as the weather is fearfully hot at this time (July – August) and one sweats all day, especially if working out of doors.

At 7 p.m., just after sunset, the well-to-do families have a heavy 'breakfast', and another at big meal at 2 a.m., and they are therefore up most of the night.

Just before Ramadan started, Bert Sutherland, who has become my chief pal since poor old Follit left, made friends with one of our two dentists – a New Zealander named King. These two dentists, King and Logan, came with the 1st Contingent, and were then attached to New Zealand regiments. When we came along, they became attached to us.

They have always kept rather aloof from everyone, and seemed to know a lot of residents in Cairo and environs. This whetted the curiosity and envy of some of us, notably Sutherland and myself, so that after a while we chummed up with them – not wholly with disinterested motives I fear, and Bert and King soon became good pals. These two used to slip out in the afternoons, and I never knew, or enquired where they were going, until after a few days, Bert told me that there was something doing!

King is a most remarkable fellow – strikingly handsome, blue eyes, dark hair and a healthy fine skin. He is absolutely natural and simple in his manner, debonair, gay and reckless! The type of man, and I have not met many yet, who absolutely attracts the other sex like a magnet!

With this extraordinary power of his, he contrived to make the acquaintance of two families (cousins) of little Turkish girls. These girls are watched and hedged around with strict surveillance, so that they are absolutely unapproachable by any man, but more especially by Christians! They are never allowed out of the House except in black robes, veiled to the eyes, and attended by a eunuch. So you can imagine the extraordinary triumph this youth had in breaking through these impregnable defences!

Even thus protected, these girls are compelled to be indoors again before sunset all year round, with the exception of Ramadan, when everyone sleeps most the day, and wakes up and eats at night. During this month it is their custom to visit their friends, closely attended by their servants, between the two night meals.

Well, Dick King and Bert Sutherland, whom Dick soon initiated, managed to come across these girls once or twice in the afternoons before Ramadan, when they visited Mme Vignol, who had a beautiful garden in Heliopolis. Of course Dick made friends with Mme Vignol, and his visits coincided with theirs.

After several such meetings, I was taken into their confidence. Ramadan then commenced and plots were laid for moonlight trysts! The girls of one family, the El Bakris, would set out in their carriage to visit the other family, the El Sabbris, taking with them a picked servant – an old man, whom Dick had 'squared'.

In a deserted part of the road, we intercepted them in our large car. A rapid transhipment took place, and the journey was continued with all of us in our car. As we approached the El Sabbri's palace, we got out, and the car went on with its bevy of veiled beauty, returning soon with a reinforcement of the El Sabbris.

We then all packed into the car and made for the beautiful Gizeba gardens, where we sat in the moonlight – five girls and we three chaps – for a couple of hours, returning in the same manner, trans-shipping the El Bakris into their carriage, escorted by their old servant.

This little escapade was repeated every few nights all through Ramadan, and many are the pounds we spent on cars, and many the narrow squeaks from nearly getting caught! The little girls were simply charmed at the stolen freedom, and were in ecstasies of delight and expectation the whole of Ramadan! They had never so much has spoken to a Christian man before and though, with the exception of Dick, our fascinations were nil, yet we all consider ourselves gentlemen, and endeavoured to make their impressions of Australian officers at least favourable.

These children live a weird life. They sit indoors year after year and read and sew, and play the piano and study. The result is they are all highly educated and extremely well read. Eventually, their father gives them to some eligible Turk in marriage – they themselves having no say in the matter! They hate and loathe getting married – and are pleased if they do not actually dislike their husbands! Falling in love is a sensation unknown to them, as they are never allowed to see any of the other sex until each is handed over to a husband as though she were a package of goods.

They speak English, French, Turkish and Arabic fluently, and can discuss literature and history of all these nations with ease. In fact they're the most fascinating and attractive little companions. Besides, with barely an exception, being extremely pretty!

Sanieb El Bakri is my particular friend, with Liada El Sabbri a close runner-up.

With these moonlit parties, Ramadan soon slipped by and after one glorious night – the last night of Ramadan, in which we stayed out until 3 a.m. and ran all sorts of risks by taking the girls to a café in the middle of the night for supper, and peeping into a variety show theatre, both of which events fill them with wonder and astonishment – Ramadan drew to a close!

During the latter half of Ramadan, a lieutenant in the Egyptian police, who was a cousin of the girls – a young Turk named Hassan – joined our parties. He is a ripping little chap, and being a special favourite of the heads of the House of El Bakri, had been allowed, on certain rare occasions, to so far infringe his national social etiquette as to meet his cousins in their own house, when visiting his aunt. He had done this for years, and was the only man whom they had ever met. Hence they took him into their confidence, and he used to keep the moonlight trysts too, and we soon got to know and like the boy immensely.

On that last night of Ramadan we were so late that Hassan persuaded me to go home and stay the night with him, which I did. It appears he is an orphan, and well to do. He lives in a huge palace with tremendously strong walls, which is buried in the heart of Cairo. I could not find it again now to save my life!

My night in a Turkish palace, sleeping in a galabiyeh, on a bed as soft as a cushion, after a drink of Soabien, was unbelievable! Washing in the morning in the true Turkish fashion, a with a servant pouring water over me out of a kind of enormous brass teapot – and breakfasting on eggs, dry toast, cheese and Turkish coffee, without knives, forks and spoons. It was an experience I shall never forget!

This evening Bert and I are going down to see Mme Vignol, for Auld Lang Syne – Dick has gone down to Alexandria.
Ramadan finished on 10 August.

23 August
The 10 days have been replete with important events.

George Cole has got married! He has been tumbling further and further in love with that little pink-haired girl from Geelong, whom he got engaged to about three weeks ago, when she arrived in Egypt as a nurse of the 1st AGH. Last Tuesday night he informed me that they had orders from his battalion to hold itself in readiness to proceed to the front. Next day, he told me that he was going to get married the following day in Cairo, and that I was to be guest, and Green of the 23rd, Best Man.

At 11:30 am, George, Green and the Regimental Padre of the 28th turned up in my room, all in full uniform. I was decked out likewise, and very hot! After some refreshments we drove off to the Consulate, where we had an interminable wait for the bride and her friends. Finally they turned up with the bride conducted by her brother, a private in the Light Horse. After much introducing, etc. and signing of papers, we proceeded to the little St Andrews Presbyterian Church. Here they were married by the Padre; covered with confetti by us, and driven to Shepherd's Hotel, where we had a table decked with roses and lots of champagne.

Then we got into cars again and drove to the photographers, where we had group photographs taken. George and his Bride then went off for a long motor drive, and Green and I took the bridesmaids home. I got home in time for a bath, and then went out to afternoon tea with the De Lanker's, a Belgian couple that have been very good to old Kay and myself. I met them through him.

The next event of importance was as follows. JW Barrett sent for me to attend his room. I went in and found him as sick as a cat – thin and pale, and in bed. I got quite a shock, as I haven't seen him lately – he is always buzzing about in Cairo.

He said in a kind way. 'Morlet do wish to go to the front?'

I said, 'You know I do Sir'.

He said, 'Well, I'm willing to help you – what to do you suggest?'

I said, 'Give me a week's leave and an AMC pass, I shall go straight to the trenches and take my chance of finding a job over there.'

He said, 'You can't do it that way Morlet, but I might arrange for you to relieve someone who has been there for some time. Give me a written statement, stating your willingness to do so, and I shall arrange it by telegram.'

This I did within half-an-hour, and have been waiting for marching orders ever since!

Twenty-four hours after this it became known among us that the odious dynasty of Barrett and Ramsey-Smith, beneath whose tyranny we have cowered for 10 long months, had at last *fallen!!!* Ramsey-Smith has been recalled immediately to Australia!

Barrett has been stripped of his military positions and is to confine himself to Red Cross work, and even in this he is now under the surveillance of a Commission, sent from Australia to inquire into the management of it.

Our dear old Colonel Maudesley, the most popular man in the unit, is now OC. It is too *splendid!* We cannot realise it yet! Everyone is smiling and happy and there is an absolutely different atmosphere in the place.

Smith and Barrett bade no farewells! Neither of them had the grace to even speak of their impending departure at mess, nor to comment on the work we have done under them all these months! They both, quietly and silently slunk out of the Palace, and no one knew they were gone until mess that night!

Well! What about the extravagant promises made to me regarding going to the front? Before calling Barrett a cur, promising what he knew he could not fulfil, I shall wait a bit. Perhaps he did it among his last acts. Time will tell!

Last Saturday, Bert and I hired a car and driver, which drew up at a quiet corner, where a closed carriage containing four sweet little girls stopped and emptied its contents into said car, and then drove off. The car then took the Suez road, away out into the heart of the desert, which it followed for about five miles. It then stopped and waited. In due course it was overtaken by an 'Arabich' with Bert and myself – and a hamper containing afternoon tea!

We got to the desert tryst about 5:30 p.m., had tea, and a stroll over the endless sand, then drove back to Heliopolis, the girls being compelled to be home before sunset. This was our last 'desert picnic'!

2 September

A boat is just going back to Australia. I'm going to send back the diary up to date, by one of the Sisters. It is probable that I'm going up to the front in a few days …

Chapter 10

7 September [1915]

I'm on the train – off to the front at last! Volunteers were called for a week ago, and I at once offered myself, and was accepted! I've had an exciting time getting away and saying goodbye! I was put in charge of seven officers for the front and of course, made a howling mess of things by forgetting utterly, at the last moment, to say goodbye to the OC, Colonel Maudesley! I have felt a worm ever since leaving, and am thoroughly worried over it. I always was a scatterbrain!

Don't know where we're going after we reach the coast. Have been put in to an Officers' Clearing Camp to wait for a boat to take us across. Expect to leave on the 9th.

8 September

I'm in a tent with Gum Plant. Sand all over the place. Down my neck – in my mouth and eyes at every movement.

Went to town and visited Turnbull and Yuille at the convalescent hospital. Met Aberdeen there are who told us we could not take kitbags across. Had lunch at an Italian eating-house and went for a drive with McKenzie, returning about 5 p.m. and getting web equipment, I managed to pack about half my things in to this, which is all carried on the person, and I must leave the rest. Had a good dinner with five of the chaps at Carlton Hotel near our camp – we thought it would be our last in Egypt.

Alex is just teeming with military, camps, horses, French, English, Australian and Indian – the streets are drab with khaki, relieved by the red caps of the French soldiers everywhere.

9 September

A boat went this morning but we were left behind – no orders yet. Loafed on the beach until lunch.

Then unpacked and repacked my kit, and having decided to leave a lot of my things behind, I placed them in kit bags and took them into Alexandria to Turnbull's hospital. I had dinner there, and then went to see several games of Pelote in Alex. A wonderful game! Returned about 11:30 p.m.

The camp where we are now is at Carlton, quite close to Ramleh, in a stretch of sand in a hollow behind a hill, which separates it from the sea. It is just a Clearing Camp for the officers who have to wait a few days for transport to Gallipoli. It is very hot, with no breeze and ankle-deep in sand. Still no news of our departure.

10 September

I am still here at Alex in the sand, getting sunburnt and having a lazy time. I feel ashamed to go into Alex as I have only very rough service clothing, while the city teems with British officers in smart uniforms, this being the British and French base. If I had any idea that we will be kept waiting so long, I should have bought some nice uniforms with me, and left them here.

11 September

Orders have just come in that all officers shall take their base kits with them on leaving Alex. Sent a wire to Bert Sutherland to send my uniform case along. Spent the day swimming and loafing on the beach then went for a walk in the evening around Ramleh. Awfully pretty place, full of charming houses and gardens.

13 September

Still no orders, and running short of cash. Went to Pay Office and got paid up to date. Saw some officers off by the midday train to Cairo.

After lunch collected my uniform case and took it to Raz el Tin. Changed into a decent uniform and felt an 'officer and gentlemen' again. Had afternoon tea at Ras el Tin and watched a Hospital Ship come in from Gallipoli. She looked clean and beautiful.

Arranged to take a yacht with Turnbull and Max Yuille and go for a sail. Just before we started, got a telephone message that orders to embark at 10:00 a.m. the next morning had just come out. Arranged to stay the night at Raz el Tin, and gave up the sail. Went out to camp and arranged to have kit taken into the ship in the morning.

After dinner at Raz el Tin, went to the Pelote, simply because I had several pounds which it did not want to take to the trenches, so I decided to gamble. Staked it all at the Pelote with the intention of losing it, but won hands down!

Met Dick King and went to the Casino Bellevue for a while. Home at 11:30 p.m., and had my last sleep between sheets.

14 September

Had all my hair cut off. My scalp now bald, white and round – a disgusting spectacle!

After breakfast, said farewell to my friends at Ras el Tin, took my uniform case to Cook's, packed one kitbag with everything I could think of that is warm, and left the rest stored at Cook's.

Drove down to the boat with the bag, saw the rest of my kit on board, reported at the orderly room and found the boat did not leave until a sunset, so I went up town again. Wilcox, Henderson and I, with our rough service jackets and bald cropped heads, had lunch at the Savoy Plaza in luxury.

About 3 o'clock, Wilcox and I got a yacht and sailed around the harbour. There were five hospital ships and a hospital yacht, two British, and one French cruiser, a balloon ship, and two transports in the harbour. We sailed over to our transport, the *Orsonia* – a Cunard liner – an old fashioned wooden tub, which until recently was used as a cargo boat. A battalion of Canadians was embarking, so we left the yacht and watched the proceedings. Close to us alongside the wharf was a huge troop ship, just arrived from England, crammed with Tommies.

By about 6 p.m. we had everything on board – the last gun, horse and man – and then the Canadian band struck up aft. The boat now seemed to be literally crawling with troops. These consisted of a battalion of Territorials, Fusiliers and a Canadian battalion of Newfoundlanders – an English General and his staff, and a full Colonel and his staff – a New Zealand dentist, and we eleven Australian medical officers.

The boat is quite a small tub, and the poor men are packed like sardines. Wilcox, Plant and I have a cabin next to the engine room – stifling and uninhabitable!

The Newfoundlanders have had an awful time. Enlisting in October 1914, they were sent to Salisbury Plains to train. In December they were sent up to the north of Scotland to camp in the snow. In February 1915 they were brought down to Alexandria. Then they were sent to Malta, then to Lemnos, but not allowed to land – then to Alexandria and then back to Cairo, where they camped in the desert heat until embarking today! They are fine looking big men.

The Territorials, come originally from Malta, where they formed the garrison. They were sent last April, on the outbreak of hostilities in the Dardanelles, to Khartoum, where they have been sweltering in the unbearable heat of Upper Egypt all through this summer! Their officers are all handsome, well-groomed English youths, immaculately dressed with fancy socks, shoes, etc., and long, well combed hair. I was astonished at this at first, but I suppose, being thousands of miles from the war, they do not realise what they are going to. In a month's time, I expect they will all look as rough and untidy as I do myself.

At sunset, the big transport alongside us steamed out, her rigging and decks a mass of troops. It seemed odd that there were no goodbyes; no one to wave to. As she steamed past us, our band struck up 'It's a long way to Tipperary'. Half an hour later, we moved out.

We have a six-inch gun aft, and a machine gun mounted forward. Not a light on board – pitch darkness. In the dim starlight with a tiny moon, we laid out our beds on the deck and turned in at 9 p.m.

15 September
Wednesday

A beautiful day. The sea is as blue as the sky. Quite uneventful. We have been heading west-northwest all day. Tonight we are about 200 miles off our course, and have never once sighted the other troopship, which started only a half-hour before us. The cruise from Alexandria to Gallipoli is varied for almost every trip, in order to avoid submarines.

Some of the Fusilier officers have had their hair cut short today, and have been roundly chaffed by their more foolish mates. Purple socks are still however, well to the fore, although we shall soon be in earshot of the guns.

16 September

Another glorious day, sunny and warm, but with a cool breeze. The sea was more blue than anything I ever saw, and as calm as a pond. Spent the day reading, sleeping and eating. Today we should be in sight of land, but saw none all day. We have been taking a most erratic course ever since we left Alex. The Territorials are still shamefacedly getting their hair cut, but the creases in their trousers are wonderful to behold!

We must be somewhere near the south coast of Greece, I should say by now. At night every porthole is covered over, and every spark of light on board is extinguished. Smoking not allowed on deck.

The food is remarkably good, and really we are having a most enjoyable and comfortable trip around the Mediterranean! Had we gone direct, we should have been in Lemnos tonight. But it seems we shall be about 48 hours late, owing to the deviations.

17 September

Woke this morning to find a driving mist. The air was sharp and cold. After breakfast it

Claude preparing to leave Heliopolis for Gallipoli

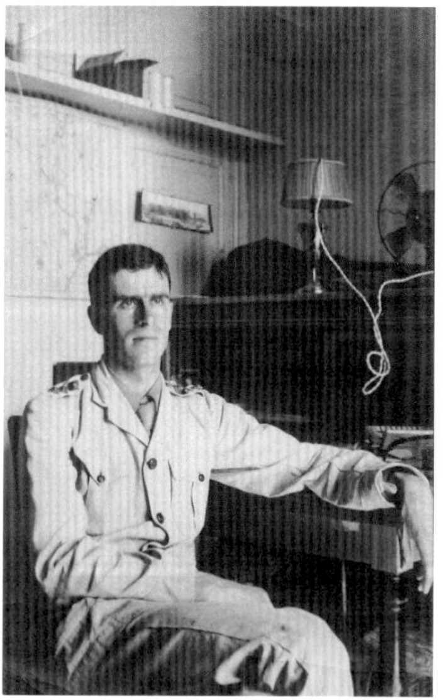

Two studies of Claude ready to leave for 'the Front', 1915.
Left, from Dr Stanley Argyle's war diary; right, taken by Captain Kay, September 1915

actually started to rain! It is over eight months since I have seen rain.

During afternoon the sun came out, and we sighted land. All evening we were threading our way in and out of the most charming rugged little islands – many of them with villages and settlements. From the course we have been holding lately, we judge them to be somewhere to the southeast of Greece.

That night a stiff breeze got up and we pitched a good deal. It was now quite cold and I had a muffler on for the first time since the *Kyarra* days. During the night a destroyer hailed us, and fastened her searchlight on us. There was a good deal of excitement, and the sailors stood by the boats. However, she seemed satisfied, and steamed away into the darkness.

18 September
Saturday

This has been the most impressive day I have experienced since leaving Australia.

Coming on deck about 7 a.m., I found land quite close on one side, while on the other, a huge battleship grimly watched us pass. It was a most beautiful still sunny morning, with a hazy mist hanging over the horizon. The sea was dead calm and deep blue. The land alongside which we were gliding was the now world famous island of Lemnos. Coming on deck again at 8 a.m. after breakfast, we found ourselves creeping slowly up to the entrance of Mudros Harbour, and among quite a number of small steamers of various sorts, coming or going.

The harbour at first glance seemed to be wide-mouthed and crescent-shaped, containing a score or more ships of various kinds – three or four hospital ships – a few transports (empty) and number of small craft. Three destroyers and two torpedo boats were in view. One of the latter dashed up to us and gave some orders through a megaphone, after which, we proceeded slowly into the harbour.

It soon became evident that there was more to this harbour than met the eye. As we crept on, approaching the centre of the crescent, a point of land jutting out formed a corner, from behind which, ominous heavy clouds of smoke arose. Reaching the corner, we found a boom right across the harbour with just a narrow gap sufficient for one boat to pass through. Traversing this, we rounded the corner. A wonderful sight lay before us! Stretching away inland, we now found a vast expanse of still blue water, which seemed to be just one mass of warships! Huge, silent, grey, and bristling with guns. Their decks all cleared for action; some of them belching black smoke as they lay in every direction still, silent, and ready!

Slowly, into the crisp bright morning we glided on, threading our way in and out between these monsters. It was very impressive – the silence of this great fleet, crowded together in this little harbour, their immense hulls not a stone's throw apart; quiet and motionless. Scarcely a word was spoken on our ship. The 2000 men crowding the decks were gazing silently at this tremendous concentration of strength.

Soon we found ourselves around another bend, and at the end of the harbour, now surrounded by transports and a hospital ship. The shore around us consisted of barren looking hills dotted with clumps of houses and white patches of tents. We were told there was no prospect of our going ashore, so we settled down for another day on board. After lunch, many of the men dived overboard to swim in the clear blue water.

We spent the afternoon sitting about and sleeping. During mess, the Fusiliers Band struck up on deck, playing bright tunes while we ate. Presently the General arose and gave the toast of 'The King'. We rose to our feet and the band on deck played the National Anthem with slow solemnity.

All the afternoon as we sat on deck, guns could be heard thundering in the distance – the first guns I have heard in this war, and I think most of us experienced a little thrill as we listened to the distant sullen boom! The men were issued ammunition, and the news went round that the Newfoundlanders were to land at Suvla in the morning and go straight into action!

The scene after dark, I shall never forget. The harbour was alive with ships' lights, and the hospital ship made a charming picture, with a row of green lights from stem to stern above the waterline, and with the conspicuous cross of brilliant red lights above the centre of the line.

The night was absolutely still, with a brilliant half-moon spreading a broad silver path on the still water, mingling with soft green and red reflections of the hospital ship lights. The Newfoundlander's band took turns with the Fusiliers, and the merry tunes crashed out over the still water, covered with brilliant lights reminding one of some water carnival, or perhaps Sydney Harbour. It is hard to believe that only 40 miles away are the trenches, and that this is the eve of a battle! The men cheered and clapped and whistled after each rousing tune, drowning the faint distant roar of the guns with laughter and noise. Echoing over the water came the lilting air of 'Cock of the North'.

It is pitiful to think that by sunset tomorrow many of these fellows will be dead, and a number maimed and in agony.

The revelling lasted until 9:30 p.m., when silence settled over the charming scene, while many brave men slept their last sleep on this earth in the peaceful silver light of the moon.

And still the distant thunder of guns.

19 September

This morning the Newfoundlanders went off to the trenches, cheering, and in good spirits. It was a beautiful still warm day, and the sea was like a pond.

We have been sitting on deck most of the day waiting for orders. About midday, four of us got a boat and pulled over to the hospital ship. Their officers welcomed us and showed us over. Most interesting.

Had a swim in the afternoon and at dinnertime, got orders to proceed to Anzac, where we are under fire from the moment we land!

The wind got up in the night, and it was mighty cold. The wind blew the sounds of the guns towards us, making them more distinct.

I slept dreaming of battle and murder.

20 September
Monday

This morning the wind is very strong and the sea rough. Soon after breakfast, we received orders to be ready to board the ship's pinnace by 1 p.m., for transport to Anzac.

About midday, was told that owing to rough weather, only a limited amount of kit could be landed, so once more, unpacked everything and arranged so as much as possible could be crammed on person. I had two suits of underclothing on, when suddenly, orders were cancelled, and we all have to stay at Lemnos! Five of us to go to the 1st Stationary hospital and six to the 2nd Stationary hospital.

Major Macdonald, McKenzie, Plant, Wilcox and myself formed a party for the 1st. The other six for the 2nd.

Well, in bitter disappointment, we boarded the launch and went ashore. The first three men I met where Alf Alcorn, Le Messurier, and Verco and it really was nice to be shaken so warmly by the hand, and welcomed generously and cordially! After the greeting they told us that they were in the act of packing up, to proceed to the Front at Suvla Bay.

The Clearing Hospital has died out – every one of its officers is either sick or dead, except one, Major Gordon, who sits there on the beach at Anzac alone in the midst of the shrapnel.

With winter coming on, it is necessary to have a hospital at the Front, so No. 1 Australian Stationary is under orders to double its staff of officers and to proceed to Suvla Bay. So we seem to have fallen after all on our feet!

I'm going to be in a tent with Fred Le Messurier. There is no one, bar old Follit who is at the Front, with whom I would rather be quartered. After afternoon tea, Verco took me for a ride. This Island it is a most wonderful place! I never dreamt that it was such a centre of enormous activity. Looking out over the harbour, it reminds one exactly of one of the busy shipping centres of the world. The Thames could not be more crammed with shipping of all sorts.

Battleships and cruisers are everywhere, torpedo boats, submarines, destroyers and monitors all over the place. The harbour branches in arms and bays in all directions, just like Sydney Harbour, and the Island consists of rugged hills and valleys interspersed with many smooth, rounded elevations – now barren and bare, but they say, green and fertile in the winter.

The inhabitants are Greeks – dirty looking devils with dusky faces (possibly due to dirt). Queer square-looking fur headdresses and black stockings. Nearly all the young women were shipped away from the island on arrival of the troops (which is a mercy). There are now all men, or old hags and children. They are living in villages made of stone and plaster – filthy, untidy and ramshackle. They have some beautiful orchards and plantations, and ride about on donkeys and mules, and herd sheep and goats about the barren hills. As in Egypt, there are no fences.

It is however the military aspect of the place that is so interesting. Thousands of troops are camped around the harbour – British, French, Indians, Australians and New Zealanders. Everywhere there is a scene of most frenzied activity – an enormous sense of urgency. Piers and wharves are being made. Roads, bridges, and railways being built. Several thousands of labourers have been brought from Egypt and Malta, and the air is filled with the sounds of hammering, clanking of chains, blasting of rock; shouts and noise of the busy thousands, mixed with bugle calls – and the ever-present distant rumble of the guns!

Our hospital consists of a large collection of tents and marquees on the side of a hill, which falls away to the sea. A stone's throw from the mess tent, where I am writing, is a large French camp, and adjoining us on the other side is a French hospital, an Indian convalescent camp, and a British hospital. We still have about 900 patients, but are gradually evacuating them, so as to be ready to move off to the front.

21 September

We were told this morning that at present there would be in no work for us to do, so having heard last month that Jim Elder was sick and on Lemnos, and not having heard of him since, I set out to ransack the island for news of him. I crossed the harbour in a felucca and found No. 2 Stationary hospital, where the other half of our party from Cairo was hard at work with their sick and wounded. There is no question of them moving, and they're all down in the mouth!

Every one of the original staff of officers of this hospital is away sick, except old Colonel White, Deakin and Clark. They have been running the hospital with the aid of officers from the RAMC and Canadian AMC until arrival of the men we bought. Had lunch there, and searched the records of this, and other hospitals for Jim without success. I was told that the whole 1st division was resting in a camp on Lemnos, on the other side of a hill. I set out to find it, filled with hope. After wading through a lagoon a quarter of a mile wide, I came across the 1st Australian division camp! I could hardly believe it!

Here in this straggling little collection of tents and marquees were the shattered remnants of that huge Mena Camp! That proud martial display that was the pride of Australia, whom thousands visited and admired a year ago at Broadmeadows. That struck the Egyptians dumb with awe and admiration as they marched through the streets of Cairo with crashing bands, and camped in the desert at the foot of the pyramids, which in their martial pride they belittled and flaunted. This little quiet camp was all that remained, after six months' exposure to the fury of the Turks and the ravages of disease!

I found the remains of the 14th battalion – 170 of them – in three marquees. They were occupied silently going through the effects of their dead comrades. Jim had left them, they said, sick with dysentery and septic hands, at the end of July. They had not seen or heard of him since. I wearily trudged back at dusk.

22 September
Wednesday

A howling cold wind is blowing over the island, sending up clouds of dust and whipping up the sea in the harbour. I sat in the mess tent and wrote up my diary and letters in the morning until lunchtime.

After lunch, Freddie Le Messurier and I went for a ride way around the harbour. Found a big French camp and a French hospital. They are wisely building huts there, ready for the winter. The British and Australians have as yet made no preparations for the winter, which is now almost upon us.

Freddie asked me if I wanted to get into an ambulance or a regiment, as some of us would have to be drafted away – he said that whoever went, he hoped I would stay, as they were so awfully glad to get me, and all thought I would be a welcome addition to their already happy party. It is a new and delightful experience for me to feel I am really genuinely wanted and appreciated!

However, there are at two reasons against my staying. Firstly, after nine months of comfortable living, I volunteered in order to relieve someone who is suffering hardships, to give them my comfort and ease. Secondly, I have cast myself adrift willingly from security and peace in order to experience excitement and adventure. I am unable to choose at present, but then, I have not yet been given the choice. Time will tell.

23 September

A freezing cold wind is thundering over the barren island. The air is filled with fine powdery dust, which fills my ears and eyes – and lies thick on my food, covering everything with white powder. There is absolutely no shelter anywhere except in the tents!

I sat in the mess tent all morning and wrote letters, then lay my bunk and snoozed after lunch until 4:30 p.m. Then when the wind died down a little, I went for a ride with Verco, around the harbour to the point where the whole plan of Mudros defences lay at our feet. It was a magnificent sight but too windy and cold to appreciate.

25 September.

Rumour – Greece is at war with Bulgaria!

There is intense excitement and enthusiasm in the tiny Greek settlement. The bell of the Greek Church – the only building worthy of a name on the island – tolled incessantly until about 10 a.m. Then the mayor of the village read a decree from the church steps to a motley crowd of Greeks, attired in filthy and discoloured rags, but none the less giving a most picturesque effect.

Mingled with the crowd were numbers of French porters, Zouaves, Singalese, Ghurkas, Indians, British Tommies and Australians, as well as English tars, French sailors, and Officers of all kinds, naval and military. After the decree, with much cheering and shouting, the Greek Standard was triumphantly carried through the little streets of the village, followed by an enthusiastic procession!

I spent almost the whole day reading and writing on a deck chair in the sun. This afternoon some nurses came from other side of the harbour for tea. Great excitement among the young officers, who scarcely ever see a woman!

Went for a stroll with Fred in the moonlight. He said that Powell, the OC, had told him I was only temporarily attached to the unit, but that he did not think I am strong enough for the hardships of a field ambulance, and intends giving me a rest here before letting me go on. Awfully sporting of him – but somewhat misdirected kindness, as I am quite fit!

26 September
Sunday

A beautiful warm, sunny still morning. Some Singalese are making a road past our mess tent in the French lines, which abut on ours at this spot. They are of course, black, with a tight black curly hair and dazzling white teeth, and sing a weird chant as they work. They're dressed in bloomers of khaki with dark blue putties, khaki jackets, and bright red caps. They are most good-natured chaps, always smiling and showing their teeth.

Crowds of Greeks have bade farewell to their families and gone off in barges to sailing ships in the harbour, en route for the army.

After lunch, Verco, Freddie Le Messurier and I went out on the harbour in a motorboat and fetched the Warrant Officer off a transport, returned to us after being invalided to Egypt. Clouds rolled up from the southwest while we were out, and it began to blow again. Freddie was seized with pain, which he has had all night. I'm awfully afraid he has a got a touch of appendicitis!

Most of us went to church at 7 p.m. after mess. It was jolly nice. The padre here is the first decent padre I have come across since I left Australia. The two specimens we had at 1

AGH, were enough to put one off church for the rest of one's life! I enjoyed the service and so did everyone else.

Monday

Freddie has appendicitis!

He is a bit better this morning, but there is no doubt about it. They will send poor old Freddie away now, and the OC told me to take on his work today. I felt very depressed, for it seemed as though I was to be kept here for good, to take Freddie's place. I would not mind stopping so much, if he were here too, but to have to stay here when he has gone – why, I would have been much better at the Palace, where my friends are, if I'm only to be in a hospital again.

So I went and spoke straight out to Powell – told him I was in a base hospital for nine months and only volunteered to leave it so as to relieve somebody at the Front. He said I was only temporarily attached here and would move on soon. This removed my troubles and misgivings, and I did Freddie's work in an easy frame of mind.

I have a feeling something big is happening! A number of cruisers, destroyers, hospital ships and transports crammed with troops have quietly slipped out of the harbour during the last 24 hours. Rumours of an Allied advance in France, and of Russian victories on the Eastern front are being freely circulated on the island!

28 September

I was Orderly Officer today, and up at 6 a.m. Nothing much to do. Went around Freddie's wards and looked at some bad dysentery cases.

At 12:30 p.m. Powell sent for me, and handed me a bundle of correspondence, which he said referred to me. He told me to take it at once to the ADMS, and said that I am wanted at once at Anzac!

I went to the ADMS and reported. He said I am to proceed at once to the front, at 2:30 p.m.! (It was then 12:30.) Fortunately however, he thought better of that and said I could go tomorrow. So I am off to the guns at last!

Chapter 11

Gallipoli

29 September [1915]
Wednesday
The wind has dropped, and it is a beautiful day. I leisurely packed my bags and haversack after breakfast, and immediately after lunch I said farewell to my kind South Australian friends, and sailed off in the ferry for the *Aragon*, the sumptuous and luxurious ship which is anchored in the middle of the harbour, and on which is located 'Headquarters Lemnos'. This comprises dozens of generals and colonels, whose chief concern seems to be their own stomachs and bodily comforts.

I got my orders checked and confirmed here, and went quietly on board the *Partridge* which had come alongside.

It is now 3:45 p.m. The *Partridge* sails at 4 p.m. – to battle for the first time in my life, and may it be a long time before I leave the guns, for I shall not slink back to the base except under compulsion of sickness, or being wounded.

Sitting here on the deck, the harbour presents a really wonderful sight. Transports, cargo boats, yachts, hospital ships and warships of every kind from mine sweepers to battleships are on all sides. The water is just alive with pinnaces, motorboats and launches rushing about with staff officers, admirals, generals, etc.

On shore just opposite me on the low rounded close is the 1st AGH – a collection of marquees and bell tents – about half a mile away. Two aeroplanes, or rather, seaplanes, are hovering around us in the still, mild atmosphere. Everybody is bustling about now, and we are about to start!

We shall not get in until after dark. I shall have comfort until the last moment, as the *Partridge* is quite a nice boat with a comfortable saloon and even a gramophone!

30 September
Woke up this morning with a splitting headache. The crackling of rifle fire seemed to be all round and mighty close! Every few minutes a terrific report would nearly split my ears, blowing a gust of air against my face and causing a little crumbs of earth to fall all round me from walls of the dugout I was in.

Last night seemed a long while ago … I had a jolly good dinner with the ship's officers, and being the only army officer on board, I became everybody's guest after dinner and the bottle went round freely, with gramophone records and laughter.

At 9:45 p.m. the engines stopped, and going out of the saloon, I discovered that we were standing off about a quarter of a mile from a high cliff dotted with lights all the way up. The sharp crackle of rifles was incessant and sounded exactly like a lot of fireworks going off – two or three single shots, then a chorus – then a pause for a second or so, then a few all together followed by a few single ones.

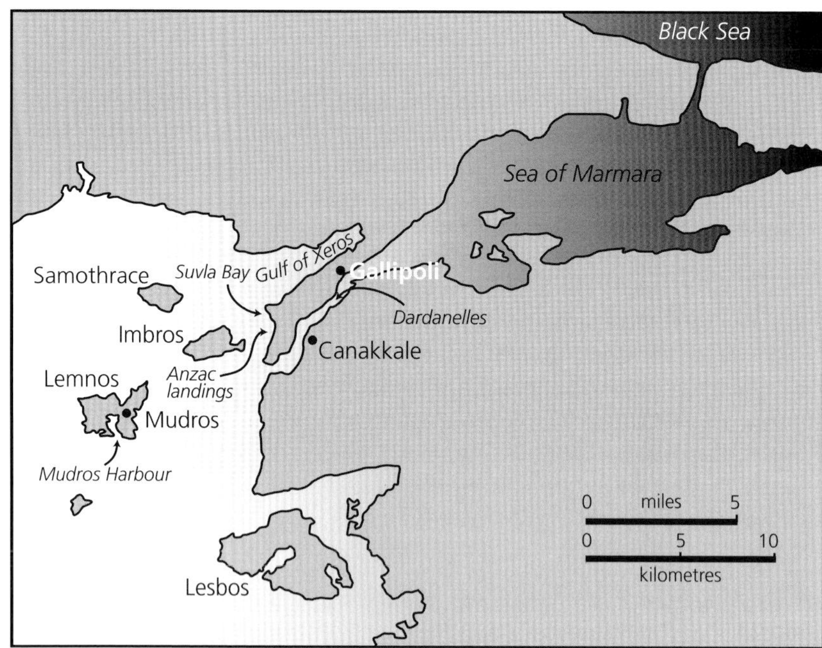

Map of the Gallipoli campaign

So this was the spot where the glorious landing was made! Where boat loads of silent men were towed up to that huge towering precipitous cliff, fringed and furrowed with trenches crammed with rifles and machine guns – up which they dashed, tumbling and treading over one another.

As I watched, a flash lit up the water for an instant. Several seconds later a terrific crash and a great gust of air blew into my face. It was a destroyer about a mile away, letting fly with a 4.7 at the Turkish trenches!

I was landed with my baggage in a lighter and got a man on the beach to help me with my swag, was directed to the dugouts of the Clearing Hospital and in turn to the dugout of Lieutenant Boddam, who I'd seen in Lemnos just before starting, and who suggested my doing this.

Well, the whisky on board must have been extremely bad last night, for I did not have such a great deal, but this morning I felt absolutely wretched, with a beast of a headache.

So this was the Front! The rattle and banging of rifle fire was absolutely incessant – even so I became used to it in the first hour. I could not eat breakfast, but reported myself at 9 a.m. to the CDMS (Lt. Colonel Howse, VC) who is a fine fellow. There I found Balcombe-Quick sitting in the great man's dugout with him! I was referred on to the ADMS, who I found in another dugout, and he drafted me into the 10th Battalion as their RMO. He was awfully nice, and gave me some sound advice.

He gave me 24 hours to get used to the fire, and I am to start tomorrow. I went back to my dugout and lay down. At 12:30 p.m. Balcombe-Quick came up and we had a good lunch in his dugout. I was taken up to the firing line to see Parkinson, who is in the 11th, and is also doing the 10th work until relieved. I must say I did not feel frightened by the whizzing of shells and the ping of bullets over my head, I was too interested and curious and excited – but I have yet to experience a bomb or a shell bursting close to me! The trenches are simply a marvel to me, beyond my expectations. Parkinson seems a decent sort of chap, and gave me some hints. I am to go up first thing in the morning to commence before breakfast.

Returned about 4:30 p.m. and had a swim. Found that 'Beachy Bill' (a Turkish battery which commands the beach and which is way back in the Turkish lines and has never been found by our guns in all these months) had been at work, sweeping the crowded beach with shrapnel. Two had been killed and 16 wounded on the beach while we were away!

Balcombe is acting OC to the 3rd Field Ambulance who are on the beach alongside the Clearing Station. He is just the same dear old thing. Tozer came down for a yarn, and we turned in early, to the accompaniment of an incessant crackling of rifles, and occasional bursts of thunder from our destroyers anchored off the beach.

1 October
Friday

This morning my new life commenced – life in the trenches, which so many thousands of men are now living all over Europe.

I was up before 6 a.m. and had a swim. Returning from this, I found that Balcombe had ordered a cup of tea for me in my absence, which I polished off. Then, with my pack on my back and my haversacks and water bottle slung on, I set out for the trenches!

I arrived after half-an-hour's climb, puffing like a Grampus! Now of course, one climbs up steps and paths to reach this position, but how on 25 April, those chaps got up there with the thick prickly bush, and all those unbroken precipices, I can't understand!

Well, I got here about 7:15 a.m. and met my sergeant – a big bluff, rough good-natured fellow and my corporal dispenser – a little Frenchman, Pierre Becker. I was delighted to find this, as I shall certainly soon speak French quite decently.

I met the OC, Adjutant and Quartermaster, the former and latter seemed awfully nice chaps – I will not yet make up my mind about the Adjutant. The 2nd in command, Major Giles is a ripping chap, and took me around the firing line with him. The trenches I will not attempt to describe until I get a bit more of the hang of them. They're just marvellous!

I then did a sanitary inspection with the sanitary corporal. After lunch I went and had a yarn with Parkinson of the 11th – about a quarter of a mile from here. Returning about 4 p.m. I found that there were two slight wounds to be fixed up. I had just finished when I met a Staff Lieutenant and the Staff Major (Ross). The latter with his eyes bandaged!

He had been looking through periscope when a bullet hit it, throwing glass into his eyes. I removed some from his left eye and bandaged him up.

All day guns had been thundering around us – shells whizzing overhead and rifles incessantly crackling, and bullets pinging and zipping about. I really am getting quite accustomed to the noise, and I'm not in the least bit nervous.

At night from our high perch overlooking the sea, the searchlights of the destroyers and the flashes of their huge guns reminds me exactly of a pantomime scene, except for the ear-splitting crash following the flash!

The OC Major Shaw and I went down to have another look at Major Ross. Thank God his eyesight is not damaged and he is not in pain now. On returning, I saw my 1st bomb – just like a firework! A comet with a fiery sparkling tail, which landed on the artillery road about 60 yards from us with a terrific crash. But no one was hurt.

2 October
I was up at 6 a.m. and conducted my first sick parade. There were 30 sick, and owing to the notorious capacity of the soldier to pull the doctor's leg, I must confess I was a bit nervous! I sent 4 to hospital and got through the lot in an hour. I then ran down to headquarters to make sure Major Ross was all right. He is severely shaken, but his eyes are all right.

After breakfast I did my round of the lines with the sanitary corporal and visited a couple of seedy officers in their dugouts, first waiting until the 'morning hate' was over. The evening and morning 'hate' consists of a bombardment of our position by the Turks which always takes place for about half-an-hour or more both in the morning about 9 a.m. (presumably when they have comfortably finished their breakfast), and in the evening just before sunset. Shells whiz and scream over our heads, bursting with a crash and a howl as the fragments fly in all directions – on the ridges about 60 yards to our right and left, or just below us on a hillside.

Our guns always answer this bombardment! The roar and thunder and ear-splitting crash, and the howl and scream and hiss of shells and fragments tearing through the air, is simply deafening!

Well, we had lunch at midday and I paid Major Ross another visit. He is getting on all right, but is still very much shaken. I then returned and had a little French conversation with Pierre, which was interrupted by the OC coming in for a yarn. Two slight wounds from fragments, and then the ADMS came up and advised me to send Ross away as he is very knocked out.

The 'evening hate' was something terrific, and commenced just as we finished tea. The din was deafening for about half-an-hour!

It was a most glorious sunset – the sea like a huge blue pond, glowing with scarlet light.

3 October
Sunday
Today is still and warm – hot in the sun, and not a breath of wind.

My gallon a day water supply has not arrived, so I had to go without a wash until after breakfast, just cadging enough water for my teeth.

The sick parade was distinctly bigger this morning! These men are just done. It's over five months since that glorious landing and charge, when the 3rd Brigade was in the lead and first on the Peninsula – and the remnants of those brave fellows, officers and men are still here in the same spot, not relieved for a day!

After breakfast, I went around to the lines with Major Giles, and saw one of our officers, Captain Todd, who was very sick with a temperature of 104° [F], and have sent him off to the Base.

The Turks are very lively today, bullets pinging around and shells crashing and howling by. Two men were slightly wounded, one by a bullet striking his periscope, and the other by a shell fragment in the leg.

After lunch, I went round the lines with sanitary corporal and then had a look at Major Ross. Decided to send him off tonight too.

The 'evening hate' was very solid! Terrific explosions surrounding us, with shells screaming overhead and bullets cracking and pinging all round. During this, I nipped over to the dugout of the 8th Battery and saw Rogers, the husband of the nurse of the Eye Department at Heliopolis. A Turk flew low over and dropped some bombs, but on the appearance of two of our planes, he departed. The bombs dropped on the beach, narrowly missing Headquarters, but did no harm.

After tea I went down to the beach with Major Ross and had a yarn with Balcombe-Quick and a swim. Such a swim! I was clean at last! Got home about 11 p.m.

4 October

Another big sick parade – a good breakfast and a 'morning hate' like you never dreamt of! It was really terrific! Shells burst within 15 or 20 yards of us, the earth and stones and fragments scattered near our dugouts! After nearly an hour of this, it subsided and gave place to a lively small-arms duel – the rifle reports forming an absolute tornado!

I went round the lines with the sanitary corporal and found the OC and the General in the trenches, and all men at the 'stand to'!

The bombardment had been so violent that an attack was suspected. Nothing happened however, and the afternoon has been extraordinarily quiet – scarcely a shot fired for nearly two hours – it had been merely 'a stunt'.

Henty and Roy Cook turned up during the afternoon, en route for the 5th Light Horse and the 12th battalion. They left Egypt over two months ago, and have been to London with the wounded since then – the lucky devils!

One of our aeroplanes is overhead now, and the Turks are firing at it with shrapnel. As she sails gracefully in the clear blue sky – quite cloudless – a ball of shining white smoke suddenly appears far below her – simply appears as though suddenly created! The ball unfolds itself gently and slowly and a faint report is now heard. Then another appears behind, and another in front. Two more below, and still the plane sails contemptuously on, steady and graceful, and utterly unharmed by the fearful but beautiful fireworks!

There was a 'stunt' tonight at 8 p.m. I have never heard anything like it! A 'stunt' is an attack with artillery, machine gun, and rifle commencing altogether and lasting for about half-an-hour, but not followed by any bayonet charge. These take place frequently so that we never know whether the attack is the precursor of a charge or not. It is simply crying wolf!

At 8 p.m., the night was pitch-dark and still, broken only by the usual dropping rifle fire, when suddenly a deafening din arose! A Turkish machine gun had been spotted in a new position commanding us. A monitor lay off Gaba Tepe, and with a searchlight playing on the Turks, crashed away with six-inch guns. One of our '18 pounders' here, about 15 yards from my dugout, lit up the whole scene every few minutes with her flashes and ear ear-splitting bangs, which brought earth down all over me in my dugout!

At the same time a perfect storm of rifle fire and furious tapping of machine guns made the night truly horrible! I had to fill my ears with cotton wool.

In half an hour, all was still, except for the usual 'crack – crack' of rifles. I guess there can't be much left of that Turkish machine gun now!

5 October

Another beautiful still day. Up at 6 a.m. – quiet and uneventful. Aeroplanes overhead most of the day – we never fire at the Turks in the air, except with rifles if they get a low enough, presumably because of the utter waste of time and ammunition. The Turks on the other hand, pepper our planes freely with shrapnel, the whole time they're over them – but their planes will never face ours, coming to earth as soon as ours heave up into sight! The bombardment of an aeroplane is one of the finest and most fascinating spectacles I have ever seen!

I finished my rounds of the lines just before lunch. Went to see George Cole this afternoon and gave him the surprise of his life! Major Giles dropped in later for a yarn. It was a beautiful still evening, and though bullets sang past our ears quite freely, the Turks were very quiet, and the evening hymn of hate was omitted.

I finished the evening with a French conversation with Pierre.

7 October

It is now a month since I left Cairo. I have had no letters and not a word of news of any kind from my people and friends during this time!

After lunch went with Rogers – husband of my eye nurse at Heliopolis – to all the guns of the 8th Battery, and their observation post, where I witnessed through a telescope some of our shells bursting over the Turks' trenches. Very interesting. Watched a Turk come out of his dugout, have a look around, scratch his head and go back – nearly two miles away!

At 8:30 p.m., there was a grand stunt all along the line! I shoved some bandages in my pockets and went up into the firing line just before it started, and watched the whole thing from our observation post. It was a most extraordinary sight!

At 8.29 the night was still and dark except for the usual dropping rifle fire. At 8.30, with a roar, a perfect tornado of rifle and machine-gun started! Numbers of rockets flew from our lines over the Turks trenches, where a little star was left hanging high above them. This suddenly burst into brilliant light, and very gradually sank onto the Turks heads – lighting up their trenches with a glare as bright as day. I could see their bayonets flashing.

I went to the firing line. The trenches were full of smoke from bombs thrown by the Turks and the noise was simply deafening! From the observation post, our trenches look like a long line of fire – flashing and gleaming red and yellow. Bombs were freely exchanged, which soon filled everything with white choking smoke, whilst their explosions shook the ground and nearly stupefied one with their thunderous crash!

A cruiser and a destroyer played searchlights up and down the Turks positions and the thunder of their immense guns was incessant!

In three-quarters of an hour, all was still again! There was not a casualty, until the last few minutes, when a bomb killed one man outright. The Turks are estimated to have used 250,000 rounds of rifle ammunition alone, besides bombs and artillery! It was a most successful stunt!

8 October

A still, warm and misty day with rain threatening. Inspection and sick parade over, I had a talk in French with Pierre.

After tea, the usual meeting of the officers of the Battalion took place in the mess dugout – every evening we come together for a little pow-wow and the OC, who is really a most excellent chap, reads us any news that there may be from the other Fronts. It seems to me that if the Russians managed to keep the Germans out of Riga for another month, the end of the war will be in sight.

Later, I talked French with Pierre and at that moment a storm burst over us! It poured with rain till about midnight and then cleared up. My dugout was quite dry all night, though I don't know how its will stand another good downpour.

The shelling has been very quiet lately, the Turk quite forgetting his usual 'evening hate'. A heavy bombardment is however taking place on the slopes of Achi Baba – the explosions being visible distinctly with glasses.

10th Battalion Infantry
Mediterranean Expeditionary Force
'Anzac'
Gallipoli Peninsula
2 October 1915

My darling Mum
Well, here I am at the Front! In the safest of safe dugouts; the shells all flying miles over my head and a good hefty mass of earth lies between me and the pinging little rifle bullets. Quite safe – quite happy – tons to eat – snug and warm at night, and basking in beautiful sunlight in the mornings. But very dirty!

Let me tell you the story of it all …

Claude told his mother of the last days in Lemnos, and his arrival in Gallipoli.

… I shall give you had a little sketch of my first view of Anzac.

The sea was dead calm – no wind, and the air a little chilly. I had my huge greatcoat on. I was sitting in the saloon yarning with the chief engineer when I felt the engine stop. We were in absolute darkness from the outset, as ships carry no lights on deck when they near the Front. I came out on the deck and lent over the side. There was no moon, but millions of stars. About 300 yards away was the outline of a great towering cliff the conformation of which was familiar to me as it must be to you from pictures. Dotted all over the cliff almost to the top were lots and lots of little lights which I found out afterwards to be caused by candles in the hundreds of dugouts on the face of a cliff!

Try to imagine several hundred boundary riders standing a couple of hundred yards away each with a stock whip which they incessantly cracked, you would have the exact sound that met my ears as I lent over the rail that evening about 9 p.m. There was just an irregular but incessant crackling of rifles. Now one, now three together, then a few single ones, and then a chorus …

A hum of voices and the sound of moving cases and barrels came over the water from the beach. As I looked and listened, and thought of those brave fellows and the wonderful landing at this very spot five months ago, a flash lit everything up for an instant and it was dark again! I was looking round, wondering where it had come from, when a few seconds later, a most terrific crash nearly split my ears! More sudden and more ear splitting than any thunder I have ever heard! At the same instant a gust of wind seemed to hit me in the face, and after an instant a rolling echo, then there was nothing but that constant cracking to be heard, and all was still.

It was merely one of our destroyers, a good three miles away, firing upon the Turks trenches, way over the heads of our own men! Then came another flash – but this time I was ready for it – with my fingers in my ears! After 9 or 10 shots she gave up, and those sharp cracks and distant voices alone disturbed the still evening.

A half moon rose over the cliff and showed us a picket boat coming off to us from a little jetty, towing a coal lighter. In this, I landed with my kit bag, my blankets rolled up in a waterproof sheet, which with the pack and two haversacks and a water bottle, constituted my worldly belongings.

When I arrived on the beach, I inquired for the Clearing Hospital, in which, as you know, Colonel Giblin, Jack O'Brien, Hildred Carlisle, Tommy Atkins, etc. had left Australia. Every one of these is now away sick, except Major Jack Gordon from Melbourne! He is in command and his officers are all English RAMC men who have reinforced the unit. Boddam their Quartermaster, whom I met at Lemnos, told me to sleep in his dugout when I arrived that first night. This I did, and was too tired to investigate Anzac any further that night.

I woke next morning and found myself in a little cave, cut out of the side of the cliff, with a waterproof sheet hung over the front. This was a 'dugout'. It was about 8 ft broad and 10 ft deep, that is, from the opening inwards, and was hung with pictures from illustrated papers, etc. The 'crack – crack' of rifles was still going on, but was now punctuated every few moments by a crash which brought fragments of mud from the walls and roof of the dugout, pattering on the floor!

I arose and had a swim in the briny, then a good breakfast – porridge, bacon and eggs, bread and jam, with Major Gordon and his officers. I then went in search of the CDMS, Colonel Howse, with my written orders in my hand. To my surprise, Balcombe-Quick was sitting beside the great man! He passed me over to his Assistant, who drafted me into the 10th Battalion as medical officer in place of Captain Nott, their real medical officer, who left Australia with them and who is now away with typhoid. He gave me 24 hours to get used to the fire and told me I could start work next morning ...

My new home is a dugout – a most comfortable one – perched up near the summit of a high ridge. It faces over the sea and the outlook is simply beautiful. Far below me, the blue Mediterranean stretches away to the island of Imbros, which rises up as a huge mountainous blue mass on the horizon and behind which the sun sets with the most glorious rosy glow, spreading warm pink all over the calm sea. A couple of cruisers, several destroyers and some monitors, besides two or three hospital ships, are lying off the landing place at little Anzac Cove, and looked just like pretty little toy vessels, reflected in the still water.

Our firing line is on the opposite side of the ridge, facing the Turks, and is approached by 'saps', which are deep cuttings, and tunnels. The crest of the ridge being swept by the Turk's guns.

On our side of the ridge, we have several guns below us, to our right and left, which fire over our heads, over the ridge and lob shells on the 'Fezz of Abdulla', who in his turn rains shells and high explosives over the ridge from his side to try and hit the guns. Needless to say, in spite of the most terrific explosions, ear-splitting crashes and the shriek and scream of shells through the air over our heads, his shells never do the slightest damage, and lob everywhere except where he wants him to! He sent over 69 shells in less than half-an-hour the other day without producing one casualty of any sort! This, may I remark, is due more to the strength of our position than to his own shooting, for the Turks are good shots!

Another thing about the Turk – he is a scrupulously fair fighter and has never been known to fire on the Red Cross flag! There are two hospital ships lying in full view of his guns, which, though they pepper the warships, have never sent a shot anywhere near the hospital ships. There is a field ambulance (British) in full view along the beach between here and Suvla Bay, and never a shot has gone near it! Everyone says the same over here – the Turk is absolutely punctilious about his respect for the Geneva Red Cross!

I am never tired of watching the aeroplanes here, which hover over us, both friend and enemy. They are very daring on both sides but never seem to get damaged!

Well Goodnight my dear Mum. I have not had a letter from you for a long time. They sent my mail on here from Cairo, but it arrived before I did, and in the meantime it was sent off to Lemnos to look for me – where it probably still is! My dugout is next to the CO's and therefore in a safest position of a lot! My fellow officers are South Australians and I get on famously with them all. Especially the CO, and the 2nd in command is a fine chap (Major Giles).

Goodnight dearest. I'm very happy and well, and strong and safe.
From Claude

P.S. 7 October
I have been keeping my mail, waiting for a post to go. Have now waited five days for mail to even start from here! The postal arrangements from Gallipoli are very bad indeed, though letters coming here are fairly regular.

You'll be pleased to hear Mum darling, that my corporal who is my right hand man, is a Frenchman named Pierre Becker. Consequently, I am never at a loss for something to do, and each evening fairly regularly, he comes into my dugout and we talk French, and only French for about an hour. Soon I hope I shall talk to Pierre exclusively in French, in the execution of my medical duties!

Mum dear, I will give you a resume of what I have had to eat since I got here – more or less. Porridge always for breakfast, followed usually by bacon and eggs two or three times a week or else fresh meat about once a week. Bread and toast about four times a week, otherwise biscuits – which are not to be recommended for delicate teeth!

Then for lunch, bully beef – which is really jolly nice – with rice – or fried bully beef, which makes a good rissole – or sometimes steak and onions. Very seldom bully beef by itself. Then we have sardines on toast, or salmon, or fried bully beef for tea and tinned butter, very good condensed milk, marmalade, golden syrup, and apricot, plum, apple or raspberry jam always on the table. Oh I forgot to say, we always have boiled rice and stewed tinned fruit for pudding at lunchtime.

So you see Mum dear, I'm not getting starved by any means! I always tuck in with relish and amuse the other chaps by having two helpings even of plain bully beef!

Our casualties during this trench warfare are extraordinary light. It is only when attacking, when our men have to actually leave their trench, that casualties are heavy. There have been an average of about one slight wound a day since I arrived and no serious wounds. Pierre tells me that sometimes a fortnight of trench warfare passes without a casualty, and yet the firing is practically without intermission night and day from rifle, machine gun and artillery. Strange and splendid, isn't it?
My best love, darling Mum to you, and Lucile and Stan and their little family.
C.M.

CHAPTER 12

The Trenches

[October 1915]

The firing line of the 10th Battalion is, at its closest point, 50 yards from that of the Turks, being much more distant than at many other points of the Anzac lines. Most firing lines in modern trench warfare consist of a deep narrow trench, with sandbags stacked on the top of the walls, so that the trench is seldom less than 9, and usually is 10 or 12 ft deep. Every few feet along the wall facing the enemy, a platform is cut, sufficiently broad to accommodate two or three men. These platforms are known as 'fire recesses' and at these points, niches are left between the sandbags for loopholes. In front of these niches are often placed iron plates with a slot covered by an iron lid, which may be slid away at will, and these form the safest kind of loophole, and may be entirely closed at will.

The 10th Battalion consists largely of miners from Broken Hill and, being accustomed to burrowing in the earth, they have, during the last six months, perfected their trenches until at present, the lines of the 10th are the 'show lines' of Gallipoli, being the best on the Peninsula!

Most firing line trenches are made zigzag, so as to do away with the terrible enfilade fire as far as possible. In our case, we have, to a large extent, done away with the necessity of this in the following way. Our firing line consists of a long tunnel sufficiently deep under the surface of the ground to ensure complete safety against the explosions of any ordinary high-explosive shells. This tunnel, not being exposed to fire of any kind, is almost straight, with a few right-angle turns. On the side facing the enemy there are, every few feet, the fire recesses, which are little forts, approached from the tunnel by steps up. Each recess is a small space surrounded by a wall about seven feet high, in which are loopholes. Three men can comfortably stand or sit in each recess.

One returns to the tunnel from the recess through a small opening, only admitting one man at a time – by descending four or five steps. On the opposite side of the tunnel to the enemy there are, every few yards, excavations for the accommodation of three men lying at full length. These excavations or dugouts are where the men in the firing line take turns at sleeping, while their mates keep watch at the fire recesses.

Then in addition to this, our firing line boasts of bomb tunnels. These are offshoots from the main tunnel, which extend as long arms, towards the enemy lines, ending in a carefully hidden opening to the surface, where a man sits day and night, watching and listening. He has his rifle, and a large supply of bombs, and in the case of attack, or attempted surprise, can scatter these amongst the enemy from this vantage point before they get anywhere near our firing line. By means of these 'feelers' also, the doings of the enemy may be secretly watched and listened to, and the alarm given quietly to our firing line in case of any untoward movement.

This powerful firing line is connected by means of several tunnels to a support line of trenches, known as the '2nd line of defence'. This line consists of the typical firing trench line, being zigzag, and with platform fire recesses facing the enemy, in which are many

— The Trenches —

The Firing line of the 10th Bttn is, at closest point, 50 yards from that of the Turks – being much more distant than at many other parts of the Anzac Position.

Most firing lines, in modern trench warfare consist of a deep narrow trench, with sand bags stacked on the top of the walls, so that the trench is seldom less than 9, & usually is 10 or 12 feet deep. Every few feet, along the wall facing the enemy, a platform is cut, sufficiently broad to accommodate 2 or 3 men:– These platforms are known as "Fire Recesses," and at these spots, niches are left between the sand bags for loopholes. In front of these niches, are often placed iron plates, with a slot covered by an iron lid which may be slid away at will – & these form the safest kind of loophole, & may be entirely closed at will.

The 10th Battalion consists largely of miners from Broken Hill, & being accustomed to burrowing in the earth, they have, during the last loopholes of the usual type. The trenches are about a dozen yards behind the firing line tunnel, and the intervening ground is a mass of barbed-wire entanglements. Now, should the enemy charge in such force as to overpower the men in the fire recesses in front of our firing tunnel, two courses are open to him.

1. He must halt in front of our line whilst he clambers down into our tunnel, there being only room for one man at a time to pass from each fire recess back in to the tunnel. This entails the holding up of his advancing columns, while the tunnel would soon become choked with bodies of Turks as they clambered singly from the fire recess. Or,

2. He must charge over the tunnel and rush our back lines, where he finds himself involved in more wire entanglements and facing an absolutely new, fully manned firing line!

It is really inconceivable that our lines could possibly be taken by storm, and one might well describe the position as impregnable! Along both walls of the communication tunnels and in the walls of the 2nd line of defence, remote from the fire recesses, excavations occur at intervals of a few feet, wherein are housed the men.

From this support trench, another series of communicating trenches and tunnels lead back further, to the rear of our position. Between these two points, a shallow valley is interposed. Were one to walk over the surface of the ground, from our support trenches to our rear, it would be necessary to descend into the valley, ascend the opposite side, and cross over the ridge and again descend a few yards to where a broad road skirts the summit of the ridge, on the seaward side known as the 'artillery road'.

The summit of the ridge is however completely swept by hostile guns, and the 10th, nothing daunted, have tunnelled right through the ridge in several places bringing our rear in communication with the supports and the firing line, by means of absolutely safe and secure channels! At the rear, situated in their dugouts are the OC, Adjutant, etc. – also I have my own dugout, the aid post, and the cookhouses, etc.

All this goes under the general name of 'Battalion Headquarters'.

9 October

A most beautiful, clear bright morning, after a stormy night.

It soon became evident how utterly ineffectual are the preparations for winter! Here, thousands of troops have lived for almost six months, with several miles of frontage, not two miles from the sea. The only landing place is that same little stretch of beach, where those poor fellows, now mostly dead, landed six months ago. That same little narrow strip, cramped up with a couple of small light jetties, has been swept daily by the deadly battery miles away – Beachy Bill – which has now accounted for roughly a 1,000 men!

Ammunition and stores are stacked to within six feet of the water's edge, separated from it by a light tramline, which is actually touched by the water. In this narrow space between the sea and the huge cliff, riddled with dugouts, the whole traffic of Anzac is done – and it is one mass of struggling mules, wounded men on stretchers, bathers, barrels and bombs – a hideous chaotic jumble on the actual water's edge!

No timber or corrugated iron is available for construction of winter shelters for the army, which lives simply in holes and dugouts. No vegetables, only occasional fresh meat or bread – and yet within a one-hour steam, actually distinctly visible, is the inhabited island of Imbros, of which we have complete command and where some of our headquarters are located!

The thing was obvious and inevitable! At the first little storm, last night, which only lasted a few hours, the jetties were smashed; the timbers and cases by the score were washed away, while the water ruined quantities of ammunition and stores! Fresh water is now landed with difficulty, and we're all on a half-gallon of water per man per day. This is the result of a little gale of wind lasting half the night – and such are the preparations for a long and stormy winter, with blizzards and snow!

In the afternoon, having heard that Follit is still with the 9th, I went around to see him. It is about five miles walk away round to the left wing. The 9th are on 'rhododendron ridge' at our extreme left. They are away up at the top of a wild, mountainous ravine, covered with scrub, very like our own Mallee scrub. The country here might well be any mountainous district of Victoria. It is a fearfully dangerous locality, and the 9th are swept daily by a deadly shellfire!

It was grand meeting old Follit again. We had a great yarn, after almost six months apart. I called in at the 8th for details of poor old Norman Tetley, and brought away his pocket book and diary, which I sent to Egypt last night by Rogers, to Bert Sutherland, asking him to forward it straight to Australia to Wilfred. I got home about teatime and wrote letters for Rogers to take across.

10 October

After lunch went down to the beach and had a swim. Also made some inquiries about my lost mail. This was sent on from Heliopolis, probably by Sutherland to me at the Clearing Hospital here, and arrived at two days before I did – where it was promptly marked 'not known' and then sent back along the lines of communication to look for me. One of the very few occasions on which the postal authorities acted with promptness!

Saw Quick, Poate and Fisher on the beach and came back in time to have tea with Ray Whitford, whose dugout is about 200 yards from here. He is medical officer for the 2nd Brigade Artillery. Had a good meal and a long yarn to him, and was home about 11 p.m.

Anzac
10 October
Mum darling

Another mail is going today, so I shall not miss the opportunity. This is my 2nd letter from Anzac. The mail is so bad from here that I shall number my letters to see which of them you get.

There is a darned gun – a howitzer, just a few yards from here which is firing now and goes off BANG! in my ear every few seconds! I hope it damages the Turks trenches, for it nearly shakes my head off and gives me a temporary earache, even with cotton wool in my ears. However it will stop in a minute then I will continue.

1/2 hour later

I knew he would! The blighter! He woke the Turk from his afternoon siesta after a while, and the latter started thundering shells across at us. Our guns joined in most merrily, and for the last half-hour there has been a terrible noise – crash after crash, boom, thunder, and screaming of shells overhead – a perfect uproar!

Shells have been bursting all over the place. I have been standing at the door of my dugout – in *perfect and absolute safety*, watching the fountains of earth and smoke and

Claude captioned this photo: 'The cliffs up which the Australians charged during the landing at Gallipoli, April 25th, 1915. Note the trenches on the summit, with regimental medical station marked by Red Cross flag.' (Arrow indicates the flag.)

'Beachy Bill' takes his toll. A shell explodes near Australian positions.

'This boot is on a Turk – the poor wretch is buried in the wall of the trench, the foot being accidentally left exposed when trench was made.'

stones flying high up in the air with fragments of shell whizzing off in all directions! It is subsiding now, and the Turk is settling down again to his afternoon nap. The shots are becoming fewer and the intervals longer.

Out of all that, we had no casualties – and only slight damage to the parapets, which will be repaired tonight. This, strange as it seems, is the rule in these bombardments!

It is almost still now, just an occasional boom – even the rifles are only keeping a desultory fire to show the Turks that we are still here.

It is Sunday afternoon – 2.45 p.m., or as we say in the trenches, 1445 using the 24 hour clock. It is bright and sunny with a light cool breeze blowing. I wish you were here to admire with me the superb view from my dugout across the blue sea to Mt Samothrace, which towers up into the sky with its wild craggy points and pinnacles, the upper one quarter of it clothed and wreathed with shining white clouds.

Away at my feet are five destroyers, a cruiser, two monitors and a glittering pure white hospital ship, like charming little toys on a brightly painted sea.

I find that I am in the very midst of friends. In the next battalion to me is old George Cole; Norton Green (of Children's Hospital fame) is next to him. Whitford, ex medical superintendent of the Alfred Hospital, is with the artillery just below me on the ridge.

I walked way round to the left near Suvla Bay, about an hour's walk, yesterday afternoon, with a guide, to see that I did not walk into the Turks' trenches for afternoon tea by mistake, and there I found the 9th Light Horse with my old friend Follit, whom I have not seen for six months. As large as life and just as merry! I then visited the 8th Light Horse and got the story of the death of poor old Norman Tetley. There I met Mervyn Higgins and Frank Beamish, both looking very well.

I feel very well fed just now, having not long risen from a hearty meal. I wish you could visit my dugout – it's the cosiest little cave imaginable, with boxes let in to niches in the wall, for one notepaper, shaving materials, etc.

I have now quite a smart trim black moustache, but the effect of this with my closely cropped hair is I must admit rather ludicrous. However, in the army one seldom takes one's cap off, especially if the weather is cold!

I find my camel hair sleeping bag a tremendous success, except that it harbours fleas and lice! However I have it thoroughly aired every day, and powdered over with insecticide, which keeps them down, and they trouble me very little. Pierre and I have great yarns in French everyday, and I think I am making progress – though slowly!

My one trouble is DIRT! We only get one gallon per man per day of fresh water, for drinking, washing and everything. The last few days, owing to some temporary trouble or other, this has been reduced to one-half a gallon per man per day.

Every now and then one can get down to the beach for a swim – I intend to this afternoon with any luck. Of course we have a lot to be thankful for in that, and the people at home in the bush in times of drought are much worse off. So you see I really had nothing to growl about and will very soon get used to being dirty!

I say Mum; the fellows here get parcels from Australia, also papers and letters quite regularly, although the mails out from here are so bad. I would tremendously appreciate anything in the nature of a box of chocolates or biscuits and some papers now and then – also a washer to wash my face! The one I had got lost in the 'lines of communication' – as did several other things on the way to the Front.

I'd also love a couple of R.L. Stevenson's books – (very cheap editions) – and a couple of magazines now and then.

Rogers, an artillery officer, went back to Egypt this morning and I gave him money to send a cable to Stan with my new address. I hope he sends it all right. I sent it to Stan on account of his short address- 'Elder, solicitor, Melbourne'.

I met a chap – curse it, I forget his name – yesterday at the 8th Light Horse who saw Jim Elder just before he left the Peninsula. He was on the beach, en route for the hospital ship, and looked hard and strong, not particularly ill, but had very sore swollen hands. Thank heavens he left just before the ghastly affair of the Lone Pine in which his regiment suffered so terribly! The Lone Pine, by the way, is only a hundred yards from me on our left.

Well Mum darling, I will stop and run down for a swim now. It will take me 20 minutes to get to the beach, and then – what-ho for a good old ablution!

It is nearly 3:30 p.m. and there is not a sound of a gun except in the far distance – just the sharp crack of the echoing rifles, and a deep steady whirr of an aeroplane coming over from Imbros, flying high and going to have a look round the Turks trenches. They will open fire on her in a minute, and our guns will open on them, and the air will be full of noise again. Sometimes, for nearly half-an-hour it is so quiet and pretty that we can hardly believe the Peninsula is what it is – but seldom for as long as a half-an-hour!

Love to Lucile and Stan and the dear children.

With a good big hug for yourself.

From Claude

P.S. I was a censoring some of my men's letters this morning. I found one who sent to his wife a row of kisses (X) with the note 'one to be taken at bedtime'.
I send the same to you my Mum! XXXXX
CM

11 October

A cloudy threatening day until midday, when a storm burst over us and it poured with rain for more than an hour. During afternoon it cleared up and I set out again to see old Follit. Found him very down on his luck, poor old chap. He has a strange temperament, rather like Jack used to be, except he is never in the high spirits that Jack ascends to on occasions. He is very sick of things and is badly in need of holiday!

Had a long conversation with Pierre in the evening, after a hearty meal, and watched a glorious sunset over Samothrace and Imbros.

12 October

Fresh and bright. Quite smart and chilly in the morning at 6 a.m. when I rose. I reckoned I should stop home for a day or two now, having been out a good deal lately. Had a nice sleep after lunch, strange to say, then wrote to Faye Maclure.

About 4.30 I strolled up and had a yarn with George Cole. George is in a pitiable state! He is desperately homesick, has no heart in his work, and spends his time longing for his wife. He speaks of shamming out of the regiment and going back to Egypt, in a half-serious way! Unless he bucks up soon, I'll speak mighty plain to him!

What is I hope, only a little temporary weakness in George, is a very great reality with hundreds and hundreds of our 'patriotic' army. The hundreds of Australian and British officers whose 'patriotism' allows them to come up with some disease or indisposition, to get sent away by the MO, and stay away from the front for weeks or sometimes months. This contemptible spirit of selfishness is not actually cowardice, but is absolutely rampant in the army, and these 'invalids' usually secure some comfortable and safe billet on the lines of communications such as 'OC Parcels', which finally prevents them ever returning to the firing line where their mates daily risk their lives for their Country, and endure hardships and disease and privations uncomplainingly, often doing extra work on account of the absence of their 'sick' comrade!

I have seen in Egypt hundreds of officers and men, healthy and strong, who are basking in the kudos of having 'been to the Front', who were originally invalided out on account of some slight wound, or some real, or often imaginary disease, and had been convalescing for months. Some of my own friends are amongst these, and I absolutely despise them for it. I say the army is rotten with it!

And who will reap all the kudos when it is all over? The man who has stayed under fire with his men for month after month, often scarcely able to crawl round his lines for sickness and weakness – living week after week without a change of clothes – a decent wash – and on a permanent and unvaried diet of bully beef and biscuits – doing three times his own work on account of these 'invalid' mates?

No, no. It is the invalided mate, poor chap, who all this time is staying in a 'country house' in England, spoilt and lionised, spending his time between partridge shooting and telling anecdotes of the Front to pretty girls. *This* is the man who will be dubbed his Country's saviour, for he is the man before the public!

13 October
Wednesday

As I woke this morning and remembered that it was the 13th of the month, the old superstition about number 13 just crossed my mind.

The Turks had indulged in heavy bombing all night without causing any casualties, and now they were trying the effect of a few high-explosive shells. It was a freezing cold morning, and after sick parade I went for a brisk walk behind the firing line to get warm before breakfast. About midday, General Walker got hit in our lines, and I was sent for in a desperate hurry!

This is the first time I have ever been sent for in the lines, and the man who was guiding me took me everywhere but the right place! I had no idea the General was so far away, and when I got there, with some bandages, I found him grey and weak. I sent for some whisky and dressed the wounds – and while doing so was told that another man had been hit at the same time!

By this time the whole Divisional staff had collected around, offering suggestions and getting in the road, and between dealing with them and seeing to the General (who had two nasty wounds in the arm and one in the abdomen) with the other wounded man still to see, I am ashamed to say I lost my head and got flustered!

I don't think it showed at all, as they all seemed to have confidence in me, but I lost confidence in myself, and had a kind of consciousness that I was doing my work badly, which made me worse! I hope I may never have this experience again! I showed to myself that I really lack the balance necessary for the work of a regimental surgeon. I shall fight with this weakness!

In the afternoon, I had a talk with Colonel Jack Knox who is OC of the 23rd Battalion on our left. He said that Kathleen Knox is in Cairo.

A talk with Pierre in the evening …

14 October

Not quite so cold in the morning. Cleared up into a bright and pleasant day.

It has been a regular day 'at home'! The 1st caller was Concert Riddell, who is camped just close by. While he was here, at about 11 30 a.m. Clowes of the 8th Battery Artillery dropped in for a while. He has scarcely gone when in came Tom Brennan and Father Fay. The latter being 'the sporting parson of the 11th' – an RC padre, noted for his bad language and gambling – a rollicking good-natured Irishman!

They had scarcely gone, when old Follit turned up, having had an hour's walk across. He stayed to lunch, and we had a great yarn. A about 3.30 p.m. he left, and at 4.30, Colonel Hearn and Poate turned up, leaving about 5.30, then tea, and a yarn to Pierre, and bed.

Up once each of last two nights with a wound – last night quite a slight one. I hear that they have taken the bullet out of General Walker, who most kindly seemed to have spoken well of me on the beach. It is more than I deserve, for having lost my head!

Got two letters today! The first I have received since leaving Egypt. One was from Mr Borrowman in Melbourne thanking me for looking after Jimmy, and the other from – of all people – Max Butler who has landed at Gallipoli with 7th Hamps! – I shall soon have every friend I possess around me!

15 October

Heavy and cloudy all day. Flies were thick and very sticky. Wrote a couple of letters after lunch, and had a yarn with Major Giles.

Went to bed very early, as there is to be a 'stunt' at 4 a.m., but dropped around to see Whitford first. He has been very sick last couple of days, but is better now. Found Concert Riddell there. Took a run up to Norton Green for a few minutes. The 'stunt' was to scare the Turks, and find their strength – also to make them waste their ammunition! It was a very big affair, and took place along the whole Anzac front.

At 4 a.m., a green rocket went up from Russell's Top, away round to the left, followed immediately by one from the Lone Pine just beside us on our left. This was the signal! Immediately, every man in the firing line along the whole front fired one round in a volley, producing one simultaneous crash and flash of fire along the whole line of several miles!

Our men then brandished their bayonets above the parapet – without showing themselves, and cheered lustily – while at the same moment, the warships and artillery behind our lines open up on the enemy with a roar, pounding shell after shell into their trenches with the sound like one long protracted peal of thunder.

The result was a complete success! The Turks opened up a most terrific fire on our trenches, expecting an attack. The noise was absolutely deafening! Rifles and machine guns keeping up one long roar, punctuated every few seconds by the rending crash of bombs and high-explosive shells. The air was alive with hissing shells, buzzing bullets and fragments screaming overhead and on all sides! Until 4.45 a.m. they maintained a perfect hell of fire on us!

Our men had not fired one shot since the initial volley, but kept up a great shouting and cheering which worked the Turks up to a frantic state of excitement and alarm, judging by their fire! After three-quarters of an hour, they began to drop to it, though still suspicious, and their fire gradually slackened, until 5 a.m. when the eastern sky was beginning to show a faint grey, they relapsed into the usual monotonous dropping fire with the occasional bomb.

In the whole of this rain of lead, there had been *not one* casualty on our side – *not one*!

I had spent the time with my pockets stuffed with bandages, dodging to and fro between the firing line and at the dressing station along a tunnel. On one occasion some earth from a nearby bomb spattered me, but I did not get hurt in the least. I went to bed again from five till 6.30 a.m. then up again for sick parade at seven.

16 October

Spent a quiet and uneventful day.

About 5:00 p.m. a man from the 12th battalion (who occasionally relieve two companies of ours in the firing line for 48 hours) was accidentally shot dead by one of his mates who was cleaning a loaded rifle! Rotten sad thing!

Dropped around to see Whitford in the evening. He is looking much better.

After tea, a wounded hand, and a talk with Pierre. The little devil is most unsatisfactory, as he will do *all* the talking! I can't get a word in edgeways, and our conversations are really a long dissertation by Pierre, and an occasional 'oui' and 'non' from me! However I should be thankful to have him at all!

17 October
Sunday

A heavy cloudy day. I do believe winter is going to burst upon us at last. Very heavy artillery duel over our heads about midday. Lasted about half-an-hour, during which everyone took cover. Several fragments of shell and shrapnel pellets struck the earth just outside my dugout. No casualties!

During the afternoon, I walked around to the 9th Light Horse (about an hour's brisk walk) to see Follit. He was in rather better spirits and looking better now. He had a letter for me from his mother, to whom I had written before I left Egypt, sending his photographs to her. It was a warm, sweet hospitable note and the first letter I have received since leaving Cairo, except for the one from Mr Warren. Follit gave me some chocolates and tinned chicken for our CO Colonel Shaw, who is suffering from a lot of dyspepsia.

Struck a new scheme for French with Pierre. I read to him aloud from a novel by Balzac, *Ursule Minomet*, and he corrects me and explains – in this way I may learn quite a lot from him.

18 October

Cool and cloudy. It's been drizzling most of the night, and it's sticky underfoot, but no rain has fallen today. Took things very quietly today, had a doze after lunch, and read a bit of French. Strolled up and had a yarn with Norton Green before tea.

Pierre in the evening – bed very late last night as a man had an epileptic fit at about 10 p.m.

Everyone is rejoicing at the smothering of 'Beachy Bill' today! Ever since the landing, the beach has been swept daily by shrapnel – half-a-dozen shots being fired per day at irregular intervals, always when things are most busy! Almost daily Beachy has his toll of casualties, and it is estimated that in the last six months there have been over 1,000 casualties here from this one factor alone!

Beachy, judging from the fragments of shell picked up on the beach, does not consist of a single gun, but of a varied assortment, showing that there are at least several batteries playing on this thickly populated a stretch of beach!

Beachy has been located at a spot called 'the Olive Grove' some four or five miles inland. This spot has been swept time and again by our artillery, but if the guns are disabled, they are very quickly restored or replaced, and anyhow, must be in a very obscure and secluded situation, for after six months, Beachy rakes that beach daily, although thousands of our shells have been expended on attempts to permanently disable him!

This afternoon, Beachy Bill spoke about 3.30 p.m. as usual, and immediately there was an awful crash as a little monitor (which no-one had noticed, but which had quietly crept close to the shore and had waited patiently for this opportunity) fired a huge 14-inch gun at the spot where Beachy's smoke – a weak, faint haze – appeared! So well directed and well aimed was it, that they must have made a mess of the whole battery, for Beachy has spoken no more today!

19 October
Tuesday
Cold and cheerless today. I do not feel too well with pains in the stomach.

Lay down after lunch and about 3 p.m., when the sun came out, I dodged about the firing line and took some photographs – some being of the Turks' trenches, by shoving the camera against crevices and loopholes in the parapet. If I were to raise my head I would be shot at once!

French with Pierre. Early bed.

20 October
Today, two officers, a Major and a Captain, who were wounded on the '1st day', returned after an absence in England of six months! They are both senior to Giles and Shaw, who will now I suppose have to hand over to them.

Major Beevor is a fat, rubicund, pompous, self-satisfied brute – quite common I should say, with boundless self-assurance and vanity. Captain Jacobs is a thin, good-looking youth, conceited and bumptious. Both have been obviously lionised and spoilt, until beside our fine officers, who have stuck grimly to their duty and facing the same risks and hardships as their men – beside these, they appear insufferable conceited pups!

A cold wind has been blowing all day, and I have difficulty in keeping warm. I have had pains in my stomach all day.

Had a good talk to Pierre and went to bed at 8:30 p.m.

21 October
My first attack 'Dardanelles diarrhoea' – and damned unpleasant!

I was feeling rather better at lunchtime, and like a fool, I took a little bully beef and some boiled rice, and was prostrated all the afternoon with violent vomiting, diarrhoea and headache!

I did not appear at teatime and slept in my clothes and boots, to be ready for a dash out into the cold night. My head ached until far into the night, and I did have several dashes.

I'm feeling fearfully ashamed of myself, as I have only been in the trenches three weeks today, and I'm already down with sickness!

Everyone said in Egypt that I was not strong enough for the life, and I was quite sure they were wrong, and yet here I am, ill after three weeks.

Lay in my dugout all day.

22 October

I am much better this morning – bundled out of bed at 6:30 am and conducted sick parade.

Went around the lines after breakfast. Felt a bit squirmy after lunch and slept in the dugout most of the afternoon. It was cold and raining, and about 3 o'clock I had a hot bath – my first on the Peninsula! It consisted of sitting on a waterproof sheet in front of a tin with two quarts of hot water, as I carefully sponged myself from head to foot.

After tea, I muffled myself up in my overcoat and went up to see Norton. I was seized with of the collywobbles whilst there, and hastened home to bed, with much dosing and French conversation from Pierre.

23 October
Saturday

Feeling fit again! Cold bleak windy day, with thin driving rain.

This morning I watched the bombardment of a Turkish mule convoy. After two or three explosions in their vicinity they scattered and vanished – presumably into a sap.

Spent the day trying to keep warm, but failed!

25 October

Just six months since that terrible day of landing on the Peninsula! Six long months and here we are, the troops on the identical spot which they took from the Turkish hordes that fearful day – with the exception of about 300 yards advance at the Lone Pine, with its awful loss – we're still in precisely the same spot!

Spent a good deal of the day sitting basking in the sun and writing letters.

The Adjutant, Captain Whitburn, a jolly fine chap, has dysentery. I'm awfully sorry for him for he is a real soldier to the core, and full of pluck.

I wrote a couple of letters – and a talk with Pierre and got into bed.

26 October

Everyone seems to be sick today! Whitburn has dysentery – Sawyer has malaria with the temperature of 104°. Major Shaw has eczema and a tummy ache. Pierre has gastritis, and Ritchie, my batmen, has diarrhoea!

I have not been too brilliant myself – with a slight headache and diarrhoea, but it may be imagination, everyone else being so seedy. My dugout is rapidly becoming a kind of consulting room!

Today has been marked by a naval bombardment overhead. An aeroplane, which hovered over the Turks, directed the shooting and two cruisers and several monitors participated. Under a leaden sky they boomed away all day at intervals, while I wrote a letter or two, and attended to my patients.

27 October

It's a miserable day and blowing a howling sou'wester – the dust was thick everywhere.

As Ritchie was sick, I got no water and was dirty and dusty all day. Whitburn the Adjutant is very sick, but is imploring me not to send him away as he loses all rank and pay at once on leaving the Peninsula. Pierre is sick with a temperature of 101°. I have no candles, and there are none to be had. Am not feeling too well myself – bowels are still loose.

Tried to draw a tooth from a poor devil with the awful toothache. The damn thing broke off under the gum! Toothache now worse, and face all swollen up. With these things all on my mind, and a sick parade of double the usual size, I am feeling a bit fed up of war and the trenches, and the 10th Battalion in particular.

In bed last night I was kept awake by centipedes, which kept knocking earth down on to my face. I kept fantasising they were crawling among my blankets!

29 October
Friday

Today our whole firing line was relieved, and the entire battalion was drawn to the support trenches! I was awfully glad as the men badly needed to rest, and they could spend the day smoking and playing cards and nursing their grievances and ills.

After lunch I took a towel, after packing Whitburn off the Peninsula, and started off for a swim, it being a still warm beautiful day.

I called up to see George Cole first. Once there I heard an explosion further round it to the left, and went round to see if I could do anything. I found that one of our tunnels full men had been blown up by the Turks! About 30 men were semi-suffocated by the fumes of the explosives – five or six never came to, and died.

Going on to the beach, I was very narrowly missed by a shell from Beachy Bill, which exploded a few yards from me!

I went to the Clearing Station where I found old crock Carlisle had returned, though still looking very seedy, also the handsome lady-killer Campbell, who has been shooting and fishing in Scotland for five months or so, on some very thin pretext of sickness.

I had a swim, and feeling clean and happy, I had tea with Balcombe at his 3rd Field Ambulance – a royal feed! Seeing the splendid way these fellows on the beach do for themselves makes me discontented with our tucker, so I bought five shillings worth of herrings and strawberry jam. With this slung over my back in my towel, I trudged home about 8:30 p.m. Found Tom Brennan waiting in my dugout to have a yarn, so walked to his dugout with him.

I went to bed about 10:30 p.m., clean and contented.

31 October
Sunday

It is cold and misty today with a thick fog blowing up from the sea, making everything damp and clammy.

After lunch I sent my batman Ritchie, who is well again now, down to the beach with a note inviting Major Newland up to see me.

He is the 2nd in Command of the 1st Stationary Hospital which has been for eight months at Lemnos, and which has at last come over to the Peninsula to set up, so as to be able to accommodate sick and wounded during the rough weather, when evacuation is impossible.

Newland, who is an awfully nice fellow, has come over in command of an advance party. About 3 p.m. he turned up and Ritchie brought us some tea. I took him all around the trenches and firing line. He scrutinised the Turkish positions through the periscope, watching Turks strolling about in their fields and farmhouses and swept the slopes of Achi Baba with the telescope. He then stayed for tea, in the course of which the 'evening hate' commenced! In this terrific affair he could scarcely eat or drink, but looked around him with wonder at the stupefying din! I walked down to the beach with him afterwards, having thoroughly enjoyed showing him around, and he was intensely interested in everything he saw.

Got home shortly after eight and turned in.

1 November

Today Imbros and Samothrace were a perfect picture. A southwest wind has been blowing all day and breakers had made the blue sea just sweetly pretty. The sunset was simply glorious.

Each evening it seems more beautiful than ever before. I yarned to my bluff old Sergeant for a while in the evening. He is a rough, hardened old campaigner, a soldier all his life – he was in an expedition in 1896 into the depths of Western Africa to subdue some native tribes – lived for eight years in the Sudan and has many strange and interesting experiences to relate!

2 November

After lunch I sat down on my bunk and finished *Dr Jekyll and Mr Hyde*. I had just finished this when the inevitable and futile deputation waited on me to discuss sanitary arrangements for the winter. This consists always of Colonel Hearn (whose niceness, futility, and weakness are well known to me), Fry (who has just been made a temporary major by a piece of gross favouritism) – also futile but conceited as well – and a harmless, aimless kind of Engineer. None of them know what they want, where they wish to go, (or when), or what to do. Neither they nor I have been made a bit wiser about anything, nor have we affected anything at all.

While they were here, I was wanted on the telephone, and who should be at the other end of the line but Max Butler! I bundled the deputation out quickly as I could and ran around to Divisional Headquarters where he was ringing from, and in a few minutes, was shaking hands with my old friend after not seeing him for 11 months! Dear old Max, in a dapper Imperial uniform, bronzed and hardened after a month in the trenches, but otherwise just the same old boy! I had a short talk to him and got Jack's address, and found where Max is camped – about five or six miles from here.

After tea, Norton Green turned up and we yarned for a good while, I then walked home with him and nearly reached an early dissolution from a bomb! Later on, as I was going to bed, an 18-pounder shell burst at the door of my dugout, sending splinters of metal into the wall! I was lying down and not touched. I started to read in bed when Tom Brennan turned up, having had a gay evening with many drinks. He sat and talked excitedly to me until midnight.

3 November

Beyond my usual parade and inspection, I have done nothing but write a Christmas letter home, sitting in the warm sunshine, while another artillery dual took place over my head, and the shells screamed through the still calm air.

After tea, Don Young came down for a chat and told me, incidentally, that he had heard from Gladys, that Mother is going to England, and stopping in Egypt for a while to see me!

I hope this is not so, most heartily, for with both Jack and I out at the Front, it will only mean that we will all get lost to one another, as Mother won't get our letters, and won't know where we are to write to us! I have written to Jack for particulars tonight.

Anzac
3 November

My own darling Mum
I am sitting outside my dugout. This Wednesday afternoon on a box, in the most glorious sunshine imaginable. Never again, I expect, shall I write a Christmas letter to you in such extraordinary circumstances! I shall just try to give you a picture of myself, and surroundings. Our Adjutant has just taken a snap of me with my own camera, so someday you'll see this letter in process of manufacture, as it is at present.

With my back against a wall of the dugout, in which wall holly is sprouting and climbing, I'm sitting on 'Artillery Road', perched up high on our ridge. The ground falls away in front of me at the edge of the road, in a steep ravine to the water's edge about three-quarters of a mile away, rising again to right and left in two rugged shoulders, both of which are lined with our guns concealed in bushes and holes.

The water is a deep blue and absolutely calm, stretching away to where both Imbros and Samothrace rise up in a kind of pale pearly grey mist. Two cruisers, three destroyers and a shiny white hospital ship are lying lazily on the motionless water. There is scarcely a cloud and the sky, and the warm sun is shining brightly.

The whole scene before me is just a charming picture, the weather perfect – exactly like one of those still bright spring days in Victoria where the sun just saves the crisp air from being chilly. The Adjutant is now writing beside me, and I had just remarked to him that I'm going to try to describe in my letter the circumstances in which we are writing. He smiled and said, 'My boy, if you do succeed in describing it, you'll never be believed.' Then I smiled, for I know that you will believe what I write to you, but I know Mum that I can never make you realise the extraordinary scene.

If were I deaf, this would be a charming and peaceful scene before me, – I but we are in the midst of murderous cannon fire! The air is full of the most extraordinary sounds that I cannot describe, and indeed were I to read a description of them not having been here, I would say that it was absurd and hopelessly exaggerated!

Anzac Beach is just hidden from me, being only a narrow strip at the foot of the huge

Claude's dugout at Gallipoli; writing a Christmas letter home

Mary Morlet reads a letter from the Front, Christmas 1915

cliffs far below me. This beach is always crowded with busy throngs of men landing stores and ammunition, and mule teams, with their Indian drivers loading and unloading them.

As I write, the Turks are vigorously bombarding the beach, trying to harass the busy hundreds labouring there. Their shells are whistling over our heads in a constant stream, making a sound exactly like the 'ssswishhh' of huge skyrockets, and bursting over the beach with a distant bang! A cloud of white smoke, which, as it rises above the cliffs, comes into our view in shining white wreaths in the bright sun.

Our guns, situated quite close on the crest of the hills to the right and left of me, are replying to them vigorously. Their reports being a series of crashes, which make my ears ring, and seem to blow a gust of wind into my face at each report!

During occasional pauses in this din, there are other noises to be heard. One of our aeroplanes is sailing serenely overhead in the clear sky – and the wisps of smoke from under her engine clearly visible, trailing behind her as she floats along, with a dreamy monotonous 'whirr', like a huge dragonfly.

Away round at Cape Helles, there is a distant continuous rumble of the naval bombardment from our ships, which has been going on for some hours. There is one more noise, besides the usual cracking of rifles, that is practically incessant, and that is the laughter and chatter of men sitting about smoking.

One other sound is the queer, uncanny rustle of bullets buzzing overhead, going away out towards the sea. One always reads of the 'zip, zip' of bullets. It's not quite like that, but I can't get much nearer to the sound except perhaps by the word 'whisp'.

Well, I have been very long-winded, and Mum I'm sure I have utterly failed to give you any idea of my surroundings as I sit here beside the Adjutant and write my Christmas letter. But I feel sure that I shall never write you at Christmas time under more extraordinary circumstances!

I only wish I could peep in on you and see what you're doing this glorious afternoon.

Well, now for some news!

Yesterday to my intense joy, who should call on me but Max Butler! By Gad I was glad to see him, after 11 months! He is in the 8th Hampshires who are entrenched about five miles from here towards Suvla. He looked awfully well, and was able to tell me that Jack has gone to France, and gave me his address. It was like a breath of Melbourne air to see him again, and his news, which was sketchy enough, but most welcome to me, as news and letters are things that I have given up hoping for. Except for this, everything has been going on as usual.

I am quite well, happy and for trench life, extremely comfortable. I shall continue this after tea.

Don Young has just come to see me – he is quite close, in the 6th Field Ambulance.

I enjoyed talking to the dear old boy until he mentioned, in a matter-of-fact tone that *you* have gone to *England!* I found on questioning him excitedly, that Gladys, in a *recent* letter to him, had mentioned that you are going through Egypt, and you mean to stop with me for a while, then to join Jack in England!! Good Lord Mum! Have you then received *none* of my cables saying I was leaving Egypt, and again that I was at Lemnos?

Oh Lord! This will mean that you will not get my letters for about four months – that you will not know where I am, and that I shan't hear from you for ages and ages. And I hope it is not true!

I hope and hope you're still peacefully at Melrose, Mum. If you start moving about too, we shall all utterly lose each other!

I am sending this to Lucile anyhow, for if Don's news is correct, my other letters will never have been opened!

This Mum darling, is my Christmas letter to you, but if you have left Australia, you won't get it at Christmas time, and probably not at all ...

I am enclosing a little sprig of holly* which grows all over the place at Gallipoli. This I picked from a plant that is creeping over the wall of my dugout – I am leaning against the plant as I write.

Well dear Mum, if you are not there, I hope *you* Lucile will read this fearfully long-winded effusion – although I'm afraid it will bore you my dear!

Anyhow, I wish you all good luck and happiness. You and Stan and the dear mites – but I suppose Elspeth and Katrine would not like to be called mites now! A year will have made a lot of difference to them, and I suppose they're quite little ladies now. Give them a kiss on Christmas morning from their old Uncle Claude, who will I hope, be there to do it for himself next Christmas!

If you *are* there Mum darling, I send you all the love I have in me – I shall be with you, wherever you are, more on that day than on any other since we have been apart.

Bless you, my darling Mother and may we all come together again before long.
From Claude

** The small piece of holly remains to this day, folded in a piece of paper in the envelope of this letter.*

4 November

Today, I fully intended to walk around and see Max, but did not as I woke up with diarrhoea, and felt uncomfortable day. Also the weather was stormy and threatening. Lay in my dugout most of the day except when I argued with Major Carter, MO of the 12th, who is taking over part of our firing line, about boundaries and latrines.

Made the greatest blunder of my trench life today – I sent a man away with an un-united fracture of the fibula that I failed to diagnose! – Poate diagnosed it on the beach, and I have been blushing with shame and misery over it all day! This, together with my tummy ache, and the bad weather, has made this an exceptionally unhappy day.

About 8:30 p.m., I was about to get into bed, when suddenly, tremendous firing started on my right, and in a few moments this spread up towards us and passed us, so that after a few minutes there was just one long continuous roar of rifle fire, punctuated every so few seconds with the crash of an exploding bomb.

I ran up to the firing line, where the air seemed to be absolutely thick with rifle bullets singing and whistling past over and around me, whilst illuminating rockets flew up every few seconds from both lines, lighting up the whole scene in a pale glare. The flashes of guns and exploding bombs gave one the impression of incessant flashes of lightning, while the thunder of reports and explosions followed each other so rapidly as to almost make one continuous roar. The whole thing sounded like a terrific thunderstorm, with a tremendous and sustained downpour of hail, were one standing beneath an iron roof!

This lasted over an hour, and we had two casualties, one man hit in the eye with a fragment of bullet, and the other I'm sorry to say, in the abdomen with a bomb.

5 November

It appears that the cause of last night's outbreak was this.

On our right wing, our men had sapped out in tunnels towards the enemy's lines, so that it only remained to burst through the crust of earth to the surface, and establish a new firing line closer to the enemy.

Our old position was about 100 yards back from the edge of a gully, on the other side of which was the Turks' position. The objective was to establish ourselves at the edge of a gully so as to command their position, and with this idea we set about tunnelling. At the same moment the Turks moved their firing line forward to our side of the gully. It seemed as though the enemy had information as to our intentions, for as soon as we started, the Turks attacked this section of our line, maintaining a heavy fire on us elsewhere to keep us all occupied.

Four times they attacked, and each time, every man carried a sandbag. These were all deposited so as to form a breastwork close-up to our new firing line, and behind this, the Turks finally ensconced themselves, and have been busy digging there all day. That put them on a level and at close quarters with us! Reinforcements have been observed coming up to them, and thus their new position is now unpleasantly strong!

We had 4 killed and 15 wounded in this part of our front, and two killed and one wounded at Lone Pine during the heavy covering fire. I feel one of my own two will die, so it totals at 7 killed and 17 wounded – 24 casualties for the night!

It is the general opinion that there will be another brush tonight in this spot. If the Turks do not attack us, we shall attack them!

It being a beautiful day, after lunch I made Norton Green walk round with me to the left and see Max Butler. It's a tremendous walk. Max was in good form and I enjoyed talking to the old beggar. He told me all about the doings of himself and Jack until they separated, and both came to the front – Jack in the 67th Field Ambulance somewhere in France, and Max sent to Gallipoli.

We got back at about 5: 30 p.m. Mess was over, and I had tea in my dugout, supplied by Ritchie. It is now 9:20 p.m. and though the firing is unusually heavy on our right, there is no sign of any attack yet. However I shall sleep with my clothes on tonight!

6 November

Nothing happened last night. I spent all morning choosing sites for winter latrines – a perfect nuisance! I hate poking around latrines.

This afternoon I went and looked up poor old Major Macdonald, who has after all pushed his way up to the trenches, and is now with the 2nd Battalion.

I am noticing a very serious change coming over me. I am getting nervous! I catch myself ducking as shells fly overhead, in a way that I never used to do! I do not like it at all. People say, 'Oh, it's just at first one is nervous, but one gets used to it'. I don't believe it! My opinion is that the longer one is here and the more one sees, the more jumpy does one become! I shall take a firm grip of myself!

I blushed several times today at the way I started as a fragment flew past me. I have lost all self-respect in my work after that awful blunder with the fractured fibula, and feel that I never want to go back to the beach again, lest I meet Balcombe or Poate. I'm ashamed to show my face amongst that crowd, and yet it was simply nothing but carelessness.

7 November

There was a meeting on the beach to discuss lice. I was not keen on meeting Balcombe or Poate, so I undertook to look after the 12th as well as my own lines, whilst Carter went down.

Wrote to Mr Hamilton Russell this afternoon in the sun.

About 4 p.m. the Turks started dropping shells on the ridge about sixty yards on our left. The explosions were a splendid sight! I took several photographs of the fountains of earth and smoke thrown up. One landed in the gun pit of one of our 18 pounders, and exploded some ammunition and set fire to the brushwood screen yet he did not damage the gun! The only harm done was to burn one man's arms slightly.

At 8 p.m., the Light Horse was to attack the Turks new breastwork. This was to have come off last night, but was postponed. I watched at our observation post from 8 p.m. to 9 p.m. but could see nothing.

8 November

I am feeling as strong and healthy as I ever did in my life, and I think I'm putting on weight.

Last night, although we, thank goodness, were perfectly quiet, things happened on either side of us. To the right, the Light Horse stole out of the darkness and occupied the Turks' position almost unopposed. Then the latter attacked with bombs with the result that, though we held position, one officer was killed, and one officer and 15 men wounded!

On our left, the Lone Pine men – 23rd Battalion – burrowing and sapping in a tunnel towards the Turks, suddenly broke through into one of their trenches. Both sides were completely taken by surprise, and the opening was hastily barricaded after the exchange of a few shots!

9 November

Another glorious day. The mist is hanging low over the sea, obscuring the islands and shading the sun, which nevertheless shines brightly through the veil onto our trench-laden cliff.

I shall never listen to people who tell me that Victoria has one of the finest climates in the world. I would not have believed that there existed a climate where one encounters such long successions of glorious days as here, and Egypt!

Had little difficulty with Carter my next-door neighbour, over latrines. Managed to strike a compromise.

Just about midday there was a sensation! Three destroyers seemed to suddenly go mad – rushing through the glassy water at a terrific pace, foam flying up from their bows and surging away behind them. They had sighted a submarine! Exactly like dogs pursuing a rabbit, they swung to-and-fro: dodged and headed off their invisible enemy, tearing off now in one direction, now in another! One of them fired twice at which the others dashed up to her, and all set off again in a new direction. The water was dead calm, and the air was still and mild. Watching with binoculars, we could see no sign of a periscope. Presently two aeroplanes flew over from Imbros and circled over the water, but the quarry had evidently escaped!

After lunch I sat in the sun outside my dugout and wrote Christmas letters.

About 3 o'clock, a cruiser came in close and fired broadsides over our heads at some point in the Turkish position. I have never seen broadsides fired before. Most impressive! Gave me a headache for a while!

Had a talk in French with Pierre in the evening – or rather *he* had a talk!

The crisis in Lone Pine has ended satisfactorily, as the Turks evacuated the trench opened by our tunnelers, and it has now been occupied in part by our own men.

10 November
Wednesday

Another big mail has come in, and as usual, there is nothing for me. It is now nine weeks since I had any mail at all!

After lunch, I got Carter to look after the battalion, and went down to the beach. I went to the Post Office again and roused, but got no satisfaction. I then wrote again to the OC Post Office both at Lemnos and at Alex, and complained.

Going along the beach, I found the 1st Stationary Hospital unloading stores, and putting up canvas, etc. Le Messurier, Alcorn, Plant, McKenzie, etc. and Majors Powell and Newland welcomed me warmly. Had afternoon tea with them, and a hearty old yarn. With the exception of Follit, Sutherland and Max Butler, the best friends I have on this side of the world are in this hospital.

Home at 9 p.m.

11 November

Busy picking sites for winter latrines all morning. In the afternoon I intended to go and see Whitford, but at 4 p.m. a man was badly hit with shrapnel, and by the time I had fixed him up, it was too late to go.

12 November

Parkinson, who is now in the 2nd Light Horse Field Ambulance, came up to see me this afternoon, and asked me, from Major Crowl, who is OC, to come down and give my opinion on an eye case. I found the eye case to be Gum Plant's brother! I removed a foreign body from his cornea, after which he was much relieved.

I then went down to the Stationary Hospital for dinner. Had a tip-top meal with them and a yarn, and then came back. As I approached home, a Turkish bomb came over and exploded quite close to me – a piece of earth struck my forehead!

Yesterday I was in a group of about 20 men, amongst whom an Indian was leading three pack mules in single file. A shell burst over our heads, and one mule was killed. Not another soul was touched!

When I got back, I found that a bomb had come through the roof of the dressing station of the 6th Field Ambulance, killing three men and wounding three others. Fortunately Don Young was not there at the time. This is about 50 yards from my dugout.

Two nights ago a bomb exploded just outside my door. I had been standing there five minutes before, and had just come inside. It made a hole in the ground and shook the floor and walls of my dugout, putting out the light. No harm was done!

13 November

Saw the sick as usual at 7 a.m. Inspected the lines thereafter.

During afternoon I read a little, and then Gum Plant, Alf Alcorn and old Major Macdonald came round to see me.

In the evening I wrote a letter, and then had to fix up two bomb wounds. These bombs are getting a little nerve-racking! The Turks shoot them out of a trench mortar, and as soon as darkness falls they began to fall promiscuously amongst our dugouts! The explosion from them is something fearful! They contain 4 sticks of dynamite, packed around with cubes of iron, and are constructed from old shell cases and have a long heavy broomstick attached to them, which fits into the barrel of the gun from which they are shot. Aerial torpedoes, we call them! They are becoming more frequent every night! One never knows when one may come, as they send them over at irregular intervals all night!

14 November

Today was supposed to be the commencement of the relief of the 3rd Brigade! From the very start, the poor old 3rd Brigade has always had the worst of it. Away back in March, they got marching orders, and left the great Mena Camp a good six weeks before any of the other brigades.

They were embarked from Alexandria on a fearful mouldy old transport – the *Ionian* – they were told that they would only be on board for 48 hours, and provisions and water were arranged accordingly. But instead of hours, the 3rd Brigade stayed on the *Ionian* for eight weeks at anchor in Mudros harbour!

The 3rd Brigade was then selected to lead the landing party on 25 April and was thus the first on the Peninsula. The 1st, 2nd, and 4th Brigades were relieved, and had six weeks' rest at Lemnos. The 3rd Brigade was left in the trenches where they have now been for almost seven months continuously! Seven times have they been reinforced, but still they are less than 50 per cent of their strength.

Ravaged by disease, torn by shot and shell, the old 3rd Brigade has been continuously buoyed up and encouraged by false hopes of early relief – which has been 'only a week or two off' for four months now! Several times a date has been fixed, but invariably postponed – indefinitely! Such a prolonged and unvaried term of service in the trenches is unprecedented and absolutely unheard of!

Well, the move was meant to take place yesterday. No one was in the least surprised when we were told that it was postponed on account of rough sea. It will certainly not take place today either! When the sea becomes calm there will be some other reason for postponement!

About 3 p.m., our guns got to work on the Turks. In about three-quarters of an hour, their parapets and breastwork looked like a shipwreck! Just a scattered collection of broken sandbags.

The Turks replied with vigour, and shells dropped thickly around us. The nice new latrines, which I'd had built for Headquarters officers about 10 yards from my dugout, were wrecked! A '75' came through the roof. This roof I had made particularly safe, with sandbags, earth, and iron bars! Within a few feet of this building, was a dugout with nothing but a blanket over it in which two men have lived for six months. My latrine roof was crumpled as though it were tissue paper, while the blanket roof next door was not touched!

15 November
Monday

A wild stormy day, with rough sea. The water is a deep leaden blue with white breakers – the wind is howling and screaming over cliffs.

For several hours, the navy bombarded Achi Baba furiously! The whole thing was plainly visible from here. Two monitors with very heavy guns lay away out to sea and fired alternately every few seconds! A cruiser lay close in, and fired broadside after broadside in rapid succession! The flashes of the guns showed out distinctly in the sombre light and wreaths of smoke rolled from them. One long continuous thunder rolled over the sea! The separate explosions, with pillars of white and grey smoke, showed up on the slopes of Achi Baba, where a cloud of dust and smoke hung low. The whole hillside seemed to be covered with these explosions!

I had a headache after lunch and lay down for a while. Arose about 3:30 p.m. and rugged myself up. I started off and fought my way through the wind to the beach, where the breakers were pounding barges and piers to bits, and ruining stacks of cases, which no one had attempted to place in safety!

Went straight around to the Stationary Hospital, and had afternoon tea, and with it, *a piece of cake!!* I returned before dark, feeling much better!

After tea, Billy Cook came round to see me, he is now a subaltern in the 4th Battalion, and revelling in the comfort of being officer, having only had his commission for 14 days!

A wild thunderstorm raged until late. Slept badly.

16 November

A beautiful day! Took things quietly in the afternoon, and read for a while in the sun. In the evening, Major Beevor came into my dugout and yarned to me until I was nearly mad!

About 8 p.m., the 9th and 11th marched past en route for the beach to embark for Lemnos for their long promised rest! The 10th and the 12th are to follow them tomorrow – so this is my last night in this cosy little dugout!

Chapter 13

17 November

'BLACK WEDNESDAY'

The great day when we were to move out of the trenches at last, and embark to Lemnos for a rest. The remnants of the poor old 3rd Brigade! This has been the most miserable and unhappy day I have ever spent ...

22 November

Monday

I take up the thread of this story, lying in a cosy berth on board the troopship *Princess Ena* in the Mudros harbour. The misery of the last five days seems now like a horrible dream! I have just had a wash and cleaned my teeth and now I think I can calmly recapitulate some of the recent hardships.

To continue where I left off.

That Wednesday when we left the trenches was a most awful day! A roaring southwest wind was howling over the sea, and over the foothills that separated us from the beach. Every inch of the ground had been dug and tunnelled with trenches, and the surface was all broken up. Consequently, apart from the fury of the gale, which made it barely possible to stand up except behind shelter, the air was thick with dust and pebbles, which got in our eyes and mouths and stung our faces!

In these circumstances we packed our clothes, with a thick layer of grit over everything, and fought our way, with our load on our backs, out of the trenches to our new quarters. These turned out to be nothing but an open bivouac on the hillside, fully exposed to the fury of the storm! There were holes two or three feet deep, in which we were to shelter from the wind and shellfire, and in these we sat, with earth streaming over us and down our backs, and ate our ration of bully beef and biscuit – and sand! We managed to borrow a little water from Brigade Headquarters, and most of us had a taste of muddy tea as well.

Then, with pegs or stones, we tried to fix a blanket over our hole as a roof, and with all our worldly goods, sat in pairs to see the night out. Shortly after dark the gale increased to a hurricane, which blew away our blanket covers, and almost immediately, an absolute deluge of rain fell! We were soon drenched to the skin, with our blankets and all our personal property. The holes quickly half-filled with muddy water, and drenched and shivering, we crawled out into the howling wind that cut through us like a knife!

Young Captain Loubet and I scrambled up the hillside, frequently slipping and falling in the slimy mud, and walked about on Artillery Road, which was then half under water. The rain had stopped, but the wind howled, bitter and freezing with increasing fury! There was no dry place – not a blanket nor a garment, and no shelter. Others joined us, and we sat or lay in the mud, huddled together and shivering. Some fell asleep, but I was too utterly miserable to think of it! I crawled about, frozen and half choked by the wind until about 1:30 a.m. when I came upon five of our men who were trying to light a fire with wet sticks.

I joined them for the rest of the miserable hours until daylight; sitting huddled over this smoking little apology for a fire.

[18 November]

At daylight, I set off for a brisk walk. The rain had quite finished, the wind died down about sunrise, and about 8 a.m. we managed to scrape together some bacon, tea and biscuits, and felt better again! It turned into a beautiful day – but all our worldly goods were buried under a mass of yellow mud!

The men were in excellent spirits after their awful night, and in the warm sunlight with their blankets and clothes spread out to dry, they laughed and sang, and chaffed one another over their bedraggled appearance!

All night long, shells from the Turkish guns had been whistling over our heads, bound for the beach, where the surf was roaring over our flimsy piers and tramline, and piles of unprotected stores!

By midday, we were all fairly dry, and the sea was calm. Everyone was full of expectation about embarking at nightfall. Our Quartermaster had been on the beach and foraged out some stores for us. Water was worth its weight in gold, but we managed to borrow enough to drink from surrounding regiments. Turkish shells screamed overhead all day, and burst on the beach where hundreds of men were at work repairing the damage after the storm!

After lunch, I went down to the beach with young Lieut. Blackburn. Two piers had absolutely disappeared! The beach was denuded of the usual stacks of cases of stores, all which had been washed away! Not a vestige of the tramline remained! The whole beach was littered with barges and boats that had washed ashore. We went along to the Stationary Hospital where Major Powell, and Newland and Freddie, etc. gave us afternoon tea. I hardly liked taking it, knowing the shortage of water. We returned about 4:30 p.m.

Coming back, a Turkish aeroplane hovered over our poor little beach, gloating over the chaos! Beachy Bill pounded our working parties with shrapnel! There were 70 casualties on the beach that day!

At nightfall we were all ready to start – but no marching orders came. We waited two hours, then mournfully unpacked again and turned in. Ritchie had worked hard at my dugout, which had been swamped, and had borrowed me a regular tunnel to sleep in, in case of need. I crawled into this about nine p.m., thoroughly worn-out.

The Turks now began to drop howitzers on us, from some battery a long way inland. Their ammunition was rotten, and only occasional ones exploded! They landed with a 'plump' in among our dugouts, and I lay awake for long while, listening to the scream of a wounded man. At length I fell asleep.

At midnight my dugout fell in on me! I immediately thought it was a shell, and I was done for! I soon discovered that I was not injured at all. I struggled from under the earth, and spent two hours excavating myself from the burial with all my goods. Shells were still falling thickly around me! I expected each one to drop on top of me, but although frequently falling among groups of men and covering them with earth, not a soul was hurt!

I slept soundly for the rest of the night.

[19 November]

The next morning, the camp was like a pigsty, and I got the sanitary squad busy digging cesspits, latrines, etc. We managed to scrape up enough food, but could get scarcely enough water for tea. After lunch, I went up to the 2nd Battalion, where old Major Macdonald entertained me royally with a basin of water, and some soap! I had not washed my hands for two days!

[20 November]

Saturday morning was another fine day with a smooth sea. Last night we packed everything up again and were ready to move off at a moment's notice. But once again had to disconsolately unpack. I wonder how long this hand-to-mouth existence, borrowing and begging the very water we drink is to go on?

Everyone was becoming sick. I have sent one officer and 22 men away to hospital already. I called up to see Major Macdonald again this afternoon, and felt better in consequence!

The wind was freshening from the North now, blowing off the land. It looked like rain. The sea remained calm so far, but I wished they would take us off, for it is sure to get rough if the wind veers at all.

[21 November]

On Sunday morning a cold wind was still blowing off the shore. The sea was calm and the sky threatening. Colin McPhee the regimental padre, turned up this morning, He seemed a nice chap, and has been in Egypt or somewhere for months, getting better from something or other. We had a church parade in our bivouac. The first Regimental Church Parade I have ever seen, though I have been on active service for 12 months! At times the padre had to stop speaking on account of the roar of the guns. A shell burst close by, in the middle of a hymn, wounding two men who were carrying water. The hymn did not waver!

Our Quartermaster had been very busy earlier in the morning and as a result, we had a sumptuous Sunday dinner consisting of roast beef and *cabbage*! I don't know where he got it but it is the first time I have seen a green vegetable since I got to the trenches!

During the afternoon, orders came to embark at 9 p.m. I held a sick parade at once, and sent off some men to hospital, who I did not think fit to stand the strain of marching with baggage.

By 6 p.m. all was ready. I took the precaution of eating a big meal at teatime, and was mighty glad of it afterwards! At 7:30 p.m. we marched off in column of route, carrying our equipment. It was cold and bleak, but by the time I had gone a hundred yards, with my heavy overcoat, haversacks, pack, and water bottle, revolver and ammunition, I was mighty hot!

Soon the clouds rolled away and the moon shone. Shells screamed over us, but there was not one casualty! With the Quartermaster and the 2nd-in-Command, I bought up at the rear, and the long column was clearly visible, winding silently along the narrow sap, like great dark snake in the moonlight. We reached the beach at 8:45 p.m. and sat down in the bitter cold wind to wait for the troopship, which had not yet turned up.

Six-and-a-half long, weary hours we waited on that beach, frozen to the bone, with the wind biting through our clothes and paralysing us! I had just made up my mind that the boat was not coming, as the sea was getting rougher by the hour, when she turned up!

Stiff and frozen, hungry and miserable, we watched her landing 500 troops before our turn came. Then we boarded two lighters, which put to sea. The sea was now very rough and the wind blowing a gale! We were packed just like sheep in the lighter, down below in the hold – crammed together so that there was no room to move or turn! It took a half-an-hour to get out to the ship. The air was thick and foul with breath of about 250 men. The lighter lurched and rolled. Several of the men were sick, vomiting over their own clothes, and their mates.

At length we reached the troopship and bundled on board. I was at once taken to a cabin where one of the men who had just arrived on the ship lay unconscious and had been abandoned by his regiment. I found the poor devil had been drinking rum until he fell asleep on the icy cold deck, where he was found comatose and nearly dead from exposure and cold!

By the time I had brought him round, all the cabins had all been bagged. I sought out the chief steward, and got a cup of hot cocoa. Oh, how welcome it was! I then lay down on the bunk above the sick man in his cabin. It was then 5:15 a.m.

I woke at 10 a.m., and found my patient better. I foraged about and raked up a cup of tea and some bread and butter for us both. The ship was lurching and pitching all over the place. I had a splitting headache and I went up on deck. Found our ship to be the *Princess Ena*, a Channel boat of the 'L& SW Railway'. The decks were littered with our men, mostly seasick and huddled together with freezing spray dashing over them! The sea was very rough and the icy wind howled over us.

In the saloon nearly all of the officers were sitting smoking and swapping yarns. About 1 p.m. our batmen got some tea and we had biscuits and bully beef. By this time we were steaming up Mudros harbour with its tremendous array of a navy and transports. The immense hospital ship *Aquitaine* lay there like a graceful clean-looking monster. The battleships lying around her, looked like mere pygmies! The enormous *Olympic* – her gigantic hull and four funnels all painted black – went past like some huge ferocious looking mammoth! She was crammed with troops who stood silently on her decks, packed together, each man with his life belt on.

All afternoon we lay at anchor in a furiously rough sea, expecting any moment to be taken off. At nightfall, cold, bleak dark and miserable as it was, we got orders to prepare to disembark forthwith. It seemed to me just too preposterous! Within the next hour, we had three contradictory orders, the last one being not to disembark. I then got a steward to get a hold of some water, and I had a jolly good wash!

At 8.30, we were to have a good hot dinner in the saloon, and to embark on ferries of some sort for the shore at 6:00 a.m. tomorrow.

23 November
Tuesday

We were all ready to trans-ship at 6 a.m. At 8 a.m. the boats came to take us off and by 10.30 the battalion had landed at West Mudros. I immediately sent a sick officer off to the 3rd AGH, who developed dysentery on the voyage and whom I had to keep under morphine for 12 hours – and my frozen man (he comes from Shepparton).

A few wagons were commandeered for the baggage, and most of the officers, including myself threw their packs on to the pile. The OC got a horse, and the rest of us marched in column of route the four miles to our rest camps. It was very cold and bleak, but not nearly as wild as the previous day. We got here about midday, and the band of the 7th came around to meet us and played us in.

I was, at my own instruction, put in a tent with Ben Leane, the adjutant, a lieutenant and a jolly nice chap. Our batman soon made us comfortable and we sat down to a hot lunch, far from shot and shell in a rest camp at the Base. Four hundred reinforcements from Australia were awaiting us here, and they did all the fatigues for us, while our poor worn-out remnants of a battalion, after seven months in the trenches, stretched out and rested after their many hardships and terrible exposure. I was busy for the rest of the day, seeing that sanitary arrangements were satisfactory.

24 November

Blowing a hurricane! Sick parade of 75 men. Almost everyone in the regiment has a cold.

Busy with sanitary problems all day. In the evening I was sent for by Colonel Chuck Shaw of the 1st Field Ambulance, and told that a case of meningitis had occurred amongst our reinforcements about a week ago! No steps re isolation had been taken whatsoever, and he now put the whole responsibility on me by telling me to do what I thought necessary! This was just before sunset, and nothing could be done that night.

Next morning, I had the tent of the meningitis case pulled down and pitched a quarter of a mile away with all the man's tent mates. In the afternoon, accompanied by Colonel Shaw I crossed over the lagoon in a Greek boat and went to the 3rd AGH to see what had become of the case himself. Met Major Martin the pathologist there, and had an interesting talk with him on the subject of the disease. The patient was dead.

Met Faye Maclure, Stewart and Sister Davies of the Alfred Hospital. Was delighted to see Faye again!

Today I had lunch with Tom Brennan at the 11th. They are a very happy party, do themselves well, and Tom is the life of the whole place!

26 November

Sick parade at 7a.m. – 86 of them! The weather is still terrible with a howling wind and dust!

After lunch I went to the 2nd Field Ambulance to replenish my stores. Found Roy Chambers there, the sole survivor of the ravages of sickness. Then went to base medical stores four miles away. No satisfaction at either!

I arrived home at 4.30, when it rained heavily. The 12th, with Major Lorenzo came in today. They had been waiting for favourable weather to embark from Gallipoli ever since we left. Now the whole 3rd Brigade are out of the trenches and they are settling down for a long rest at the Base.

27 November
Saturday

Having got through my work by 10:30 am, I set out for that harbour to see the world. I crossed the lagoon in a Greek boat and walked across to South Pier to catch the ferry. The weather was at this time still and cold with a fair breeze and choppy sea.

I met Tom Loubet and Young Hooper at the ferry and we all embarked for the *Mimetonka* (the Ordnance Store ship). Got there about midday, and bought some clothes, collars, puttees, etc. – everything absurdly cheap. Then we all had a rattling good lunch on board with civilised crockery and cutlery, for the sum of two shillings!

After lunch I thought I would try to get a boat to East Mudros and interview the Post Office people about my mail. I found there were two French officers on board from Mudros East with a yacht, and I asked them for a lift, which they immediately gave me.

As soon as we started, it teamed with rain! We were all wet to the skin at once. Landed at Mudros East. I made careful inquiries as to when the last ferry left for the other side, and I was told 4:30 p.m. Then after being misdirected, and rushing off on a wild goose chase in the mud and pouring rain, at length I found the Post Office. All I was able to extract from them was extravagant promises!

I fought my weary way back through the mud to the pier in good time for the ferry, only to find that owing to rough weather it had left three-quarters of an hour early! There was absolutely no chance whatever of getting a boat of any kind to take me across that night. It was now dusk, the sea furiously rough, the wind howling and the sky heavy with storm clouds. Five miles of raging sea lay between me and the opposite coast and our camp was five miles inland from there! I had not a friend, not even an acquaintance on this side of the island! To walk around one would have to go about 15 or 20 miles!

In this predicament, I saw an official naval pinnace struggling in to the wharf. She was to return immediately to the *Aragon*. By assuming an authoritative air, I managed to bluff my way on to her and so reached the *Aragon*. Here I had the priceless luck to find the West Mudros Camp Commandant had been marooned, and was to be put ashore at West Mudros in a tiny boat!! I stowed away on the boat and reached West Mudros in the pitch-dark in a raging storm! I fought my way up to the 3rd AGH where I was put in to warm dry clothes by Faye Maclure, had dinner there and went to sleep in a cosy bell tent.

All night the wind howled, and before daybreak I rose, left my overcoat and most other wet clothes there, and fought my way around in the murky light of dawn and the bitter wind to our camp. Three-quarters-of-an-hour's walk. I arrived half frozen at 7 a.m., in time to hold Sick Parade and avoid questions being asked. Never will I venture out in that treacherous harbour again!

28 November
Sunday

Church parade was held at 9 a.m. At that time I was unshaven, frozen and miserable. Also had still some sick to see. I did not go to church.

All day the icy wind has howled over us, biting our ears and numbing our fingers and toes. Snow began to fall in the afternoon, driven into our faces with smarting force. Spent all day doing my work, and sneaking back into blankets for a short intervals until the shivering stopped – then went out again into the fearful storm.

29 November

It is still frightfully cold! The snow has been falling lightly all day, except for about two hours. It melts however, as soon as it reaches the ground. I was Brigade Medical Officer today, and managed to get warm once or twice for short intervals, walking about the camp inspecting. I never dreamt wind could be so cold! Have not got my overcoat back from 3rd AGH where I left it soaking wet, and doing without a coat is simply killing.

Seven cases of diphtheria appeared in the Regiment today, and six others in the Brigade! I expect we shall all be quarantined tomorrow!

In bed shortly after tea, shivering violently. Feet still feel like ice!

30 November

A frosty morning – ice all over the place. Found four more cases of diphtheria in the lines. I fear the Brigade will be quarantined.

Had afternoon tea with Faye Maclure at 3rd AGH – met Bess Ferrier and Sister Davies over there, both Alfred girls. Have not spoken to a girl for nearly three months before this!

Took things quietly after duties next morning. Just before lunch, dropped in to see Tom Brennan. He opened a bottle of champagne, after one of beer, with the result that I had a splitting headache all afternoon and night! I went to bed at having had no dinner.

2 December

I'm better this morning, but still a bit headachy. I lay down after lunch for a while, and then wrote a long letter home. Sent off some Christmas cards in the evening.

The next day there was nothing doing! Lay down after lunch until 4 p.m., and then Tom Brennan persuaded me to run across the lagoon in a boat and call on some nurses who were to have dinner with the 11th. Found Colonel Stawell, just returned from England and looking, for him, very well! Returned in triumph with three nurses about six p.m.!

4 December

Today, I decided that being 'medical', and therefore immune and exempt from quarantine, I would go in search of the hot spring 'Thermia'. I hired a mount and a guide. The former turned out to be a tiny shaggy Shetland pony, and the latter, a small boy. I soon put the boy on the pony and walked. Noticing a pained expression on the pony's face, I removed the boy and the saddle and found the poor wee thing had a sore back. I made the boy lead the pony and soon dropped them both far behind and lost them!

Following a little bridle track, I wound in and out of the rocky barren hills, getting steeper and bigger as I went inland. After about one-and-a-half hours' hard walking and scrambling, inquiring my way by signs from Greek shepherd boys, who tended their little flocks, I came on a deep ravine with precipitous rocky walls rising on either side. Nestling at the bottom was a rambling old homestead, half hidden by enormous old fig trees. I descended to this place, which was very like a country boarding house in Australia. Under the beautiful giant fig trees were tables and chairs, and there were several suites of sleeping apartments available for a prolonged stay.

I was at once shown into a large bathroom. The floor was of marble flags, and the atmosphere full of steam. At one end, the floor was scooped out to form a deep bath full of steaming hot water, as clear as crystal. Into this, from a hole in the marble wall, flowed a constant stream of water, exactly the right heat for a good hot bath without being scalded! The water comes from a natural hot spring and runs night and day. It was then 4:30 p.m., and although mess was at six. I could not resist the chance of plunging into the delicious hot water just long enough to soap off my grimy limbs all traces of the trenches and my earthy life therein!

At 5 p.m. I started home. By 5.30 it was quite dark and I missed my way! Sometime after seven I arrived back in the camp weary, footsore and fagged out! I went straight to bed.

Chapter 14

5 December [1915]
Sunday
Woke with a bad headache, which passed off during the day.

After lunch I wrote a letter and then went over to the 3rd AGH and had afternoon tea with Faye Maclure, Sister Kennedy, Ben Leane and two or three other nurses. Got back in time for mess. Not much appetite.

Had a short French conversation with Pierre then went to bed with a headache.

7 December
Not feeling very well. I always wake in the morning with a bad headache.

Reveille is at 6.30. – I crawl out about 6.45 and hold sick parade at 7 a.m., then come back to my tent, shave and wash before breakfast. By this time the headache is beginning to subside, but I can't eat much.

8 December
Took young Tom Loubet and Shaw, two captains of our regiment, over to the 3rd AGH this evening and introduced them to Faye Maclure, who invited us all to dinner. It was a ripping dinner, but I couldn't eat somehow, and had a headache whole time I was there.

9 December
Woke with a splitting headache and did not eat breakfast. Six of us had planned a donkey ride to Thermia for a hot bath today. At 12 o'clock we were to start, but the Greeks let us down over the donkeys, so after waiting until 2 p.m. for the animals to turn up, we abandoned the trip.

I came home to find, of all people, Max Butler sitting in my tent! The poor old boy had come through the most fearful hardships owing to the awful mismanagement of the withdrawal of the remnants of the Fifth Division from the trenches. We had a long yarn, and although my head ached a lot, I loved seeing the old chap again. He told me the romantic tales of his own and of Dick's engagements – and showed me a letter from brother Jack. I walked part way home with him, and came home feeling ill, so I didn't have much dinner.

10 December
Woke with a splitting headache again.

Held a sick parade and then crawled back to bed for the rest of the day. No meals. Temperature 100° in the morning, 102° evening. Felt miserable all day. Head splitting. The Colonel was very kind, came in and sympathised in a ponderous fashion.

11 December
Had planned to walk to Thermia with Ben Leane the Adjutant, and stay the night, coming back early on Sunday morning, having had copious hot baths. Of course this was out of the question. I felt worse instead of better, and my temperature was still high. I crawled out of bed and held sick parade, then crawled back to bed where I have stayed all day feeling utterly miserable. I could not get anything to drink but tea, they made me some arrowroot, which was disgusting! I couldn't touch it!

In the evening the Colonel looked in again and insisted on getting Max Butler to see me.

He blew in like a fresh breeze at 9 p.m., made me some Bovril in his own tent and arranged for my evacuation to hospital.

12 December
About 10 a.m., Colonel Chuck Shaw turned up and said he had arranged to have the Ambulance wagon brought up to my tent. There happened to be a meeting of officers at the time, and they were all standing around in a group when I was put in to the wagon. You would really think it was my funeral!

Well I drove off in the fearful ramshackle old market cart of an ambulance. After a long wait, several stops, and a frightful jolty lumbering drive around, we got to the 3rd AGH where we waited for an hour before I was admitted to a ward. I found that I was shoved into a convalescent ward, owing to the shortage of room. My head was then splitting, and temperature 102°. My bed is in the corner of a marquee, which is pitched on a hillside. My feet are higher than my head! The other patients are mostly up and playing cards – roars of laughter and anecdotes all day.

My impression is that the place is hopelessly short of nurses and orderlies – probably this is only because I am in a convalescent ward – but, anyhow I felt sick and miserable and longed for my own quiet well-managed ward at Heliopolis …

3rd Australian General Hospital
Lemnos
20 December 1915

My own darling Mum
Everything seems to indicate that you are in England, so I am chancing it and writing there.

Lately I have been writing to you care of Lucile at Blairgowrie, Toorak, not knowing in the least where you might be. Lucille being the only stationary member of the family!

You see, Mum, I have never received a word or line from *any* member of the family from Australia or England for nearly four months! The only letters I have received since leaving Heliopolis on 7 September have been one or two from friends in Egypt. I have kept on writing a steady stream of letters home to you and Lucile all this time, always once a week, often twice, until I got ill.

Yes Mum, don't get anxious or frightened, for I am all right now! I have been in bed for 10 days in hospital with a high temperature and a splitting headache. I have had 'Para Typhoid Fever' which is a mild and attenuated form of typhoid, but much shorter and less serious than typhoid.

To set your mind at ease at once, let me tell you that my bed has been carried outside the tent, that I'm sitting up, well wrapped up, and writing with a block on my pillow, and I have just – (note this carefully) – I have just had a meal of chicken, potato and arrowroot. There now! I am feeling thoroughly pleased with myself, for this is the first time I had been allowed to sit up, or to eat chicken.

Now let me tell you all about it, such as there is to tell.

We left Gallipoli before the actual evacuation commenced, and thank heaven, before that fearful storm! Not that we missed the storm, but we had just got comfortable under canvas when it burst upon us. So we had no shot or shell as accompaniment to the snow, sleet and howling cold wind!

Well the weather calmed down again and has been just glorious ever since. About 8 December I began to feel sick and headachy and miserable, and a few days later they bundled me in here, where for a week I could scarcely raise my head, and don't remember much about those days. Now however, I'm convalescent and will soon be back with my regiment again – probably just about Christmas. I'm going to beg them to let me go back to duty on Christmas Eve.

Faye Maclure is an officer of this hospital and has been to see me several times. I really feel very highly honoured, for I have had frequent visits during my sickness, from Colonel Maudesley (dear old chap) and Colonel Stawell. The latter has been perfectly sweet to me, lending me books and Melbourne papers!

The former has been an old father to me just as he was in Egypt! He comes and talks to me in a really paternal fashion. He told me that 'He had heard while in London of the fine work I had done on the Peninsula' – a remark which is almost absurd, as I never had an opportunity of doing anything out of the way, much less did it!

However he seemed to have made up his mind and refused to be convinced otherwise. It is very nice to be told these things, even though one knows that they're not true!

I have an excellent batmen (personal orderly) and he comes over from the regiment every day and shaves and washes me. He is as gentle as a nurse.

Now that I'm allowed to eat again, he scours the village in search of fresh eggs and butter for me, also little biscuits and things.

So you see Mum, I am practically well again – in excellent hands and well looked after. I am tired now and will stop, but will write again in a day or two.

Max Butler is at Lemnos too, and he has a letter from Jack who says that you will be in England by now, so I hope you will get this all right! Be sure that whether I am here, or whether I'm allowed to go back to my regiment, I shall not be under fire at Christmas, and I shall be well enough to have a jolly good time.

My address, which will I hope be now permanent, is the 10th Battalion, 3rd Brigade, 1st Australian Division. I long for your letters, which will probably turn up in a heap some day!

Meantime darling Mum, I know you will write to me frequently and think of me always – as I do you. The thought is very comforting, and will be especially so on Christmas Day.
From Claude

22 December

Am now well on the high road to recovery! It seems that I am to be sent to Egypt to convalesce – though heaven only knows it is not necessary!

Yesterday, Kent brought me over a letter from Sam Crevelli. It has taken seven weeks to get here, but is full interest, and his news of Jack, who's with the 67th Field Ambulance in a village by a river, a few miles behind the trenches in France.

24 December
Christmas Eve

So here I am on a hospital ship bound once more for Egypt!

All Wednesday afternoon and Thursday I felt very miserable and completely lost my appetite, felt nauseous and rotten. Could not look at the eggs and butter that Kent brought, my temperature went up to 99° again!

On Thursday morning Captain Anderson, medical officer of our ward, informed me that I was to leave for Egypt at 4:00 p.m. the same day on the *Delta*. I wrote notes to Max Butler, Ben Leane, and Colonel Beevor, telling them of the fact. When Kent arrived I sent him straight back to camp with the letters, and to get my things together. He returned at 3.45 with the nicest and warmest letters from both the Colonel and Ben.

I was immediately hustled on to a motor ambulance and run down to the wharf. Oh the luxury of that motor, after that awful stagecoach which brought me to 3rd AGH! There I was carefully placed in my stretcher, on the deck of a trawler. Blankets were placed over me, and I was made quite comfortable. We sailed immediately. The sea was calm, sky heavy with clouds, yet with a pink glow touching the tops of the tent-covered barren hills around us. As the trawler wended her way through cruisers, battleships, monitors and destroyers, there was a bitter cold wind, felt even through my blankets.

At last we came alongside the *Delta*. All who could walk went up the gangway. There seemed to be a lot of them! Then after a long wait, our turn came. A crane was swung over the side and a wooden tray lowered. My stretcher and kit were placed on the tray and away aloft I was swung into the empty air!

Before I had time to feel surprise, I found myself smoothly lowered into the bowels of the ship. My stretcher was picked up, and I was carried along to the officers' ward, a spacious saloon. In a few minutes I was tucked into a cosy little bunk, and here I am!

Everything is clean and fresh, and the orderlies wear operating gowns and rubber gloves.

So this is the old *Delta*! How many brave men dying of wounds and sickness have travelled in this very bunk of mine, during that disastrous Gallipoli campaign! At 7 p.m. they brought me a menu. – Oh what luxury! What a banquet! I was allowed to have soup, fish (FISH!!) and a delicious caramel pudding!

Everything was so dainty, so inviting, I found my appetite almost at once, though I viewed the soup with suspicion, lest it should smell of beef tea! But it didn't!

The next day, about 8 a.m. we moved quietly out of the harbour. There was a long swell, which made us roll a good bit. At 9 am I ate a tremendous breakfast, and in the afternoon I was allowed to sit up in a chair, but not for too long. The sudden change to decent food is playing up with me! Tonight I'm distended, and my temperature is 99.5°. Could only eat a little fish for dinner.

They have been decorating the ward all afternoon and it is now gay with red and white bunting, Emus and kangaroos and lizards in cotton wool. Wish I felt well, like most of those on board! The sea is calm and weather is getting warmer every hour. Last Christmas Eve I was on the *Kyarra*, with a cut lip, sewed up by Colonel Syme!

25 December
Christmas morning
A most beautiful calm, warm day, with the sun streaming in through the portholes. Everyone is bright and happy. But my temperature is alas, just on100°. However the RMO, a nice Canadian Lieutenant ('Mr') Montgomery, allowed me to have fish for breakfast, thereby showing his good judgement.

I wrote to Mother in the morning, and was put into a warm bath before lunch. I ate a carefully picked but deliciously dainty lunch, and was then carried up on deck. Lying there on a lounge, well wrapped up – the sun streaming on me, with a mild sea breeze fanning my face.

The sea was as blue as blue, with a slow swinging swell. Oh it was delicious! I could feel myself getting stronger, and I could think of nothing more delightful – no way of spending Christmas more charming than this. Afternoon tea was brought to me, and I was carried down after watching a glorious sunset.

Christmas dinner was at 7 p.m. It was carefully arranged so that almost every patient would find on the menu some delicacy appropriate to his illness. My temperature was taken before dinner – normal! I had a most varied and delicious meal, including a taste of champagne, in which I fervently toasted absent friends, after my own little scattered family.

So tomorrow, Egypt! Slept like a top!

26 December
Sunday
Morning tea at 6 a.m. as usual, and up at 7 a.m. Engines stopped and a pilot came aboard.

It was a beautiful bright sunny morning when, about 8:30 am, I espied through the porthole a mass of square buildings with a group of palm trees in the bright sunlight. We were anchored out in the harbour, and remained there all day. There are three hospital ships being disembarked just in front of us, and two more came in behind us!

I was taken on deck to my lounge again for three hours in the afternoon. Little boats and yachts sailed by tarabouched Egyptians gaily flying the 'Star and Crescent' fluttered around.

I thought of the two previous occasions on which I had watched this scene from a deck – 12 months ago full of wonder on the *Kyarra*, and three and a half months ago, when it might have well been my last glimpse! We remained all day and night at anchor.

27 December
We moved up to the wharf soon after breakfast and commenced disembarkation. A hospital train came on to the wharf alongside the ship. Considering that more than half of the patients were able to walk down the gangway, that the weather was perfect, and that hundreds of ships had been disembarked from the same wharf by the same staff in the past nine months – surely one would expect a little efficiency and expedition to be shown! But no! The thing was bungled, blundered, and mismanaged just in the same old characteristic British fashion!

We eventually were taken off about 5:00 p.m. – flung about the wharf like sacks of wheat – hurled into an ambulance, after an eternal period, and trundled off to the 21st General Hospital at Alex – a RAMC hospital. I was bitterly disappointed at not being able to get up to Heliopolis. I had been eagerly looking forward to meeting all my old friends again!

Geoff Wilkinson – who had been worse than I, but is now equally as well – old Colonel Cudmore from the 3rd AGH – who has been worse than either us, and is now better – and myself. All having the fatal word 'Enteric' on our labels, we were all packed off together! So, here we are now in the 'Officers Enteric Ward', and it has taken us all our time to convince the nurses and orderlies that we're able to sit up and eat decent food! Such is the power of that sinister word 'Enteric' on our labels!

The hospital was originally a barracks for some regiments of the army of occupation. It was to have been taken over by the Australians as a hospital, but was condemned by the Royal Army Medical Corps, who then took it over themselves – in characteristic British fashion!

It is right on the seashore, and is really very comfortable and well managed. Colonel Cudmore, Wilkinson and I found ourselves in a nice airy apartment with another Australian and three Englishmen. One of them was a Baronet. ('2nd Lieutenant Sir Michael Bruce'.) Not a bad kid – a mere brat of a boy, of about 20. Everyone seemed to think we must be desperately ill with an awful 'Enteric' brand on us, however we got a dainty supper, served by a pretty nurse – with real milk in our coffee!

28 December

Tuesday

This morning I got out of bed, put on a dressing gown and slippers and walked about the ward. It was a truly beautiful Egyptian day. I found I could walk fairly well with a stick – with rests! The doctor came round and said we could all have baths, get up, and if we liked, and go for a drive in the afternoon! I had a fine hot bath, put on my uniform and sat down to a jolly good lunch.

Last night on arrival, I posted my letter to Mother, which I wrote on Christmas Day, to London care of Bank of New South Wales, taking on the weight of evidence in favour of her being there now. I suppose this ridiculous 'Enteric' scare will be cabled about the world, so I tottered into a carriage to send off a cable to Mother at the same address, telling her the truth of my condition.

I then went round to the BPO to see if I could not find out something of my mail. They were quite obliging, and to my surprise it seems that my whole mail was sent over to Lemnos about 14 days ago after lying here for three months and that it might turn up here again any day!

At the last moment, they found two letters that seemed to be lying about at random – both for me! They did not attempt to explain their presence, and it did not bother them. One was three months old from Mr Hamilton Russell, and the other, fourteen days old, from Mother - *IN HELIOPOLIS!*

I went to the phone and rang up Pension Montrose at once! Mother was dressing, but I spoke to Lorna Cooke – little Lorna Cooke! I could hardly believe my ears! So Lorna and Mother are together in Heliopolis! What a most delightful situation!

29 December

Got up and had breakfast in my dressing gown. Read some letters, and had a haircut by the hospital barber. I then had a hot bath and lunch in the dining room like a Christian.

Drove up to town after lunch in a motor ambulance. Went to the BPO – no more mail for me yet. I drove down to Raz el Tin Convalescent Hospital and had afternoon tea with Max Yuille. Dick King had a row with him and had gone back to Cairo some time ago – no one knows where he is! Home for dinner.

Mary wrote in her diary:

'I left Melbourne on 2 Nov. 1915, and reached Egypt on 1 December …

At the time I sometimes wondered what I was going to do, but all the same I thought it was right for me to go. And now I can see it was Divine Guidance that led me to go when I did!

I had only been 4 weeks at Heliopolis when Claude was invalided back from Lemnos with Para-typhoid. He had been very ill for 2–3 weeks, and landed in Alexandria on a stretcher, but he quickly recovered, and when we met, I shouldn't have known he had been ill!

During the 4 months he had been away from Egypt, he had not received a single letter from me and only heard in a round about way that I had left Australia! He thought I must have gone to England, and it was the greatest surprise and delight when he found I was in Heliopolis, waiting to receive him!

He arrived on 31 December, so we were able to spend the New Year together, and spent such a happy month together, which he called our "honeymoon".'

Chapter 15

29 February 1916
1st Australian Stationary Hospital
Ismailia

And so the war [in Gallipoli] is over!

Sitting here on the broad veranda of this comfortable house, surrounded by tall lebac trees, and the whole traffic of lines of communication streaming to and fro past the gate, I look back over that awful campaign which has just terminated for us, in complete defeat.

What utter waste. What appalling frightful waste! To think that just 12 months ago, here in Egypt, we could look around with pride on our magnificent Australian army, fresh, well trained, untried – fretting to beat the foe – thirsting to prove themselves and win glory for our young Country. And now – where is this army? 38,000 casualties from sickness, wounds and death! 38,000 brave men, victims of the fatal Gallipoli fiasco!

And here in Egypt once more, I am a surrounded still by our army – but how different! An older, wiser army, having fought like tigers, done their level best, struggled and sweated and battled for eight long months – and been beaten! They have returned to breathe a while – to smooth their ruffled feathers, to reorganise …

I left off this narrative of my experiences the day before I returned to Cairo, which I reached on New Year's Eve.

For two months then I have lived in Egypt, since the Gallipoli war – and looking back over these weeks, I feel that what hardships and discomfort fell *my* lot in the disastrous campaign are now compensated for, a hundred times over …

I shall never forget that day, 31 December 1915 when, after four months' absence, I returned to Cairo again. The excitement and expectation of the railway trip up from Alexandria through the beautiful the verdant Nile Valley – now so familiar – with its vista of brilliant green fields and palm groves, with peasants labouring patiently with their primitive quaint farming – so little changed in method from the times of Father Abraham.

The arrival at the busy railway station, where Follit and I had watched the troops entrain for some mysterious destination – which proved for so many to be a grave on that fatal coast – nearly 12 months ago –and when we longed to accompany them, and cursed this dear old Cairo!

The drive out to Heliopolis in the motor ambulance, every inch of the road is familiar as home. The arrival at the dear old Palace, glistening in the sunshine just as it did that eventful Sunday a year ago when we first entered its great iron gates and were astonished at the vastness of our new home.

I was duly admitted, just as I had admitted thousands myself, and ensconced in a luxurious apartment in the officers' ward. Wally Summons was the MO in charge of me, and he informed me that I should be invalided back to Australia when convalescent! News that I received with horror, and a mental reservation to do all in my power to avert such a calamity!

Mother was living immediately opposite, at 'Villa Montrose', and each day I spent with her going for drives, motoring and strolling. For 10 days then I was a patient, able to go out every day, sleeping at night in my ward, and having breakfast in bed. The warm winter sun streamed in my window each morning and aeroplanes gambolled over the town from the aerodrome close by.

After 10 days, I called on the DMS, and protested against being invalided. He agreed to keep me, but doomed me to work in Cairo for a time! I was sent then to Luna Park, where I did 10 days penance among its convalescents! I always hated Luna Park, and was thankful when recalled to the Palace to take over my old Ward 12. Lorna Cook was nursing there, and it was just too quaint to see pretty little Nurse Lorna in my own old ward! The work was very easy, a shadow of the old strenuous days of last summer.

Well, Freddie Le Messurier was still a patient at Gazireh, and I went see him there. His unit, the 1st Stationary Hospital, was at Ismailia, and they were understaffed. He promised to speak for me when he returned there, and thus it came about that after a month at the base hospital on 'light duty', I got orders to proceed to Ismailia and report for duty to Colonel Powell!

While in Cairo I had taken Mother to every place of interest and seen every sight. Had various trips with Lorna and Marjorie – the two 'Belles of Cairo' – and danced with them at the Continental.

Fit, strong and well, fatter than I had ever been in my life, I reported for duty on the 2nd of February 1916, at the 1st Australian Stationary Hospital, then stationed with the Australian troops on the Canal.

Ismailia is the most beautiful little town I have ever seen. Situated on the banks of Lake Timsah, through one end of which passes the Canal, the town is the headquarters of the Directors of the Canal Company, all of whom are French. Fifty years ago the site of the town was arid desert. Now it is a network of the most beautiful shady avenues with great leafy lebac trees, so close together on both sides that the roads are converted into veritable tunnels, with walls of green tree-trunks and creepers, and a massive high roof of dense foliage. The streets and avenues are flanked by delicious, cool gardens and lawns where the graceful date palms are festooned and linked together by showers of creepers – brilliant with Bougainvillea bloom, and the gorgeous rich hues of tropical flowers and shrubs.

The houses are large, airy, two-storey buildings with broad verandas and almost invariably surrounded by beautiful gardens sparkling with bloom. There is a roomy Club, with its gardens filled with poinciana trees under which are tables and chairs. The Tennis Club is surrounded by massive foliage, and consists of four courts, all in good condition. The lake is lined by rows of bathing boxes and bestrewn with yachts and feluccas. The brilliant blue water is surrounded by pure white sandhills gleaming in the bright winter sun.

The hospital was a convent with several adjoining houses. It is roomy and comfortable and excellently appointed. Our own mess is a four-roomed house in the midst of the annexed buildings, and is cool and airy. The staff, of course, I know well, having travelled in the *Kyarra* with most of them. This then is my new home. I'm going to very happy here.

28 August 1916

So now I take up this narrative again after an interval of six months.

I have spent the whole of this time in Ismailia, on the strength of the 1st Australian Stationary Hospital, which is still my Unit at this moment. Of the 21 months in which I have now been on Service, the last six had been far and away the most delightful and enjoyable. In fact it is difficult to believe that the war is still on! So peaceful and calm and delightful was our own sojourn in that charming village on the Canal. So quiet and comparatively uneventful was our life there – so blissfully happy, that it is difficult looking back over the time, to pick out the different little incidents that made up so delightful a period in my life.

I can best do this by dividing up the whole time into three periods – irrespective of the actual length of them, but considering only the incidents that are grouped in them.

Period 1 – From 1 February until end of April 1916

Immediately I reported for duty I received orders to fit up an Eye and Ear Department and to do all this work myself! After 48 hours, in which I made up my mind as to what was required, I was sent up to Cairo again for two days to get equipment, and had two more happy days with Mother. Very soon, on my return, my wards filled up, and before long I was the busiest man in the hospital!

The 1st and 2nd Divisions of Australians were at this time on our section of the Canal, from Ferry Post to Seropuem. The weather was glorious – the evenings and mornings very cold. In our spare time we took walks or played a little tennis, the latter also often in the mornings before breakfast. While on the courts one day I spied a pretty little brown-eyed girl, whom I found out later, was Dutch. I got introduced to her and soon after this at a little dance, I danced with her. On this occasion I noticed that she spent most of the evening with a good-looking young English Major, and thereafter found that the two were almost inseparable! The child invited me to her house for tea where I met her father and mother – charming people with perfect refined manners, living in a big and beautifully furnished house. The young Major (Dodd) was of course there, and monopolised the little girl who seemed to greatly appreciate his attentions!

For the next two months I saw little or nothing of the Dutch people, as Major Dodd and the little lady were inseparable, making it difficult, and bad taste for a third person to enter the lists. I was disgusted. She is a sweet child, and he is a married man with a baby, which he has never seen! If the family knows this I am annoyed that they allow him to flirt so openly with their daughter. It is the talk of the town!

About the end of March, the 1st and 2nd Divisions went to France, and their place was taken by the 4th and 5th, after an exhausting march from Tel el Kebir, over the desert, which put hundreds of men out of action for days. The Light Horse and artillery also came to the Canal, so there we had over 40,000 troops to look after single-handed, and were very busy indeed. Especially me!

Each day our hospital barge, which is one of the Nile Touring steamers, plied down to Seropuem and came back loaded with sick. Each day a hospital train took 40 or 50 of our worst or chronic cases up to Cairo.

The weather was glorious, and we hired a yacht and went out sailing, and also played a lot of tennis. The Dutch girl's mother came frequently to the hospital to visit the patients. I met her there occasionally and one day she told me that if ever I got permission for Mother

Claude and Mother

Mother and Jack

Claude and Mother

Claude and Mother

to come to the Canal for a day or two, she would be glad to have her stay in their house.
I applied for permission, and was refused.*

[* Mary's diary. *'For some time, no women have been allowed in to the Canal Zone without a special permit.'*]

Meanwhile, Jack had been invalided from Salonika with a broken arm, and had been sent to Cairo, where he stayed with Mother for several weeks. I had a few days' leave and stayed there with them. We had great times together the three of us, and Max Butler was also there. We saw him at his 'School of Instruction'.

Amongst my patients was Major-General Campbell, Quartermaster General of Egypt and Salonika. I ask him about a pass for Mother, and using his influence he got one for three days! Mother duly arrived at Ismailia, and I motored her around to the Dutch people, with whom she was charmed. They were awfully good to me, and I had many meals there while Mother was with them. Although Dodd always monopolised Meis, their daughter.

The Prince of Wales was at Ismailia at this time, and Mother and I met him in the street twice, and also I saw the Commander-in-Chief out riding one day.

After a happy three days, I saw Mother off again to Cairo, about the commencement of May.

(Extract from Mary's diary.
'Claude and I were strolling about one afternoon, when we suddenly came across the Prince of Wales and another young officer walking towards us. Claude of course saluted, and he returned it, but with some little difficulty, as he had a stick in one hand and a huge parcel under his arm. They were both dressed in shorts, puttees and helmets.')

Period 2 – from 1 May to be the end of June 1916
The 4th and 5th Divisions were still on the Canal at commencement of this month. Follit was at Ferry Post, as DADMS, Fifth Division. He dined with me two or three times, and I dined with him, but saw comparatively little of him altogether. Although it was always very nice, I could never get back to our old terms of friendship with him somehow. He now has such different interests, and numbers of his new friends are amongst the Englishman on the staff.

After Mother went back I was on much more intimate terms with the Dutch family – the Van Konijneuburgs, and saw a great deal of Madame and a certain amount of Meis –in spite of the married Major!

About the middle of May the two Divisions had embarked for France, leaving only a thin line of English troops on the Canal. Before this, however, Jack had come down with me from Cairo, where I had another trip of about 48 hours, and stayed a couple of days at the hospital. I took him around at to the Van Ks, who were very kind to him and motored him out towards the trenches from Ferry Post. We had a fine time together!

With the two Divisions went Major Dodd, and also most of our work, which dropped to a mere shell of its previous amount. The barge only went down the Canal twice a week, likewise the train to Cairo.

Each day I saw the Van K's who were kindness itself to me, and I became almost one of the family. I went for bicycle rides with Meis in the early morning, to the amusement of the Mess, and our friendship became closer each day.

The weather had now become frightfully hot. The temperature scarcely dropped below 100° degrees for nearly two months – (June and July). And frequently rose to 116° in the shade! The heat and monotony told on us and we all lost weight and got sick of the Canal.

About 20 June, the Van Ks, except Mijnheer, left for Holland, and I saw them off at Port Said, staying the night with them there. It was very pathetic as Mijnheer was refused a passport and had to remain in Egypt by himself! He and I returned together to Ismailia, and thereafter we were close companions until we left the canal.

Very hot, very monotonous, very little work. All our friends in France – Englishmen with their aloof, discouraging manners were all round us. June drew to a close without a hint of us leaving Egypt!

Period 3 – From the end of June to the end of August 1916.
Jack and Mother had just spent a delightful week together in Alexandria in the Casino San Stefano Hotel, and had scarcely been back in Cairo more than a week, when Jack suddenly got orders, and entrained for Alex en route for Salonika! Mother was now by herself in the awful heat of Cairo. Nearly all her friends having gone to England, there was nothing for her to do, as all the Australian hospitals at Heliopolis had just closed down. Well, I got leave from the Colonel and spent five days with Mother, in which time I was able to persuade her to take the next boat to England, and to help her with her passport, her packing and final purchases. I accompanied her in the train to Port Said, and actually saw her into her cabin on board the *Arabia*.

I was back on duty after exactly five days' absence. The monotony of the next six weeks was broken only by my daily and nightly visits to Mijnheer, and the frequent dinners and supper parties that he gave me. Almost daily, we played tennis at about 4:30 p.m., and afterwards went swimming. The swimming was at its best, however, before the Dutch family left for Holland, when we had daily mixed bathing parties, followed by tea in their cabin.

On 11 August [Claude's birthday], we got word of our approaching departure, and on the 12th I went up to Cairo for a last visit, returning the same day. The weather began to get a little cooler about this time, though still very hot. For the next 10 days we were occupied in packing and other preparations. I was able on two occasions, to send a case of beer out to Max Butler in the desert, and had him stay with me for a couple of days.

On 24 August we entrained with our men and all our baggage, and finally left our beautiful little home on the Canal with its many delightful associations. After 16 hours train journey, we reached Siddi Gaber shortly after daybreak, and were quartered in a comfortable camp at Mustapher – where Jack had spent 10 days en route to Salonika.

Looking back over these seven months, the first five were almost without a hitch – absolutely glorious!

I had the most valuable experience of being the only specialist on our section of the Canal and did many mastoids, excised eyes, removed pterygia, aural and nasal polyps by the score and of course, lots of tonsils. I did much laryngoscopy, and quantities of refracting. I numbered amongst my patients six Generals, numbers of Colonels and many other more junior officers. Altogether I saw 1,350 patients and supplied 230 pairs of glasses! Such was the work. The last two months were very hot and we became rather sick of it all, as all other Australians from around had gone to France. The truth was we had not enough work at this time.

Early in August, the hospital suddenly filled up with wounded Light Horse men from the Battle of Romani. Everything was now changed and we will all pleased and happy, rejoicing in attending our own wounded boys.

No sooner had the excitement of this subsided, than our marching orders came! Personally, even at the hottest time, when we were a bit depressed and discouraged, I always had the diversion of Mijnheer's company and free use of his beautiful cool house and bathing box.

I never expect to experience such delightful conditions again whilst on active service.

[This is the end of Claude's First World War diary]

Chapter 16

1st Australian Stationary hospital
Ismailia

11 July 1916

My own darling Mum
So when this reaches you, you'll be safe in London! Fancy, after 20 years!

What a most extraordinary difference you'll see in the old place now. I do hope your journey was as comfortable and happy as it promised to be Mum dear. At present moment you must be about 24 hours out from Marseilles, and tomorrow, I hope to get your cable telling me of your safe arrival there.

I have written to Lucile giving her full details of your exit from Egypt, besides sending the cable we agreed on, as soon as I got back. I of course, cabled to Ella of your having started, and also wired to Jack at Alexandria that you had got away comfortably. He was still at Alex on the 7th – perfectly happy and comfortable, but still with no news of a ship to Greece.

Freddie and Pitcher went down to Ramleh for a few days leave yesterday, and I wired to Jack of their going, so that if he is still there they should have a good time together.

It is of course still very hot here, but I am quite well. The new uniform arrived today, and I think it will be all right. I have spent nearly every evening since you left with the old Dutchman, and have dined with him twice. He dines with me tomorrow.

I am not very busy, but just have enough it to keep me going comfortably till about midday – that is all. Still no news of our going, but I'm getting quite resigned now.

I will not write any more at present Mum darling, but will wait 24 hours hoping for the cable from Marseilles.

12 July 3 p.m.
My darling Mum
The cable has not yet arrived but your letter written on board the *Arabia* the morning you sailed has just come – opened by Censor – five days after written!

My room at the Eastern Exchange (the one that Meis had when I saw them off) looked over the harbour, and I awoke at 7 a.m. and saw the ship still in. I went down to breakfast at 7.30, noticing that the ship was still there, but at 8 a.m. as I drove to the station I saw that she had gone.

It was a great success getting that man 'Henry King' to look after the baggage, as we were first on board, of all the passengers who came by that train! As I passed the Customs House on the way back, I saw piles of luggage there and a number of distracted people clambering around Cook's man trying to get it sorted out!

I do hope you're having a comfortable trip Mum dear, and I am much relieved to think that you have left this climate. It is awfully hot today!'

I shall wait until leaving before closing this in case the cable comes – if not I must post it for the mail.

30 July. The cable has come Mum darling! It arrived at 9 o'clock last night. Thanks so much. I am most thankful that you have finished with the Mediterranean. May you have a safe and comfortable trip through France.

Goodbye Mum dear.
From Claude

Claude's mother arrived safely in Marseilles, after an anxious trip from Port Said, during which time the passengers had their life jackets constantly with them, for fear of a submarine attack. She travelled through France on the P&O Express, and arrived in England to be met by her friend Ella Foster at Victoria Station. She was taken to Ella's flat where a room had been engaged for her. This proved to be a most satisfactory arrangement, and with no household worries and only her share of the weekly account to pay, Mary stayed in her Chelsea home, surrounded by her friends until she finally returned to Australia in 1920.

Claude embarked for UK on 14 September, and was posted to the Camp Hospital, Dartmouth, Kent, only an hour's train travel from his Mother, so they were able to meet frequently.

Claude was appointed 'Oculist to the Hospital', and his Mother *'had the happiness of spending Christmas Day with him there. Great preparations had been made for and by the patients, and the decorations in the different wards were quite wonderful! About 40 patients were able to sit up to a long table in one of Claude's wards, and he carved first one huge turkey, and then another, which we handed round with all the proper trimmings. Then came plum pudding and other sweets; beer, and finally Claude's little personal gift of cigarettes to each man.'*

On 30 January 1917 Claude was promoted to the rank of Major, and received orders to proceed to France, where he was posted to the 1st Australian General Hospital. Once again, he was appointed Oculist.

His mother recorded. *'I frequently came across men in the hospital I visit at Chelsea, who had been treated by him, and it was delightful to hear the way they spoke of his kindness and skill, especially one man who was nearly 50, (Jones) and had lost both eyes.'*

Mary travelled round England, once again visiting her relatives, and spent time on the Isle of Wight with her, Jack's sisters, Lucile, now in her 70s, and Goldie.

On 31 March 1917, Claude was detailed to the 4th Australian Division, and on 8 April was taken on strength of 13th Field Ambulance 'in the field', where he was to serve for the next eighteen months.

The details of his service were carefully recorded in his large leather-bound diary, which was regrettably lost many years later, by a family acquaintance who had borrowed it! However, anecdotes remain, and a couple of letters, as well as service details.

Claude's time with the 13th Field Ambulance was colourful, and varied, and he served with distinction through these months close to the Front Line. In September 1917 he was temporarily detached to serve with the 10th Casualty Clearing Station, close to the firing line.

Details of his activities were recorded and commended by Lieutenant-Colonel Fry, CO 13th Field Ambulance.

'During the day and night of 21/22 October 1917, Major Morlet was in charge of a section of the Dressing Station at Ypres when it was being heavily shelled. He carried on with the treatment and evacuation of wounded all day in spite of the shelling, which was causing heavy casualties among his own personnel, until about 10 p.m. when orders were received to evacuate the Station as the shelling had increased to an extent as to render it untenable. He personally supervised the clearing of all wounded from the Station and was himself the last to leave the place.

'Temporary arrangements for the care of the wounded were promptly instituted by him, until the Dressing Station could be re-occupied next morning, when he went back with a diminished staff and carried on until relieved.

'By his coolness under extremely trying and dangerous conditions the evacuation and care of the wounded was carried on without delay, in spite of the difficulties caused by the impossibility of using the Dressing Station. At this time, many wounded were coming through, and had to be treated and evacuated.

'Major Morlet has done excellent work with this Unit since April 1917, and has been with it in all its turns in the Line at BULLECOURT in April, MESSINS in June, PLOEGSTRAAT and KANDAHAR Farm areas in July and August, and YPRES in October 1917.

'Major Morlet left Australia with the AIF in 1914 and did Specialist work in Egypt as Ophthalmic and Aural Surgeon for some months. He then volunteered and went as RMO to the 10th Aust. Inf. Bn. on Gallipoli where he rendered valuable service…'

(Record is illegible after this.)

On this commendation, Claude was 'Mentioned in Dispatches' by General Sir Douglas Haig in his dispatch of 8 November 1918 '*Submitting names deserving of special mention*'. (Promulgated in *Commonwealth of Australia Gazette* No 61, dated 23 May 1919)

In November 1917, Claude returned to England on leave for ten days, which he spent with his mother, then returned to his Unit. This was followed by two weeks leave in January, which he spent in Paris. He kept a diary of this time, and described how he met a charming French girl, and escorted her about the city for the whole leave. The diary was regrettably destroyed.

Some 40 years later, an extraordinary event of coincidence occurred, when Claude's old friend and 'Best Man' at his wedding, Doctor Ralph Crisp, was travelling to Scotland with his wife by train.

Sitting in the same compartment was a little old lady, who turned out to be French. In the course of the conversation, Claude's friends revealed that they came from Australia, upon which the French lady told them how she had met and fallen in love with a dashing young Australian doctor in the Great War. His name was 'Claude Morlet'. Could it be remotely possible that they knew of him?

(As Claude was then a widower, and the French lady had never married, we, his children, urged him to contact his 'old flame' – but to no avail!)

Claude returned to his Unit at the Front, and further distinguished himself 'in action' as described in his Commander's commendation.

'This Officer has shown marked initiative and skill in the organisation of Advanced and Main dressing Stations. On 27 March 1918 he performed wonderful work and exhibited great courage and coolness under severe hostile shelling while in charge of the Advanced Dressing Station at HENINCOURT, west of ALBERT. On 5 April, while attending cases in the Main Dressing Station, in WARLOY, west of ALBERT, the village was heavily shelled, and the Dressing Station received a direct hit, the ceiling falling in, and a wall being shattered. There was a large collection of stretcher cases at that time but Major Morlet's skill, courage and initiative were equal to the emergency. He reorganised the dressing station and, inspiring all ranks by his gallant and cool behaviour, successfully attended to all cases and removed them out of danger.

During the month of June 1918, Major Morlet was temporarily in command of the 13th Field Ambulance and the whole of the preparation of evacuation routes for the battle of HAMEL east of CORBIE, fell on his shoulders. This entailed many reconnaissances of the forward area under shellfire.

I consider this officer worthy of special recognition for gallantry and devotion to duty during the period 25 February to 17 Sept. 1918.

Signed, Kenneth Smith. Colonel.

ADMS 4th Australian Division.'

Albert Church, 1918, destroyed by the German offensive

'Some of my officers of the 13th Field Ambulance, 1918'

Lt Colonel Claude Morlet leading the 13th Field Ambulance in France, 1918

Following this commendation, Claude was awarded the 'Distinguished Service Order'. London Gazette dated 1 January 1919. *'Relating to the conspicuous services rendered by the undermentioned member of the Australian Imperial Force'.*

AWARDED THE DISTINGUISHED SERVICE ORDER
Major Claude Morlet.

The above was promulgated in *Commonwealth of Australia Gazette* No 61 dated 23 May, 1919.

There were lighter moments in the war, as recorded by his friend Tom Louch, in his memoirs of the Great War.

'On 22 July the 4th Division Race meeting was held at Allonville … There was concern that a large crowd collected for the races might attract enemy shelling, but this did not happen. The only casualty of the day was Captain Kemmis, ADC to the Divisional Commander, who in the first race, was thrown and killed.

The races however went on, and among the riders was Major Claude Morlet of 13 Fld Ambulance.'

In his personal communication to Claude in 1970, Tom Louch, in reference to his 'Memoirs' said. *'I have made no mention of the fact, which you may have forgotten, that after a very successful dinner at Bovelles, in October 1918, you insisted on turning out the Brigade Headquarters Guard at midnight, and inspected it – a privilege only exercised in daylight by General Officers exclusively! The Guard was highly amused.'*

At the end of September 1918, Claude was detached from 13 Field Ambulance and temporarily appointed 'Deputy Assistant Director of Medical Services' (DADMS) 4th Division, but returned to his Unit a month later for his final posting in the war. He was appointed Commander of the 2nd Field Ambulance, with the rank of 'temporary Lieutenant-Colonel', but soon after, his promotion was confirmed, and he became a 'substantive Lieutenant Colonel'.

At this point of time however, the Armistice had been declared, and the war had just 'fizzled out'. Claude wrote unhappily to his Mother.

2nd Field Ambulance
France
November 1918

My darling Mum
It is days and days since I wrote to you. Such crowded days they have been – so full of anxiety and responsibility – of petty troubles and serious problems! It seems years at least, since I got my promotion and my command!

I have come in to a very arduous task – a job with responsibility I never dreamt of – and with insurmountable and multitudinous difficulties I never realised. For nearly two years now, I have lived in a Unit, which was a paragon of harmony, where the officers were all friends, and most of them had a true and sincere affection for one another. Where the non-commissioned officers were loyal and trusty, and in whom officers had confidence and admiration, and for whom the men had most genuine affection and respect, and who were themselves a happy family. The men were like one large family of boys, who stood by each other and their superiors, and pulled together, taking pride in themselves and their unit.

In such surroundings I have pursued the even tenor of my way for nearly two years, when I'm suddenly put in command of a very different type of Unit! After the first 10 days I began to notice that things were not quite as they should be, and during the last week I have seen my new command in its true colours! There are ten officers, of whom seven are splendid fellows, and three are hopeless mischief-makers. Instead of the happy Mess I have been used to, I have had to settle arguments, bickering and quarrels amongst medical men older than myself – old enough to know better! I find a spirit of dissatisfaction and jealousy amongst the non-commissioned officers who are all pulling different ways and who have little respect for some of their officers. I find an ominous, smouldering discontent among the men – a kind of passive surliness, which hints at a readiness to open mutiny if given the opportunity!

As the 'Commanding Officer' of such a thorny and ugly proposition, I have begun to see that my position is both a difficult and responsible one! I am the 'Court of Appeal' to settle all arguments, pacify all quarrels and crush all murmurings of discontent! If ever inexhaustible patience, a clear and well-balanced head, and above all, infinite tact were demanded of a man, it is of the CO 2nd Field Ambulance! A man of personality is required – a strong man – I am neither!

Oh! If ever I realised my weakness – my moral instability, and above all my lack of patience and of tact, my total want of decision and character – it is now! I have had sleepless nights, and days that are a maze of perplexities. There have been times when I have despaired and longed to become sick, so as to get away from it all! Now you see what a fine specimen of a son you have!

I know what you will say dearest Mum – 'trust in Him and it will all come right'. Well, I do try Mum dear – not nearly enough of course, but a little more day by day and tonight, I feel truly that God is helping and that I am not quite so alone as I have been feeling lately.

Do you know I believe I shall be the better for all this, even if I go under and make a complete failure of everything? I feel tonight that this experience will (morally) make a man of me. I see more of my faults and weaknesses day by day, and try to rectify. This moral struggle is infinitely harder for me than was the strain of controlling fear when in personal danger under fire! If I can learn to trust in God one 50th as much as you do Mum, I think it will be far easier to face the problems and difficulties of civil life when I get back to it.

Well, come now, I have rambled far too much! During this advance day-by-day towards the frontier, mail arrangements are dreadful, and I hardly ever get letters. The last I heard from you was 8 November 1918, just after getting my wire re promotion. I suppose they will all come in a heap one of these days!

My 'leave' has gone by the board! I shall not get it after all!

Good night darling Mum.

From Claude

Claude Morlet in 1918, at the end of World War 1

There is no further record of Claude's time with the 2nd Field Ambulance, nor do the family ever recall hearing Claude speak of it, though he occasionally mentioned the 13th Field Ambulance. His brother Jack was still in Macedonia, where heat and ravages of malaria made life unpleasant. As he was anxious to return to France, he finally and reluctantly, signed off with the RAMC with whom he had served for three years, to join the Australian Army Medical Corps.

Mary wrote in her diary.

'It was quite a wrench parting from the Regiment (the 2nd Northumberland Fusiliers or the famous 'Fighting Fifth' as they were known) where he had so many friends.'

On 5 May 1918 Mary met her son Jack at Waterloo Station, after an absence of two years since they parted in Egypt. He had crossed the Adriatic, and travelled overland from Salonika, through Greece, Italy and France.

On reporting to Headquarters, he found to his dismay that it was impossible to transfer to the AAMC with out returning to Australia! In spite of this disappointment, he decided to do so, but did not get back to England until March 1919.

Claude left France in May 1919, and at a Ceremonial Parade at Buckingham Palace, attended by his Mother, he was awarded the DSO by King George V. He was then granted leave from May until the end of August with full pay and thereafter, leave without pay whilst he became a House Surgeon at the Royal Eye Hospital London.

In spite of his earlier efforts to get away from the eye work in Egypt, it seemed that this was now his destiny, and so he decided to continue his training to become an Ophthalmologist.

On 25 June 1919 the Peace Treaty was signed, and five days later Claude received a letter written in French from his Father's cousin Christine, Comtesse de Sommyèvre telling him that she had been present at Versailles, where it was signed in the famous Hall of Mirrors.

On 19 July, Peace Celebrations were held in London. There was a Grand Parade of all Allied Troops who took part in the Great War, and Claude with a party of friends watched the Parade from a room overlooking the route.

In early 1920, Claude completed his training at the Royal Eye Hospital, and obtained a position as Senior Medical Officer on the *Megantic*, which was commandeered to bring 1,600 passengers – mainly returning soldiers and their families, including his Mother – back to Australia. Jack had decided to stay on in UK to further his studies. He remained for the next two years, completing his Fellowship of The Royal College of Surgeons of Edinburgh (FRCSE).

When the ship arrived at Fremantle in Western Australia, Claude found a letter awaiting him from Colonel Barber, the Principal Medical Officer, asking Claude to call on him. The Colonel told him that there was a very good opening for an ophthalmologist in Perth, and that he should consider 'setting up' there! This was most encouraging, though Claude could not commit himself at that point of time, and needed to give the matter some thought.

They reached Melbourne, where Lucile and her family met them, and Mother disembarked. Claude however, was obliged to continue on to Sydney with the ship. There he received his official discharge from the AIF and a month's leave, in which he went up to the northern rivers and Brisbane, and then spent some days at Bontharambo before returning to Melbourne.

It was there that he once again met his nemesis Dr James Barrett, who informed him, in no uncertain terms, that there was no room for another Oculist in Melbourne!

At that moment, Claude decided to go to Perth where he would be welcome.

CHAPTER 17

PERTH

On 14 May 1920, Claude commenced practice in Perth. He had obtained rooms in Lister House, 250 St George's Terrace, where he put up his brass plate.

DR CLAUDE MORLET, DISEASES OF THE EYE

The rooms were spacious, so in the interests of economy he set up living accommodation in the curtained-off back rooms of the suite.

Immediately, he found himself busy, and from knowing only Dr Barber, and his three daughters, he soon had a great number of friends, and was swept up in the busy social life of the young city. He was made a member of the Weld Club, and was appointed Ophthalmologist to Fremantle Hospital, as well as Consultant to the School for Deaf Children, from whence he later wrote an important original paper on Congenital Rubella Disease entitled 'Rubella Retinitis in Western Australia'.

In August of that year, Mary travelled to Perth and spent *'a delightful four months with my dear old Claude. It was so nice to find how well he was getting on considering the short time he had been there.'*

His friend Tom Louch had returned to Law Practice in Perth, and had a large comfortable apartment, which he offered to share with Claude. This proved to be a most satisfactory arrangement. Over the next couple of years Lister House filled up with professional people, and the Post Office Directory recorded:

Ground Floor

Morlet. Dr Claude. Eye Specialist
Grave. Miss Octavia. Masseuse
Johnson. Dr A Syme. Radiologist
Crisp. Dr Ralph. H. Medical Practitioner

Second Floor

Henderson. G.B. Dentist
Gill. Frank. Surgeon
Gill H. Baldwin. Medical Practitioner

Claude rejoiced in the warm climate, which reminded him so much of

Egypt. Often in the early mornings of summer he would swim in the ocean at Cottesloe beach. Many years later he related an incident to his children.

He had gone for his early morning dip, and as the beach was deserted, he neglected to wear his bathing suit and swam naked. When it came time to come out of the water he was astounded to see two Nuns sitting on the beach beside his towel and clothes! He crouched in the water for the next thirty minutes, quaking with cold, with the Nuns showing no inclination to move!

Finally he plucked up courage, made a dash from the water, and gathered up his belongings, bidding the Nuns 'Good morning' as he rushed past! 'They sat', he recalled, 'with their heads bowed, and said nothing'.

In 1921 Claude wrote to his Mother, and invited her to stay a few months. Mary recorded:

'On 26 September I started for Perth. This time I went overland, as I was anxious to see that almost unknown part of our great Continent. Leaving Melbourne on a Monday afternoon, I reached Perth on Friday morning, having spent 4 nights in the train. It was a most interesting journey, and the train most comfortable. At different stopping places we saw a number of aborigines, which is now a very unusual sight in most parts of Australia.

Claude and I had a delightful time together, the dear boy [aged 33!] always so kind and thoughtful for me. He seems to be thoroughly established in Perth now, and his practice steadily increasing ... I saw quite a lot of West Australia, as we went about 300 miles north to Geraldton, where Claude was 'Best Man' at Evie Percy and Eric Guttridge's wedding.

At Christmas time he motored me down to Bunbury, more than 100 miles south.'

She returned to Melbourne by sea at the end of December.

Jack returned from London in February 1922, to take up a country General Practice in Camperdown, Victoria. A beautiful house came with the Practice, and before long, Mother gave up her room in South Yarra and moved in with him, where she then lived for many years to come.

Meanwhile, Claude took flying lessons at Maylands airfield. He progressed well, but one Saturday as he drove out to the airfield, he was surprised to see all the tramcars at a standstill. When he reached the airfield he found to his horror that a student pilot had crashed the aeroplane into the Perth powerhouse near the airfield, taking with him the instructor! That was the end of Claude's flying career!

In 1923 Mary visited Perth again, and while there she and Claude planned a trip back to the 'old world' so that Claude could 'keep up to date with his profession'. This was to take place in two years time.

Meanwhile Claude continued to live in the social swirl, and was considered a most eligible bachelor. He was greatly attracted to the sister of a colleague, and was on the verge of proposing marriage, when, knowing she was a Roman Catholic, he discussed the matter with the Catholic Archbishop, with whom he was acquainted. He was assured that marriage was in order, however any children would have to be brought up in the Catholic Faith. Claude had second thoughts.

At a Government House Ball he met a beautiful girl named Mildred Milbank, who to Claude's great disappointment, was already engaged to be married.

About this time, Claude and his mother sailed for UK on the SS *Thermistocles*. Mother boarded in Melbourne, and Claude joined the ship in Fremantle on 16 March 1925.

Mary wrote in her diary.

'It was a delightful arrangement, that after having been separated so much from Claude, I was now able to come away with him on a long sea voyage … Everything was so comfortable and home like. They only take 100 passengers in the 1st saloon, with the consequence that one gets so much personal attention.'

They travelled via Durban, Cape Town, and Tenerife, reaching Southampton after a smooth voyage on 24 April. They took rooms in Lexham Gardens on Cromwell Road, Kensington, and from there Mother met and called on all her friends and relatives, while Claude visited different Eye Hospitals, and got in touch with his old teachers, who invited him to assist at various operations.

Claude flew to Paris, where he described having spent a delightful ten days, renewing his acquaintance with his father's cousin Christine, Comtesse de Sommyèvre, whom he addressed respectfully as 'Aunt', in view of her age!

In July, Claude and Mother started out on a seven-week tour in his new 'Bean' motorcar. They drove to Bath where there was a Meeting of the British Medical Association. Claude attended medical and ophthalmic meetings, and was accompanied by his mother on '*a wide variety of delightful entertainments and excursions, including a Garden Party at "Longleat" the beautiful home of the Marquis of Bath*'.

Claude and his Mother received invitations to attend Their Majesties' Afternoon Party, at Buckingham Palace, on 24 July. Unfortunately however, they were away from London, and their inability to attend was recorded in *The Times* newspaper, as was the custom. After the Congress, they travelled on, visiting Claude's cousin, Daisy Frossard and her husband, Dr Frossard, and also their musician son Philip and his wife. They spent time with Goldie Morlet and her two daughters living at Ilfracombe, and then toured the Southwest district. They travelled in Wales, and then Scotland, returning to London on 6 September.

Mary recorded their travels in great detail in her diary, noting that they had only one rainy day! Early in October, they left for Paris, and stayed a week.

'We had some delightful excursions to Versailles, Malmaison, etc. and one day

had tea with Claude's old 'Aunt' Christine, the Comptesse'.

From Paris they travelled to Geneva where they stayed in a hotel by the lake, and then on to Montreux, to admire the autumn tints and the snow-capped mountains. They travelled on by train through Interlaken, Lucerne, then through the St Gotthard Tunnel to Lugarno, stopping a couple of nights at each place, and touring the sights. From Lugarno, they travelled south by steamer, and went on to Milan, Venice, Florence, Rome, and Naples, where they ascended Mount Vesuvius in a funicular, and strolled around the ruins of Pompeii, before they finally boarded their steamer the *Orama* bound for Melbourne. They stopped briefly in Egypt and had a last look at Cairo.

Jack met them at the Pier in Melbourne, and drove Mother to Camperdown in his smart new Vauxhall motorcar. Claude joined them a few days before Christmas and they 'were a happy trio for about three weeks'.

Claude returned to Perth, finding to his delight that his practice had not dwindled in his absence, and if anything, he was busier than ever! As he stepped off the ship at Port Fremantle, he was surprised to find Mildred Milbank on the wharf, waiting to greet a friend. He had heard that her engagement had been broken off, and on the spur of the moment, rather lost for words, all he could think of to say was 'Whom are you engaged to now?'

Mary spent time looking after Lucile's family while she and Stan travelled overseas, and she records: *'In letters I had from Claude about this time, he told me a great deal about Mildred Milbank, whom he had seen very frequently for some months, so that I was not very surprised when I had a wire from him on 12 August, "Engaged to Mildred today". Needless to say I was greatly delighted, for though I had never seen her, I felt sure from his description and snaps he had sent me, she must be a very sweet girl.'*

Mildred received a letter from one of Claude's patients.

'The Old Farm'
Albany. WA.
27 Nov. 1927

Dear Miss Milbank
I am sorry to be so late with this letter, which I've been trying to write for several weeks.

Being an adventurous old person, I wrote to Dr Morlet congratulating him on the happiness and change of vision you have brought into his life, and he, very kindly, sent me your address so that I might offer you all the very best and nicest I can think of.

My only trouble will be not to seem effusive, because I regard him with so much gratitude and affection you may doubt my sincerity if I try to express what I actually feel!

I can never, never forget his sympathy and interest in an ordinary, stone deaf, half blind old woman. Although I always wished he were my son, may I still constitute myself a kind of unofficial grandmother?

Well, he has the gentlest hands; the kindest heart; perfect skill, and that unbuyable gift of making the homeliest of his patients happy by his warm understanding of human needs. I am quite sure you will be very happy indeed, both of you, and I hope to be allowed to keep in touch with your future while I may?

No doubt you may have to be very severe with him sometimes, for his own good, but that is your privilege, and part of the fun.

You know what Tennyson said so beautifully.

'Champion lover that he was –
Love took up the harp of life and smote on
All the chords with might.
Smote the chord of self, that trembling, passed
In music, out of sight.'

Isn't that exquisite? Plain truth too.

You see, Love to me is actually God, and you two possessing this must be one, and content till the end of your days. So easy to congratulate two wise and happy people. So believe, dear Miss Milbank, in the warmth and truth of our good wishes for now and always.

We have been so interested in reading in the Weekly Times *of a 'Dr Morlet', a scientist in Vichy who lately assisted in a discovery of some wonderful prehistoric remains there, and who is enjoying a wordy battle with a dozen other experts regarding them, and we are wondering whether your Dr Morlet belongs to the same family. I think he must!*

Wishing you both a Merry Christmas and ever so many Happy Years to follow it.

Believe me dear Miss Milbank,
Yours most sincerely,
A. Maude Bird.

PS. I thought out this little 'Acrostic' on Anzac Day 1924, I think, the day Dr Morlet performed his first operation on my eye, and hope you will not consider it an impertinence to send it on to you. It does not scan properly.

C*onfidence inspiring,*
L*ectures always free.*
A*rdour for profession,*
U*ndoubtedly.*
D*ogged and determined*
E*nthusiast is he.*

M*ovement very graceful,*
O*xford in his speech.*
R*omancer hidden fathoms deep*
L*ove will someday reach.*
E*verything that's good and kind,*
T*rained to lead and teach.*

– *I had to put that in about 'lectures' because he used to scold me terribly! A.M.B*

CHAPTER 18

Claude purchased a large block of land in Cottesloe, later to be renamed Mosman Park, on a steep hill, where the road led down to the Swan River. There, over the next six months, they built a beautiful Tudor style house, with gables, a she-oak shingle roof, and sweeping views over the widest part of the river. The house was not completed by the time they married, but was ready when they returned from their overseas honeymoon.

Mary Morlet's diary records.

'Early in March 1928 I went to West Australia, and spent three delightful weeks with Claude and Mildred, and on 10 April, Easter Saturday, I had the great joy of being present at their wedding.

Old Archbishop Riley married them quietly in the private Chapel at Bishop's House. It was a most delightful little wedding. Mildred was the sweetest bride in her wedding dress and veil, and I have never seen Claude look so nice and so absolutely happy.

There were only 16 present all told. Mildred's Father and Mother; her bridesmaid Daphne Byron and her mother (who is the sister of the present Governor, (Campion), Sandra Chase and her mother (who is the widow of a former Aide); Mildred's great friend Mrs Gilmore and her husband. And on Claude's side, his nice Best Man, Dr Crisp and his friends Dr and Mrs McGlashan …

After the wedding we went to the Esplanade Hotel, where a delightful little Wedding Breakfast, or lunch, had been arranged, where we sat at a round table covered with a mass of lovely roses. There were no speeches, but just a friendly gathering of happy people.'

Claude and Mildred left the next day on the S.S. *Oronsay* travelling to UK and spent their six-month honeymoon in England and Europe. Sadly, the detailed diary that Claude kept of their travels, together with the diary of his romantic 'Fourteen days leave in Paris,' were destroyed. Fortunately some anecdotes remain, and a couple of letters.

Ye Olde Pheasant Hotel
Bassenthwaite Lake
near Cockermouth,
Cumberland
20 July 1928

Dearest old Mum
Well here we are in the Lakes!
I chose to stay at Bassenthwaite, as being rather off the beaten track, I thought it would be quieter and easier to get accommodation. I was right.

This is a very quiet old English Inn, very comfortable, sewered, with hot and cold water and an excellent table. There are only four or five others here, and we are staying three or four nights, then moving on to Scotland.

We left London on 9 July in glorious sunny weather, with a suitcase each, and a hamper basket. We stayed a night with the Beaumonts, a night at Winchester, one with Daisy at Bishops Lydiard, and one at Clovelly.

We delved into Cornwall, called on Aunt Goldie and had tea with her and Violet and stayed a night at Ilfracombe. Then we headed north – stayed a night at Winchcombe, a charming old place in the Cotswolds, then visited Stratford-on-Avon and Chester. We went to Liverpool and went all over the Cathedral, then came on here to the Lakes. Today we went to Grasmere and lunched just where you and I did at Rydal three years ago. After lunch we drove to the Langdale Pikes where you and I went in a horse dray 11 years ago during the war.

We got back at 8 p.m. and had an excellent dinner then took a boat, in which I have been sculling Mildred around the lake. It is now 9.45 and just getting dark.

We shall have four or five days in Scotland, and then down the north road to London. After five days there we *fly* over to Paris and start our final Continental tour on the way home!

Mildred is as fit as a fiddle and looks prettier than ever! Her complexion has been perfectly rosy in England, and her hair more golden. Alas, she is longing to have it shingled like other girls! They nearly all are over here. I don't think she will be happy until she has it done, but won't do so as long as I persist in hoping that she won't! I would rather have her shingled and happy, than un-shingled and regretful, so I fear It must be!

Her little car, a smart Morris Coupé, my wedding present to her, is running splendidly. We have already been 2000 miles in it without the slightest trouble.

You'll be glad to hear Mum darling that we went to St Paul's on Sunday before leaving London, and had a little private service to ourselves in Salisbury Cathedral. Also we always say our prayers together every night! So your upbringing has not been all in vain!

Home on the *Orsover*, leaving Toulon on 24 August and arriving in Perth on 18 September.

Mildred sends her love to you, as I do my dear old Mum.
From Claude

As children, we remembered our mother (Mildred) telling us that Claude had taught her only one little sentence in French, to use if approached by a Frenchman: *'Demandez a mon mari s'il vous plait Monsieur'*!

Another anecdote passed on to the children by Mildred occurred in Naples where a street vendor pestered them to buy a souvenir, which he assured them was 'genuine tortoise shell'. Claude then flicked his cigarette lighter, and the 'genuine' tortoise shell burst in to flames!

Claude wrote to his Mother from Paris towards the end of their time, telling her of their travels, during which time they seemed to have retraced the path that Claude took with his mother on their trip in 1925!

Paris
7 August 1928
My Dearest old Mum
Once more in Paris, and on our way home at last!

There is so much to tell you since last writing, I hardly know where to begin. The motor tour finished as it began, in glorious weather, and was a complete success! We were motoring for exactly three weeks to the day. In that time we travelled 2100 miles and had only one wet morning! But even then the sun was shining at 3 p.m. and we had no more sign of bad weather.

After leaving the Lakes, where I wrote to you last, we drove up to Scotland, stayed 2 nights at Luss, on Loch Lomond where you and I stayed together. The intervening day we spent in the Trossachs. We caught a little steamer from Luss at 10 a.m., which took us to Inversnaid where you and I stayed during the war.

Here we caught the same 'four in hand' coach to Stronachlacher, and passed the same old man playing the bagpipes that you and I did 11 years ago! Here we caught the little steamer, which takes one up Loch Katerine where we walked to the Trossachs Hotel, had lunch and returned the same way. Unfortunately it was dull and overcast. The mountains were purple and blue with clouds rolling over them. Ben Lomond and Ben Venue were half hidden in cloud and little Ellen's Isle looked far from her best! Still it was a ripping outing and well worth seeing.

Next day we drove on the way that you and I went. Over that tremendous hill to 'Rest and be Thankful' on through Inverary to Loch Awe. Here we had lunch on the banks of the Loch. Do you remember how you and I took a steamer trip on it together?

We then turned east instead of going to Oban. Before sunset we reached Loch Tay, which you and I never saw. The scenery here was really beautiful, and we stayed the night at a little township called Killen at the head of the Loch.

Next day we turned south. Passed Callender and after a most charming drive of 1½ hours, we reached Stirling at midday. Here we went all over the castle with a guide, just as you and I did, then turned towards Edinburgh.

Arrived in Edinburgh at 3.30 p.m. and drove straight to the same boarding house at 20 Royal Terrace, where you and I stayed together! We received a great welcome and got a nice room at once. We just left out bags there and drove straight to Roslyn. Here we went all over the beautiful little Roslyn Chapel with a guide, and heard first hand, the story of the Prentice Pillar. Mildred was thrilled, and insisted on touching the pillar with her little hands so that our picture of it will really mean something to her!

Next day we went all over the castle in the morning. Since you and I were there they have built a most amazing War Memorial Chapel in the Castle. It is called 'The Shrine' and is beyond question the finest War Memorial in existence!

After lunch we went all over Holyrood Palace, and then drove out to see the Forth Bridge. We then had a look at St Giles, where I told Mildred the story of Jack and the soldiers in church. There was still time to motor all round the streets and have a real good look at the city.

Mildred about to fly to Paris on the 'Silver Wings'

Next day we started for England, setting out from Edinburgh in pouring rain, which continued until we got to Berwick-on-Tweed at lunchtime. This was the only rain we had in three weeks! We drove on to Yorkshire, but instead of stopping the night at Thirsk, where you and I did, we turned aside to Richmond, where we dined and drove to Ruth, a most beautiful drive by twilight. Here we had a comfortable night and then went on to York, where we went through the York Minster.

This was our longest day, and we drove on to spend the night at Stamford, 90 miles from London, having driven 200 miles in the day! Our last stage took us through Cambridge, where we stayed about 2 hours poking about.

We reached Earls Court at 5.30 p.m., in bright sunshine, not having had the slightest misadventure, not even a puncture, over the three weeks tour!

Our next few days were a whirl of packing and farewelling. We called on the Fosters one day, Aunt Lucile another, drove 150 miles to see Aunt Rosina on another, and saw the Beaumonts in the same day. Made final purchases, got our washing done; shipped the car to Australia and sent our heavy boxes to be put on the ship in London so that we will pick them up at Toulon.

We dined one evening with the Griffiths at Mayfair, and on the sixth day after our return to London, we got on board an aeroplane called 'Silver Wings' with a suitcase each, and flew to Paris. And so, here we are!

Mildred had never flown before, and was a bit sick, but she was not the least bit frightened and actually slept in the air for about half an hour! When not feeling sick, she thoroughly enjoyed the flight, and anyhow, it was an experience she will always have to look back upon. Wasn't she a game little girl to do it?

It was a wretched day for flying, drizzling with rain when we started, and heavy clouds low over the Channel. We kept right down between 200 and 300 feet above the water, to avoid the clouds, and could see the ships so very plainly as we flew over them! A steward in a white coat passed around cups of tea and drinks during the flight, and showed the passengers our position on a map at intervals.

We made a beautiful landing in Paris, which filled me with envy, and here we are in our old quarters (originally my bachelor quarters in 1925) in Paris.

We had intended going to Switzerland, but there are only 16 days left, so we have decided that it would be too much of a rush. We are living quietly in Paris, going about leisurely seeing the sights, and going to bed early. After another week here we will move on to the south of France again and have a few days 'rest cure' at the seaside and some sea bathing before embarking on the 24th. We both feel that by rushing madly for the last few days we might spoil the trip and finish up dead beat.

And so we are as happy as two schoolchildren. More in love with each other than ever, both as healthy as can be, and enjoying ourselves tremendously!

I will go back to Perth having spent all my savings except a couple of hundred pounds, but fit and well and ready for work, with the sweetest wife in the world and a most charming house to set about leisurely furnishing as my practice starts paying again!

It is warm in Paris, but not really hot. Aunt Christine has fled to a cooler clime for the summer, so there is nothing and no one to worry us.

Mildred joins me in sending love to Jack and tons of it to your dear old self.

From Claude

CHAPTER 19

Home again!

Oceanic Hotel
Cottesloe
Sunday 30 Sept

My own Darling Mum
Here we are, safely home again, after a most hectic scramble!

I wrote to you last from the *Orsova*, just before reaching Albany. Well we got ashore there, with all our bags and luggage, and were met by my old friend Ted Balston, who looked after us all day. He took us to lunch, inviting Mrs Hamblin, Tom Louch's sister too, and we had a happy day together. It was freezing cold – a bit of a shock after a very hot trip through the tropics!

We boarded the train at 5 p.m. and had a most uncomfortable sleeper, after the beautiful Continental trains, but it was the best available! At 11 a.m. on Friday 21st, we pulled in to Perth Station, where Mrs Milbank and dear old 'Dad' and my old friend McGlashan were awaiting us.

Mildred went off with her parents, and Mac drove me up to the Surgery. Almost immediately I was interviewed by a reporter, and then had morning tea with Miss Tickell (secretary) Ralph Crisp and Dr Johnson.

I joined Mildred and her parents at their house in South Perth for lunch and went back to the Surgery at 2.30 p.m. and saw 3 patients! That was pretty brisk, wasn't it?

Dad, at my request, had taken rooms for us here at the hotel, which is only ten minutes walk from our house, and here we have been ever since. On Sunday morning last, we were prowling round our house in lovely sunshine, and no less than ten people turned up! Car after car stopping in front of the house. We took everyone all over the absolutely empty house, and the view from our veranda was superb!

We drove to South Perth and lunched with the old people and spent the afternoon with them. Since then we have had a frantically busy week. I have had each day full of patients, and have been interviewing contractors and gardeners in every spare moment.

Mildred has had an awful week. Each morning she has come to town and spent the *whole day* in furniture shops, pricing and inspecting suites, carpets, electric stoves, bath heaters, patterns for curtains, etc., etc.

We met each day for lunch, and talked hard for an hour, and then separated until 6 p.m., when, tired out, she would come to the Surgery, and drive home with me.

The week finished up with a big Ball at General Hobbs' home, where Mildred had every dance booked and I got only 2 with her! Last evening we spent with the old people again, and tonight, we will have supper with Dr Atkinson and his wife.

Clovelly nearing completion in 1928. Grandfather Milbank is on the left

This morning we went to Church together at what is to be our own Parish Church, St Luke's in Cottesloe; such a pretty little place! Our Guardian Angel has watched over us to the last! Mildred has found a really splendid woman, a Mrs Brown, who is doing the curtains for her, and who turns out to be a priceless jewel! She is a woman of about 50, nicely spoken and respectful, and really attached to Mildred. She is an expert interior decorator; knows all the fine points about furniture and prices, and the virtues and vices of different kinds of carpets and linoleums, and what is more, knows all the furniture shops and manufacturers like a book! She can say just the best place to go for everything, and is not only the greatest help in this way, but she has really good taste, and gives the most excellent advice. She and Mildred meet almost daily, and go about together.

It is such a comfort to me as I can't leave the surgery, and there is really no one to help my poor little girl in this colossal task. Dear old Mrs Milbank would not be the slightest assistance, kind and good as she is! Mind you Mrs Brown only *helps*. It is Mildred who *chooses* everything, and it is all her own taste!! Things are now beginning to sort themselves out. Mildred has a book full of lists and prices. The motor driveway is to be started tomorrow, and several suites and carpets are already ordered. The colour schemes are all decided upon, and the good Mrs Brown has the curtains in hand!

The weather has been disgusting, except for two days, ever since we got back, raining and miserable. Mildred's new car came in on the *Zealandic* from England, which stayed in Fremantle a week, then sailed away, taking the car with it owing to the strike! Heaven knows when we will see it now!

I don't think we will get in to the house for 3–4 weeks yet, the way things look, but mean time we are fairly comfortable here, and very handy to the house.

By the way, Mildred is *not* shingled! And has no wish whatsoever to part with her beautiful hair!

Thank dear old Jack for his wire. Tell him Mildred is longing to see him!

Tons of love from us both.

From Claude

Sweeping views over the Swan from the balcony at Clovelly, c. 1929

Mildred's car finally arrived, having been put ashore at Albany, and cost £16 to bring back to Perth! Fortunately it was in splendid condition and Mildred was very delighted and proud of it.

They remained in their hotel for a further two weeks, while Mildred organised the house each day, and Claude coped with his increasingly busy practice.

In their honeymoon travels they had visited the village of Clovelly in Devon, where a steep 'donkey road' led down to the water's edge. They were so struck by the similarity to their location by the Swan River that they named their Tudor home 'Clovelly'.

'Clovelly'
Glyde Street
Mosman Bay
Cottesloe
5 November 1928

Dearest Mum
What a life! It is a whole fortnight since I last wrote. The joys of matrimony!

We have been picnicking in the House, without help ever since I last wrote. Little by little, things have been gradually sorting themselves out and our troubles are nearly at the end.

It is just six weeks since we came home to an absolutely empty house, in half an acre of hopeless looking scrub. Not even a gate existed then, and the land was nothing but a mass of sand hills and thorny scrub. Now we have a white painted fence, and a gravel drive up to the house. The land is all graded and terraced, and we have planted the lawn. Gardens full of pansies, roses, phlox and Lord knows what else surround the house, which is now almost entirely furnished!

The electric stove and electric bath heater and shower are installed; every room is full of furniture. We have an electric kettle; an electric toaster; charming inverted electric light bowls in every room; pictures hanging, and – crowning triumph all, our maid-of-all-work comes the day after tomorrow! She is a Scotch girl – an immigrant, and her sister is the general servant of our great friends Reg and Molly Forbes who live next door. Her name is Margaret, and her brogue is so broad that we can hardly understand her! However we are hoping for the best! It should be an easy place, as there are only the two of us – and we have an Electrolux vacuum cleaner!

All this time, I have had a terrible rush of work. No time to put my nose outside the surgery all day! On Saturdays and Sundays, when there are 40,000 things to do, our friends incessantly poke their noses in and have to be shown around and entertained. So you see, life has been pretty strenuous!

From now on, when Margaret arrives, and the endless stream of plumbers, electricians, contractors, etc. begin to leave us alone, things should be a little more settled. But really we have had a rush, and we're both most thankful that the worst is over!

Tomorrow is Mildred's birthday, and her mother is coming to spend the day with her. In the evening we are going to a Variety Show.

I will really try to be a better son from now on, and write regularly.

Good night my darling Mum. Mildred sends her love.

From Claude

Mary's diary continues:

'April 1930. Jack and I have had the great pleasure of a visit from Claude and Mildred and their darling little Pamela, born on 4 September 1929. They came over by sea, and after a few days in Melbourne with Lucile, came on here for the rest of their holiday. It is delightful to see Claude so happily married, and the darling babe is a joy to us all. Claude could only stay for a week, but he thoroughly enjoyed a quiet loaf and the sea trip back completed a restful holiday. We all love Mildred, and she and baby were able to stay about three weeks longer, and caught the next boat.

Last October when Pamela was about one month old, I went across to Perth by train and spent a delightful 3 weeks with Claude and Mildred in their charming home "Clovelly", overlooking the beautiful Swan river at Cottesloe.'

Lister House
St George's Terrace
Perth
28 April 1930
Monday 5 p.m.

My dearest precious girl

I am sending this by air to try and ensure that you get it at Adelaide. I shall also send a few lines tomorrow by the train, which will probably also catch you – but might miss you.

I have just read your letter written from Camperdown on Easter Sunday. It was a topping letter darling! You really do write jolly good letters now.

Am most excited about Pamela's tooth, and I tell the news to everyone who asks after her!

The De Latour's have bought the block above us! Geoff Maxwell has bought the one back to back with Hubert Parker, and old Sam Elliot is said to be going to build on the block just above Hubert.

Molly and Reg Forbes welcomed me back by coming in and having a drink with me, and the Milnes by asking me to dine with them tonight, which I'm going to do. I worked all day Thursday, after arriving home on Wednesday, and the next day was Anzac Day, so I had no appointments but unpacked my new instruments in the surgery.

On Saturday after work, I lunched at the Club and then bought Sid Bloxham home for the weekend. Meantime, the Mannings asked me to dinner, which I had to refuse. Sid and I had a few drinks with Bunny at his house, and then at Hubert Parker's during the afternoon. That evening Margaret gave us an excellent dinner (chicken). After dinner, Hubert and Cam Milne were invited to play bridge, but though they came at 8 p.m. and stayed until 1:30 am, we never touched the cards but yarned and drank all night!

Sunday was a lovely day, so Sid and I drove up to town and left the car there. Then we called for Tom Louch, and we all sailed down to Mosman Bay in their boat. We had an excellent lunch at Clovelly (roast lamb) and then sailed back to Perth. I had supper at the Club with Sid, and drove myself home at 9:30 p.m.

Today I have had a fairly busy time at the surgery and will just have time to post this before going to dinner at the Milne's. John Downer, of Adelaide Steamship Company told me to wire you and tell you to mention his name to the Purser of the *Manunda*, and ask him for absolutely anything you want! He thinks you should be perfectly comfortable. I hope to Heaven that this is so!

Old Dr Kelsall is getting about now, and the Milne's baby has not yet arrived. I forgot to ask about the Roe's one. Saw Eve and Flora Bunning in the street, and both asked all about you.

I don't think there is any more news dearest. Margaret is doing everything quite OK, and I have not seen or heard of Stella.

All my love to you, my darling wife and baby. I am longing to hold you both in my arms again.

Mother and Father seemed quite OK, though the latter suffers somewhat from 'wind'!

Don't do any packing until you reach Fremantle. It's not worthwhile messing about in the cabin with trunks, etc., until Stella and I arrive, when Stella can look after Pamela, while you and I pack.

Goodnight my darling
From Claude

The 'Depression' hardly touched Claude and Mildred, as they lived comfortably in their beautiful new home by the river. Claude worked hard in his practice, and drove the 12 miles to and from work each day. By this time he had turned in his old Bean motorcar for a Dodge Coupé.

In September 1931, Claude was made a Fellow of the Royal Australasian College of Surgeons (FRACS) and his Certificate, No. 480, was signed by his old friends, H.S. Newland, President, and R. Hamilton Russell, Censor in Chief.

Sailing on Fremantle Harbour in the 1930s

Claude and Mildred had many friends, and lived a busy social life, entertaining frequently in their elegant home. Their second child, Geoffrey Claude was born on 3rd October 1932. He, like his sister Pamela, was born in their home by the river. Claude celebrated the arrival of his first son with enthusiasm, and neglected to register the birth until six weeks later. He then recorded the day incorrectly as the 4th, a fact not discovered for more than 20 years, and which caused a multitude of problems!

Just prior to this event, Claude and Mildred had their architect friend Reg Summerhayes draw up plans to have the house enlarged, adding a second storey, with attic rooms that looked out over the wonderful river view.

They bought a black cocker spaniel puppy, which they named 'Don'. He was a great companion for Geoff, who played with him in the garden. Don slept on the veranda outside Claude and Mildred's bedroom on a hessian bag, and in the cold early hours would whine to come inside. This usually prompted Claude to thunder, 'Lie down you brute!'.

Granny Morlet visited them again in 1934, and stayed a few weeks, which must have passed uneventfully, as no other record of the visit was made.

Later that year, Claude and Mildred travelled to an Ophthalmic Meeting in Hobart, and called in to stay with Jack and Mother for a few days on the way home. They had left the children with the nursemaid and housekeeper, and found 'all well' on their return.

In 1935, Jack went to England, leaving a Dr Robert Officer as locum in charge of his practice, with Granny still in residence in Jack's home.

'It has made all the difference to his holiday having the practice in the hands of one who is so efficient, conscientious and hard working, and no one could be nicer in the house. He might be one of my own sons, he is so considerate to me in every way.'

On his return, Jack left the ship at Fremantle and stayed with Claude and Mildred for a week, then continued his journey overland by train. On his return to Camperdown, Jack announced his engagement to Enid White, a New Zealand girl whom he had met on the ship going to England, travelling with her mother and brother. They saw a good deal of each other in London, and Jack had travelled on to New Zealand to propose to Enid before returning home to Camperdown. They were to be married in January, and congratulatory messages came from far and wide.

Jack set out for Sydney to meet Enid, who was arriving from New Zealand by steamer. He was waiting on the wharf when the ship berthed. When they met, Enid told him, to his total astonishment, that she could not go through with it, and the wedding was off! At first Jack could not believe it, but as they talked it over for the next few days, he finally accepted the situation and sadly returned to Camperdown alone.

As Granny said in her diary, *'He is now back at work, and has been so splendidly resigned, feeling that it was Merciful Providence that allowed them to make the discovery before, and not after their marriage – but it was a sad disappointment.'*

In March 1936 Granny visited Perth again, and stayed with Claude and Mildred for the next three months. They had bought a small house in Beaufort Street, in the suburb of Inglewood, as an investment property, and also a beach cottage at Busselton, which they purchased from the local Catholic Church for £650. This was to be their holiday house, and they named it 'Sans Souci'.

Towards the end of March, Claude drove his mother and the two children down to stay for two weeks, whilst Mildred remained in a boarding house at Keane's Point, near their home. The next baby was soon due and she needed to rest.

By now, her old Morris Cowley coupé had been replaced with a smart new six cylinder Vauxhall that was roomy and powerful.

'Sans Souci'
Busselton
31 March 1936

My dearest girl
It was so delightful hearing your voice today. They took about 15 minutes to get through to Cottesloe, commencing at 10 a.m. and that is how I missed you. Both then and at 12 o'clock, the children were with me to speak to mummy, but at 2 p.m. when I finally got through, I left them lying on their beds with Connie reading aloud to them.

I met Yates, the doctor, in the Post Office and asked him about whooping cough. He said it was a very bad indeed in Busselton, and asked if I would bring the children along to him tomorrow, to be injected against it, as a precaution. I accepted his offer (I could not do

Mildred with her car, the Morris Cowley brought back from England

Mildred standing next to Claude's car

'Sans Souci', the beachhouse at Busselton, south of Perth, with Ford and Vauxhall cars in the drive. (circa 1938)

otherwise) and so we're for it tomorrow I fear! I shall have to send him some cigarettes or something, as I have no wish to be under an obligation to him down here.

So far, the children have been awfully good, have had two swims with me and have had no communication whatever with any other children. The Duffield baby from next door came through the fence this morning and I immediately shepherded our little ones indoors, shut the door on them and put the little stranger back through the fence. Yates tells me that the Duffield's have not had it anyway.

All went well, without incident, on the drive down. The little ones went to sleep before Rockingham and woke up near Pinjarra. Passing through Waroona, after slowing down to, at the most, 30 miles per hour, a cabbage bearded village policeman in the centre of the town held me up and took my name and address for 'exceeding the speed limit in the town'. He added that the limit was 20 mph. The village was deserted, and apparently uninhabited, being Monday morning, and the thing was so preposterous. I could have hit him on the jaw! However, I am by this mail writing to Eric Sandover to see if I can, by pulling a string at that end, escape another conviction for 'speeding', as I was up for this charge only three months ago, and it might go hard on me! You might help by getting Kath Sandover to have tea or lunch with you at the Adelphi or something, to sweeten Eric up!

I have had a lovely day with the children, and a slightly difficult one with Granny, who *cannot* realise she is a guest in the house and not here to run the show! I most fully sympathise with you when she is at Clovelly, and I am at work all day! You must be terribly tactful and self-controlled as she thinks you're a most wonderful little housekeeper!

I am doing my best, but am humiliated and *overruled* about 20 times a day in matters concerning the children! It is of course, the natural result of having managed and controlled Jack so absolutely for all these years, and I shall simply try to subside, but it doesn't suit *my* nature!

The blankets are all right, and were in the tin box placed there by Bovell. The house is like a 'new pin', but the roof will need another coat of green paint after the winter. The tanks are all very low, as are all in Busselton, but it looks like rain tonight.

No more now dearest one. The enclosed note was dictated, and partly spelt out by me, but entirely written by Pamela!

Granny sends best love. The babes are sleeping peacefully – Mrs Simpson is a *jewel!!*
Love from Claude

Busselton
2 April 1936

My dear old girl

You have really no idea of the joy that the mail brought us all today. The train got in about 4:30 p.m. and I drove the children around to the Post Office about 5:00 p.m. As the place was full of children – presumably all the mothers in Busselton send their children around to the Post Office for the mail – I kept ours in the car while I slipped in for the letters during a lull in the rush. The delight, when I got back to the car with a letter for each, was just indescribable! It was good of you dear.

This morning, a still warm day, I fixed Granny up with a deck chair and the newspaper

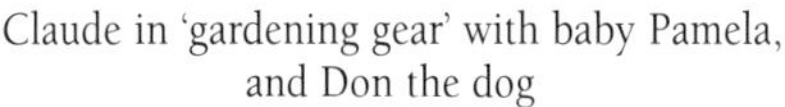

Claude in 'gardening gear' with baby Pamela, and Don the dog

Pamela with grandparents, William Frederick and Amy Elizabeth Milbank

on the beach, while I made sandcastles and ships for the children until 11 a.m. I then took them back to the house, where Connie put them in their bathers and we all had a swim, which Granny surveyed from her deck chair.

Mrs Simpson is a champion cook and housekeeper. She gives all her own orders to the trades people, and gives me a short shopping list when I go to town. She feeds us on a delicious hot scones and homemade cakes. She is a champion cake maker, and makes sweets and cakes for the YWCA. We have dainty lunches and slap up dinners of soup, meat and vegetables and pudding such as apple pie, or marmalade pudding – as good as anything we ever had at 'Clovelly', and better than most times there!

She has no interference whatsoever from Granny or me, and seems perfectly contented. Connie is having an easy time, and is very willing. The children are handed over to her about 2.30 p.m., and she reads to them on their beds until about 3.30. She then dresses them, and takes them out for a walk until 4.30, and I look after them until 5.30, when they have a warm splash and get into pyjamas for tea at six. She then reads to them while we have dinner, at which Mrs Simpson waits on us quite efficiently, and then Granny and I hear them say their prayers while Connie and Mrs S. have their dinner, wash up together and either write letters in the kitchen or go for a walk together.

At 2 p.m. today I it took the children to Dr Yates, and he gave them both the first of three injections against whooping cough. Geoffrey as usual, was intensely interested in the whole ceremony, remarking delightedly to me as a teeny bead of blood followed the withdrawal of the needle. 'Look Dad it's bleeding!'

Meanwhile Pamela, also as usual, clung to me trembling like a leaf, waiting her turn as she tearfully refused to be first. She bellowed and howled all throughout the process, and

'The Reluctant Groom'; Pamela and Geoffrey, 1934, in front of Clovelly

the moment it was over, ran out and sat in the car, while Geoffrey remained chatting with Dr Yates and me.

However I don't think they will be the same trouble next time, as she informed me after thinking it over, that she did not cry because it hurt, but because she thought it might, and finally when she got home, told me that she liked Dr Yates!

He is really being most kind and decent over the whole thing, I'm so glad that I didn't ask him to do it, but it was his own suggestion. The next injection will be Monday at 2 p.m.

There is no whooping cough in our street yet, as far as I know. The neighbours certainly have not got it. Nevertheless, I have so impressed it on the children to keep away from all others, that Pamela shrinks from a passing child in the street, as though all other children were something unclean!

Everything is running smoothly, and Granny seems at last to be realising that I thoroughly understand the children, instead of being one myself, which seemed to be her impression for the first 24 hours!

I'm so glad you seem to be comfortable dearest. I was impressed by the thought of old Don sleeping at your door. That must be a great satisfaction. Don't allow the ladies to bluff you into wasting your time playing bridge with them!

You would be delighted if you could see the way the children empty their plates with practically no persuasion, and do their poos quite regularly. Pam weighs just 3 stone, and Geoff, 2 stone 3 lbs – only 11 lbs less than Pam!

Good night darling, and many thanks for letters, cookery books and picture books, all of which arrived today.
Love from Claude

PS. don't forget the window boxes!
PPS. I found the missing keys of the house in the car when we arrived. – C.

Busselton
6 April 1936
Sunday evening

My Dearest Mildred
Your letter card and parcels arrived safely yesterday afternoon. The train was more than half-an-hour later, so we messed around in the car for an interminable time, waiting for the mail to be sorted. The joy, when I emerge from the Post Office carrying a parcel, quite made up for the long wait.

It was quite a hot on Friday, and again yesterday, so we had two swims each day. Yesterday, even Granny came in for a few minutes! Pamela can swim quite well now, and is full of confidence in the water.

Today was much cooler, with a chilly wind, and none of us have been in the water at all. This morning Granny and I set out for church at 11 a.m., only to find the Service over, having been from 10 a.m. to 11 a.m. on the 1st Sunday in each month. (I fear I was not broken hearted!)

... Tomorrow afternoon at 2 p.m. we have another injection with Dr Yates. I hope not to have as much trouble this time!

For the most part, the children have been perfect darlings, not a bit of trouble, except after lunch, when Granny and I both lie down and read for an hour or so. One or the other of them always seems to play up at this time, when Connie tries to read to them in their own room. It was Geoff's turn today, and Pam's yesterday – but I think they will be all right now.

The water in the tank is holding out all right, and we can be more lavish with it now that only a week remains of our trip. The time has simply flown by and we are all feeling splendidly fit!

Mrs Simpson is turning out quite a gem and manages the whole of the housekeeping without assistance.

Do look after yourself darling, and drive carefully!
From Claude

On 17 May 1936, their third child was born, a boy, whom they named Neville Anthony. Unlike his sister and brother, Neville was born in a small nursing hospital in Claremont, which ensured that Mildred had a good rest, and was well cared for.

About this time, Claude resigned from Fremantle Hospital, and had been appointed Honorary Ophthalmologist to the Perth Hospital.

Geoffrey, all togged up, takes the salute; 1937

Mary's diary

June 1937

And now I have to tell you of a very happy happening. My dear old Jack's marriage to Nora Bell. She is an English girl whom he first met about 3 years ago, when she was travelling out here with a friend. Strange to say, when passing through Camperdown, they had lunch with us on their way to Melbourne. Little did I think that I was entertaining my future daughter in law!

They were married very quietly in the Chapel of his old school, Melbourne Grammar.

... And now I have come to live in Melbourne, at 'Trawalla', Orrong Road, Toorak. It's a large house, which like many of the fine old homes in Melbourne, has been converted into a Guest House.

I am within a few minutes walk from Lucile on one side, and on the other, about the same distance from St John's Church, which seems an ideal spot to make my headquarters for the evening of my life.

In September 1939, after a brief illness, Granny Morlet passed away in Melbourne, and her ashes were placed in the rose garden at Springbank Cemetery.

***

Claude bought a new car in 1937 – a Ford V8, which he drove gleefully, with abandon, and at high speed, causing him to have further disagreements with the law! On one occasion, when pulled over for a breach of traffic rules, the policeman – according to Claude's version – poked his head in the driver's window, and had it shoved out again. The policeman on the other hand, maintained that Claude had punched him in the face! The Magistrate's verdict is not recorded.

On another occasion when he was pursued by the law, he drove at top speed up to the nearby Perth Hospital, where he left the car and fled inside. When finally apprehended, he said that he had to attend a medical emergency, and was quite unaware that the police were following him!

Pamela now attended school at St Hilda's Church of England School for Girls, which was conveniently located in Bay View Terrace, less than five minutes walk from their home in Glyde Street. Later, Geoffrey attended the kindergarten there too, as did other little boys from the neighbourhood.

In the Christmas holidays, the family would set out for Busselton, a distance of about 120 miles, with two motor cars, three children, nursemaid and cook, plus all the luggage. Occasionally Mr Richter, a local carpenter and odd job man would accompany them, and carry out house repairs, painting and maintenance over the vacation.

On one such hot trip south, the Vauxhall car broke down. At Claude's suggestion, Mr Richter cut a length of wire from the roadside fence, and made a makeshift 'towrope', connecting the Vauxhall to the back of the Ford. They were about to get underway when a very angry red-faced Station Master confronted them, and accused them of stealing Government property – the fence belonged the local Railway Station! Claude responded in his characteristic manner, and a shouting match followed, after which Claude drove off at speed with Vauxhall in tow, leaving the enraged Station Master shaking his fist after them!

Mildred and the children went to Busselton as often as possible, sometimes with only the nursemaid to help with the children. Claude however was heavily committed to work, and would drive down with them on a Saturday, and leaving them there, would return the next day. He would then drive down again to stay in the weekends.

By 1938, the storm clouds of war were gathering in Europe, and their blissful life style was drawing to a close. Claude became ill, having developed a duodenal ulcer, and was ordered to hospital by his friend and colleague Gilbert Troup. He spent a few weeks resting, then returned to his usual lifestyle!

Claude was joined in his practice by John Day, a recently trained ophthalmologist, and had relocated the practice from Lister House, to the modern, brand new Mercantile Mutual building in the heart of St George's Terrace, with sweeping views of the Swan River. The Ophthalmological Society of Australia was formed in 1939, and its Inaugural President was none other than Dr J.W. Barrett! Claude did not travel east to attend the occasion!

At the beginning of 1939, Pamela commenced school at 'Kobeelya' Church of England School for girls, as a boarder. The school was located at Katanning, about 200 miles south of Perth, and was a popular girls' school with lots of horse riding – which Pam loved. In the August school holidays, 1939, Geoffrey caught the mumps. So instead of bringing Pamela home and risk her catching the disease, Mildred went to Katanning and collected her, then drove further south to stay at 'Bolganup', a popular boarding house in the Porongurups, by the Stirling Ranges, close to Albany.

Mrs Laker, the housekeeper, looked after the boys all day while Claude was at work.

'Clovelly'
30 August 1939

Dear old girl
Just a line tonight as it is getting late. I have been devouring the paper, and listening to news items on the wireless. I am quite positive that we're in for war, though it is possible that it may be postponed a while, thanks to the influence of Mussolini. The impression at the Club seems to be that Italy is likely to be quickly overpowered and overrun by the French army and the British Navy, and is certain to move heaven and earth to keep the peace. Hence Hitler's pause at the 11th hour!

The house is running apparently like clockwork. Everything is like 'a new pin'. The floors and brass are gleaming and the kitchen – in the evening, at all events – is as tidy as it could be!

Baxter came today, and started by picking me a beautiful armful of flowers for the rooms. What he did after that – if anything – I don't know, as it was dark when I got home.

Geoffrey has been sitting out in the sunshine for the last two days. Ralph Crisp came to look at him today, and last Saturday. He is getting stronger each day, and eats and sleeps splendidly. Such a patient uncomplaining little chap, he amuses himself contentedly for hours with books and pictures, etc. He is to go for a short walk in the sun tomorrow with Mrs Laker and Neville. The latter is a lusty, noisy, ball of health and exuberance, and shows not the slightest sign of mumps or any other disease!

I sent Pamela's birthday cake and parcel by Jane, who left today. They will not get to Bolganup until Friday or Saturday. Miss Tickell could not get a cake tin, but she has packed it quite securely in a box. I trust it arrives all right.

Will stop now and go to bed. Love to my darling little daughter.

Do try to get her to walk with straight feet! Whenever she goes horse riding, remind her of what daddy said about keeping her feet pointing *forwards* and not outwards!

Goodnight my dear girl. God bless you both. The boys are both snoring softly and peacefully – so is Don!
Love from Daddy

CHAPTER 20

World War 2

On 3 September 1939, the day before my sister Pam's tenth birthday, war was declared. Pam and Mum were staying at the Porongurups, as I had the mumps and they didn't want to catch them. I was nearly seven, and I remember sitting with Dad listening to the announcement on the radio. I recall that I asked him would he go to the war again, and he told me yes, he would, if he was needed.

I had started at Christ Church Grammar School, Claremont, in the Primary School, whilst Neville still attended Alston Kindergarten. Father continued his busy practice in the city, watching the deteriorating scene in Europe. It became obvious that he should volunteer for service, particularly as John Day, his partner, was unfit, suffering from asthma. On 23 December 1940, he went to the Recruiting Centre and enlisted.

The next day he was posted to the 2/3 AGH, from the Reserve of Officers as a Medical Specialist, with the rank of Major. Even though he had been a Lieutenant-Colonel at the end of the last war, all Medical Specialists were to hold the rank of Major, except when in positions of command. Claude accepted his downgrade without comment.

He put his business affairs in order and packed his uniforms ready for departure, including his old Webley 45 revolver, which had lived in his wardrobe since the first war.

Claude's Diary

Monday 10 February 1941

The ships are in!

I did not go to see them until late afternoon, after packing since lunchtime. Netta Hislop brought two New Zealand medical officers in about 4 p.m., and stayed nearly an hour. About 5:00 p.m. we all went down to North Fremantle and saw the ships from a sand hill.

We returned for the last evening swim at Grant Street. Mummy and Dad and the two boys, Geoffrey, aged eight and 4 months, and Neville aged four and 10 months. Packed until late that night. John Day and Molly called in for a few minutes.

11 February

Last breakfast – all ate well. Both boys return to school this morning. At 8.15, an ambulance car called for my luggage and me. Just a fleeting moment with my dearest girl in my dressing room. Said Goodbye to Mildred and Neville at the front steps – took Geoffrey along to the next bus stop. Put him on the bus and shook hands with the little man. A wave from the bus window and I had lost my family.

I reported to the OC Troops on the *Mauritania* at 9:30 a.m. Found Major West talking to him and was introduced to the four medical officers travelling to the 3rd AGH like myself. They were Major Brook Moore, Major West, Captain Hone and Captain Gearin. We were allowed ashore again in the afternoon. I took all four brother-officers home and then for a swim. Rather a wild and noisy set out! We went to the Oyster Beds for evening meal. No time for sentiment!

Finally had a last glimpse of two small sons asleep, and left Mildred alone with them at midnight. Gilbert Troup drove me down to the harbour. The *Mauritania* sailed the next day at 1 p.m. Distinctly picked out Mildred, Geoffrey and Neville through my field glasses on the sand hill at North Fremantle with the beach umbrella. Waved a towel at them until out of sight. Last I saw was I think, Geoffrey, standing alone.

I well remember that morning, when my Father, in army uniform, took me in the car to the bus stop in Glyde Street. I waved to him from the bus as we pulled away, and I tried hard not to cry.

Mummy picked me up from school at the end of the morning, and with Neville, we drove to North Fremantle, and walked to the sand hill overlooking the ships on the south side of the Harbour. We put up the beach umbrella and sat and watched the great ships. Dad had told Mum which ship he was on, the second one from the end. As we watched a towel was waved from the crowded deck. We knew it was Dad, and we waved back!

One by one the ships steamed out of the harbour, with Dad still waving to us. Neville started to cry, and a couple of nearby wharf labourers laughed at us. Mum angrily put down the umbrella, and walked to the car, but I stood and watched, then told the men that 'We are waving goodbye to my Dad, who is going to the war'.

We went home, then, with our next-door neighbours the McKellar Halls, we drove to the ocean beach at Grant Street, and sat on the sand, watching the convoy of ships disappear over the horizon. We then all drove to the 'White Spot', a little seaside café and had tea.

13 February

At sea.

We are sailing in convoy in a calm sea, with HMAS *Canberra* ahead, followed by *Aquitania* and *Queen Mary* abreast and then our *Mauritania* and *New Amsterdam* abreast. The ship is teeming with troops – 4500 men! No room to move. No work to do. Every night there is a full blackout. Very homesick!

Claude sent this lighthearted snap to Neville, captioned 'This is Daddy getting fat on the ship, on the way to the war'

1941

Colombo, 1942

'For Geoffrey'
Jerusalem, January 1942

Ceylon

20 February

The *Canberra* departed, and was replaced by HMS *Leander*, which then released an aeroplane that cruised around the convoy. There are many rumours about our destination.

21 February

Anchored off Bombay at midday. A 10,000-ton ship came alongside and took the contents of our forward holds. Transhipped at 9 a.m. next morning, and landed in Bombay. Lunched at the Taj Mahal restaurant and boarded the train at 3 p.m. for Deolati Camp. The Camp consisted mainly of huts, and a few large tents. Very dusty!

There is quite a comfortable Officers' Mess. Natives on contract do all the cooking, with native stewards waiting in the Mess. A native bearer has been assigned to each two officers as personal servant. Bathing and lavatory arrangements are very primitive. No officers' latrine. There is no work to do.

They remained in Deolati Camp in total boredom until the second week of March, then returned to Bombay by train, and once again boarded ship …

Anchored off Bombay

Ship is an 11000-ton Dutchman, which used to ply between Sydney and Singapore. She normally carries 150 passengers and would then be very comfortable. Now she has 370 English troops from India, and 500 Australians. Even so, a she is not overcrowded as troopship go. Not nearly so crowded as was the *Mauritania*.

13 March 1941

The ship's officers, who are Dutch, are very nice fellows and all speak English quite well. The crew appears to be Indians, nearly all black, with ornate skullcaps or fezzes. The stewards are Goanese – chocolate coloured, and wearing white uniforms.

There are five ships in the convoy. Three are Dutch and the others are the *Windsor Castle*, and the *Empress of Australia*, escorted by one cruiser, the *Cape Town*, which keeps ahead.

14 March

There is a full moon tonight. I sat alone and gazed at the moon path, and thought back over 13 years of blissful married life. Is this the end?

18 March

Yesterday, during breakfast, the convoy slowed up, formed a line, did an 'about turn', then steamed rapidly back towards India until 4 p.m.! Then another 'about turn', after forming a line again, and set out for the Red Sea once again.

This morning, about 10 am two more ships, and a new warship joined us. One of our Dutch ships, the *Joanne De Wit*, broke down for several hours and we had to wait for her. Land appeared on the horizon – evidently Arabia. News of recapture of Berbera yesterday. Does this account for our hasty retreat from the vicinity, which we must have been approaching?

At 5 p.m. a large convoy – 12 or 13 ships – emerged from the mist ahead of us, and passed us going the opposite way.

19 March
At 10:30 am there was a long blast from the ship's siren. We passed about 300 yards from a floating mine! The cruiser stood by it until the convoy all passed, and dropped out of sight astern. Don't know what happened to it then. Very cool, and dead calm, unusual for the Red Sea.

23 March
Sunday
Up at daylight to see Suez. At least 50 ships of all sizes, mainly British freighters, anchored around Port Teufik. I attended the Communion Service at 7 a.m. The long voyage is over! The Information Officer came on board in the afternoon and told us a bit about Palestine.

24 March
Awoke with a fearful attack of hay fever, and my nose and eyes streaming. We received orders to leave our tin trunks and kitbags behind, to be sent on after us. We disembarked in lighters after lunch and entrained at 7 p.m. I was feeling ill. I had a miserable night on the train. A soldier fell into the Canal when crossing at the Kantara ferry in the blackout. They had an air raid here a few nights ago.

We arrived at Gaza at 9 a.m. and had breakfast at the Training Wing 'Gaza Ridge'. Then went to bed for the day as soon as a tent was given to me. My temperature was 100.4°. After three days in bed with a sore throat and temperature, and now feeling better, I joined a party of 6 bound for Jerusalem. Arrived after midnight.

Reported to Major Armstrong at 1AGH to assist in the eye work. Went with him to Tel Aviv in a Utility truck. Purchased a camp bed, chair and cushion – cost about three pounds.

8 April 1941
For the last week, I have been doing eye work at 1 AGH – mostly trifling little cases. I assist Major Armstrong who is a very nice lad – a bachelor from Wagga. He is very enthusiastic, and has an awful lot of cases with minor diseases of the eye, for which he gives a frightful lot of treatment, and takes them very seriously.

Spent a morning at the ADMS office, trying to locate trunks and kit bags that had not arrived.

Went to Tel Aviv yesterday with Major Armstrong, with whom I am getting quite friendly. Nice lad.

Worked all day till 5.30, then returned to camp where I found my missing luggage, and *my first letter from home!!* It was dated 23 Feb.

12 April
Sunday
We have been given two days leave. Williams, Pittar, and I took a taxi to the Construction Depot, where I had a yarn with Lindsay Male. We picked up Majors West and Salter, and drove to Haifa where we stayed the night.

Next morning, now six of us (picked up Chapell, dentist, at Haifa) left by taxi, and drove along hills beside the valley of Jezreel, an old battleground of the Israelites, Crusaders, etc. Went to Nazereth, and explored the caves where the Holy Family hid from Herod. We drove to Tiberius on the Sea of Galilee, then on to Capurnaum, by the Sea of Galilee where we had a nude swim, then a lunch of sandwiches.

We drove up steep mountains to Safed, passing the site of the 'Sermon on the Mount', then drove home. Cost £1-13-6 each for the taxi. Arrived home to find 5 letters from Mildred!

14 April

Heard of the death of Major Schwartz, Oculist, and Major Chambers, Physician, of 4th AGH at Tobruk. ADMS tells me that I may be wanted at short notice!

17 April

At 4 p.m. received orders to proceed to Alexandria tomorrow with a draft of reinforcements. DADMS says I am to return here, going no further than Alex. I feel there is more to it, and wonder about replacing Schwarz at Tobruk? We had a weary day in the train – 24 hours to Alexandria. I discovered the train returned to the city after leaving reinforcements at Amoriah Staging Camp, so I stayed in the carriage and got to the Hotel Bouvard, Place Mohammed Ali at 1:30 a.m.

19 April

Had an interesting day in Alexandria. Met Richie and West at breakfast and later drove to Amoriah, 16 miles away. I found John Gearin and drove to 9 AGH, which was just opening up. Got some kit from 3 AGH, after seeing Colonel Beare, and drove back to Alex, then took a taxi to Ramleh. San Stefano is now a school!

Met Athol Hobbs in the evening and dined with John Gearin, Ted Ford and Jones, all from the *Mauritania*. I heard that Major Scholes has been sent to Tobruk! I am to remain in Gaza at least one month.

21 April

Yesterday, after some shopping in Alex, I caught train at 3.45. p.m. and sat up all night, but there was good food in the dining car. Arrived in Gaza at 7 a.m., with a stiff neck. There were six of us in the carriage.

I unpacked all my kit and rearranged it, after having packed and locked everything last Thursday in case of Tobruk. Now that is out of the picture.

25 April
Anzac Day

There has been very bad news from Greece over the last few days. The campaign there is drawing to a close!

Five of us took a taxi to the beach and swam in the afternoon. After supper walked to 1st AGH and had 'Swan Bitter' beer with Gar Hone and David Allsop. Felt almost like home!

28 April

Watched Armstrong operating. He is a very good surgeon – much better than me! More confidence. (Youth probably.) Spent the afternoon reading.

No news from Greece since the Germans entered Athens. There is a rumour that the 5 AGH is captured, with Brook Moore, who came on the *Mauritania* with us, and came to

'Clovelly' the day before we sailed. The hospital has been emptied out in preparation for casualties from Greece.

1 May 1941

There is still very little work. Just heard that Colonel Kay, CO 5th AGH has been killed, and that Brook Moore and 5 others were definitely captured! They stayed with the wounded.

I went to Jerusalem with 4 officers of the 1st AGH and attended a Clinical Meeting at the Hodassa Hospital. I met Dr Faiganbaum, Professor of Ophthalmology, and was shown over the Hospital.

On the way home we visited the beautiful ancient Crusader Church of Abu Gosh, used for centuries by the Turks as a stable.

Over the next few days, letters arrived from Mildred, and one from the Superintendent of Mails, Perth, explaining the delay of early letters. Mildred had tackled him!

[Her father had been the Inspector of Mails, GPO Perth]

Found out from Don Cleland, back from Greece, that Tom Louch was also back, and slightly wounded.

The next two weeks were fairly uneventful. I visited Tom Louch who was convalescing from an arm wound, and he told of thrilling adventures in Greece. He looked very thin. On Sunday 10th the temperature reached 115° at Gaza – hottest day for 25 years!

The 3rd AGH arrived, and were bombed on the way up the Canal! Met the Matron one evening. Captain Joyce, one of the new arrival medical officers was killed in a motor accident while 'on leave' from this camp. The whole Unit attended the funeral, but I missed it, as I was having breakfast when they left. Felt very bad about it.

We just received news that Rudolph Hess had landed by parachute in Scotland! Much discussed!

26 May

At lunchtime today I received a Movement Order to leave tomorrow midday with Gar Hone and Alan Lendon. We were given a send-off from the mess at dinner that night. Next morning I missed breakfast, packing furiously, and sorting out my effects until 11 o'clock. I said goodbye to Armstrong and caught the train to Gaza at 12.30. We had lunch on the train, and dinner at Kantara at 8 p.m. with Joe Stubbe and Norman Robinson. We crossed the Canal and caught a train at midnight bound for Cairo where we arrived at 5 a.m. I slept on the floor.

It was good to see Cairo once more, after just 13 years. We drove to the Continental, had a bath, shave and breakfast. We then took a taxi to the AIF Headquarters in Heliopolis, and visited the old Palace Hotel. At midday and we caught a train for Alexandria and had lunch on board. We arrived at 4:30 p.m., and were met by Colonel Beare, who drove us out to Amiriya, where we had a comparatively comfortable night at Headquarters. They have Italian prisoners-of-war as cooks, mess stewards and batmen.

Colonel Beare drove the three of us to Alexandria. There we heard of the defeat at Crete! After lunch, he drove me with all my kit to the 9th AGH, about two miles across desert, and I was very decently welcomed by the officers of the 9th, to which I am now attached, awaiting shipment to Tobruk. Hone and Lendon were left at the Staging Camp.

Last night, Hun planes were over Alex between 2 and 3 a.m. There were scores of searchlights and a heavy anti aircraft barrage. Very pretty, but noisy. No bombs were dropped. I made my tent comfortable, and remitted £25 to Mildred. A Hun plane came over while I was writing letters.

Next day I was ordered to open up an Eye Department at 9 AGH, and had it all ready by 4 p.m., with 20 patients booked for the next day. At 5 p.m. I was ordered to proceed to Tobruk at 10 p.m.! After many farewells, I arrived at the Staging Camp by 9 p.m. I was then informed that the move was postponed for 24 hours! John Gearin made me welcome and comfortable, and put me up in his tent.

I heard from Brian Beresford of Perth, Staff captain of 14th Brigade, that the whole 11th Battalion was captured at Crete, including Les Le Soeuf! I asked to return to work at 9th AGH, and saw a few cases in the morning. I went into Alexandria in the afternoon with Lendon and Hone and bought some books, and some nice comfortable rubber soled shoes. They were stolen out of our car before we left Alex!

That evening at dinner, I was ordered to entrain for Mersa Metruh at 8 p.m.! John Gearin and Ted Ford saw us to the train, which pulled out at 11.30 p.m. At 3 a.m., a coupling broke, and our carriage, with five others, dropped off the train, and was left behind. Fifteen minutes later, a Hospital Train crashed into our stationary coaches! Eleven were slightly injured, and were carried out of the smashed carriages, and transferred to the Hospital Train. All the troops were then ordered to camp beside the wreck in the desert. It was a cold, still, star-lit night. At dawn we cooked sausages and tea. The train returned for us at 11 a.m., and we travelled slowly all day in the crowded hot dusty carriages, arriving at Mersa Metruh exhausted and dirty, at 9 p.m.

After a reasonably comfortable night billeted in the Egyptian Army Barracks, we were paraded at 10 a.m. ready to board the destroyer, which did not arrive! We were returned to the billets and waited in suspense all day. The ship did not turn up, and once again, we slept that night in the billets.

5 June

We are all packed up and ready for the move to the wharf, but no orders have come.

After lunch I set out to find my nephew John Elder. I made many enquiries and walked about two miles, then found HQ 8th Field Regiment. The CO, Major Green, drove me to the 1st Battery, where I found John, looking very well. He drove me round in his truck, visiting the wagon line, then after mess, took me back to camp.

I sat down and wrote to Lucile, and his wife Anne, telling them I'd spent the day with their John, and recalled how I had toasted his birth here in Egypt, during the last war!

The next evening, Friday, the 2nd Machine Gun Battalion, our transit host, gave a Cocktail Party, as we were to leave the next day.

For the next two days, we paraded with full kit at 9 a.m. for embarkation, only to have the order cancelled fifteen minutes later! We swam in the afternoons, weary of the inactivity. At 5 a.m. on Monday morning there was an air raid. The noise from the AA battery was tremendous! I heard no bombs, but was told some were dropped on the aerodrome two miles away. That afternoon, the men had a cricket match.

The next morning at 4.30 there was another raid, with bombs falling about a mile away. One man was killed, and the British 17th Casualty Clearing Station had stores destroyed, and also an X Ray power truck. I went over in the afternoon to see the damage.

11 June

Two destroyers were in port this morning. We stood by for orders to move, but none came. Fed up with inactivity, I called on the Adjutant of the Machine Gun Battalion to see if we could break away from the draft and proceed independently. This was met with helpful courtesy, and he made enquiries. The next morning, the Adjutant took me to the wharf side, to interview the Movement Control Officer. A very nice young English gentleman named Wilkinson from Maidenhead. He rang Desert Force Movement Branch, and obtained permission for us to proceed at midday the next day! I cabled Mildred my new address.

That evening I presided at a buffet dinner and beer-up in honour of the Officers of the MG Battalion who had entertained us in their Mess at Mersa Metruh.

CHAPTER 21

Tobruk

Friday 13 June [1941]

A lucky day for a sea voyage on a destroyer through dangerous waters! I packed early and boarded the destroyer *Waterhen* at 12.15 p.m. We sailed at 1 o'clock, leading the way out of the harbour, followed by the *Voyager*. We had a smooth and uneventful trip, racing along side by side at full speed, and had two comfortable meals at sea.

About 11 p.m., in pitch darkness, we crept silently into Tobruk Harbour, and tied up to a wrecked hulk beside the wharf. One after the other, in the pitch black of a moonless night, we stumbled over the hulk, and on to the wharf with our kit, together with ammunition and supplies that were manhandled from the ship. Wounded to be evacuated were then put on board, and the two destroyers silently slipped away into the black ocean, to make a dash for Egypt. The whole process took a little over half an hour, in silence and in total blackout.

Almost as soon as the ships left, an air raid commenced, and I was bundled in to a shelter by the waterside where I spent the night! It turned out to be a large cave with a deep concrete-lined tunnel that belonged to the 2nd Casualty Clearing Station, and was known as the 'Docks Hospital'. It had been fitted out to accommodate 70–80 stretcher cases, and from here, the medical evacuations took place. Through the night I heard strange rumblings, and was told next morning that quite a bad air raid had taken place, and that many bombs had fallen around the 4th AGH, with one motor ambulance destroyed, but no casualties.

I arrived at 4th Australian General Hospital at 10 a.m. and reported to the CO, Colonel Spiers. I was then shown to my quarters.

The Second 4th AGH (2/4 AGH) had been sent to Tobruk on 28 March. They set out on a small, poorly equipped and ill suited ferry ship, the *Knight of Malta,* with all hospital stores, equipment and personnel aboard, except for their nurses, who had unavoidably missed the ship. No sooner had they left Alexandria, they ran into heavy seas and bad weather that turned into a severe storm. The little ship battled on through mountainous seas for the next 48 hours, then just before dawn, as the storm seemed to be abating, the ship ran aground on the lee shore! When daylight came, they found themselves some 200 yards from a sandy beach, in a barren stretch of coastline. The ship was listing badly, and firmly aground. Only the shore-side lifeboats could be lowered, and as the sea was still rough, boarding the lifeboats was hazardous.

Ultimately all reached shore safely, and over the next few days, all the stores and equipment were taken off the ship and piled up on the beach. They were somewhere on the coast of Libya between Bardia and Tobruk, in an area that was well inside Allied lines, but they were unsure of their exact position. They set out on foot, heading south across some 14 miles of rough ground in search of the Bardia/Tobruk road, leaving a rear party on the beach to continue the salvage operation.

Exhausted, they finally reached the bitumen road, and flagged down a truck, which hastily returned to Bardia and alerted the British Hospital. After five days of hardship, they slept well that night. On the beach however, the rear party endured cold and miserable conditions as they continued to unload the ship and wait for help. Over the next few days, and with the aid of the Royal Engineers, all the equipment and stores were rescued, and the 4th proceeded on to Tobruk by road.

The war by this time had taken a turn. Greece was under threat, and it was decided that the 7th Field Ambulance, located at Barce west of Tobruk, currently immobilised and acting as a field hospital, was to be relieved by the 4th AGH. The 4th AGH, limited by insufficient transport, moved to Barce, to relieve the 7th Field Ambulance, under the command of Lieutenant-Colonel Les Le Soeuf. They were waiting to leave for Greece!

Over the next ten days, the 4th AGH settled into the scene at Barce, coping with the ever-increasing load of casualties from the front. The situation in the western desert, however, deteriorated rapidly, and the 4th were ordered to draw back to Tobruk. General Rommel's Afrika Korps was advancing rapidly! On 26 March, the 4th returned to Tobruk, leaving only a rear party in Barce. There they set up the hospital in what had been the Italian Barracks, a group of stone and concrete buildings on the edge of the shattered town.

Two days later, the Nursing Contingent of the 4th arrived in Tobruk, and immediately set about cleaning and preparing the old barracks for its role as a 1000 bed hospital. By 3 April the hospital had taken shape, and the rear party from Barce had arrived, with the Germans not far behind! Benghazi and Barce both fell to the advancing enemy, and the Luftwaffe were starting to appear over Tobruk.

In view of the increasing threat, orders came from Cairo to evacuate all the nurses immediately. Colonel Spiers objected most strongly, pointing out that the nurses had a vital role in the running of the hospital, both in the management of the wards and in the operating theatre. His objections were overruled however, and on 7 April, the nurses boarded the hospital ship *Vita* and departed.

Orders came from High Command that Tobruk must be held at all costs, against the advancing German Army! The three Australian Brigades outside the perimeter drew back and strengthened their defences as the Germans quickly encircled them. By the 9 April, all land routes were cut off, and

Fortress Tobruk was under siege.

The following afternoon and without warning, German planes dived on the hospital, attacking it with bombs and strafing machine gun fire. In the attack, two medical officers were killed. One was Major Chambers, the physician, and the other was the ophthalmologist, Major 'Zacky' Schwarz. It was to this well tried and now battle-hardened Unit that Claude was posted.

Major Scholes of the 9th, who has been here for six weeks since Schwarz was killed, showed me around, and introduced me to his arrangements for an Eye Department here. I decided to make radical alterations, but not until his departure so as not to hurt his feelings. I shared a room with him. At 4 p.m. I watched as he removed a destroyed eye.

There were several air raids in the night, and many bombs fell around the officers' quarters. Some of our rooms were filled with smoke from an incendiary. I went around the wards with Scholes in the morning. There were some shocking eye wounds, and at least two were obviously blind in both eyes!

In the afternoon I walked around the ruined town by myself. Tobruk Harbour is a narrow tongue of blue water cutting into the barren coast, with rocky yellowish earth all round, completely devoid of vegetation. The nearby town, though largely in ruins, is of gleaming white stone, in contrast to the tawny coloured surrounding desert. In the centre of the town, amongst the ruins, there is a church with a tower, which has not been touched!

The waterfront is referred to as 'the docks' but there are no dock installations in use. The harbour is fringed with wrecks and hulks, ships of all sizes that have been sunk by air raids and were aground in the shallows near the shore. Newcomers tie up in the darkness to these wrecks, nestling close hoping to avoid the watchful eye of reconnaissance planes that are often overhead. The nearest German aerodrome is only 32 miles away!

The Surgical Units of the 4th AGH are on the slope of a barren hill, overlooking the town, and about 400 yards from the water. They consist of a large group of white concrete and stone buildings, erected around a spacious quadrangle of bare earth, dispersed over some acres of stony ground, and surrounded by a stone wall. This was originally the Italian Barracks, and included a 'hospital wing', the roof of which was heavily sandbagged against a direct hit. This is now used as an operating theatre, while the spacious barracks accommodation is taken over as wards of up to 100 beds, quarters, and administrative offices. Whilst all the walls are substantially built and afford good protection from shrapnel splinters, the roofs of the buildings, with the exception of the operating theatre, consist only of a layer of tiles, and give no protection from falling bombs or bullets.

The Medical Wards are in tents that are well dug in to the stony ground, so that patient stretchers are below ground level and protected from shrapnel. They are located near the ocean about 2 miles from the main hospital. The medical staff live near their patients, in dugouts and sunken tents. This is known as the 'Beach Hospital'. Overall, the hospital is capable of holding about 1000 patients.

There is very little fresh water. The navy brings in drinking water from Alex for the 30,000 odd troops here. Washing and cooking water is brackish, and is de-salinated seawater that is heavily chlorinated. There are no baths or showers, and rationing was strict. Six pints per man per day was the official ration, though the hospital is able to supplement this to some extent. There are no fresh vegetables or fruit or meat, no alcohol and no eggs. Tunics are never worn. Sanitary arrangements are good – compared to the atrocious conditions we had at Gallipoli!

On Monday morning I took over from Scholes, who with Captain Quail, returned by destroyer that night to their unit (9 AGH) in Alex. I sent some letters with them to post in Alex. I discovered that the Sergeant Optician – Morris – is a cousin of Charlie Leedman in Perth. There were more air raids during the night, with bombs very close! I spent the next day re-arranging the Eye Department.

18 June

Alan Lendon now shares the room with me, and we were woken by another air raid at 4 a.m. I spent a quiet day still re-organising the Eye Clinic, and after lunch, I killed a six- foot cobra-like snake on the veranda outside the Clinic! I went for a walk to the ruins of Tobruk by myself about 4 p.m. A very dusty day. There was much artillery activity in the evening, with rumours of bad news on the Egyptian frontier.

With the Eye Department re-organised, the next week was busy with a steady flow of eye injuries, fortunately minor for the most part. Each night there were air raids with bombs falling close to us. Mostly the air raids took place in the small hours, but for the last few days, Stuka dive-bombers have been attacking the Port.

On Sunday, I went to the Beach Hospital on the waterfront to visit Gar Hone, and had a swim, having spent the morning in the operating theatre. The mail arrived that afternoon, with letters for every-one, except me.

1 July 1941

Over the past ten days we have had frequent air raids, and finally I decided not to go into the shelters, but stood and watched the fireworks at night, and the screaming Stuka dive-bombers in the daytime. (*And therefore was dubbed 'the mad major'!*) I heard today that dive-bombers had sunk the destroyer *Waterhen* that brought me to Tobruk. The crew had been saved, but much mail was lost. (Probably mine!) Last Wednesday we had an air raid at about 5 p.m., and the planes were very low. Bombs fell right outside the gate – I could see them falling! I decided to take cover.

During the week, Colonel Spiers inspected the Eye Department, which is now running smoothly. After a quiet morning, there was a terrific air raid on the harbour at lunchtime, as two small ships had come in with stores. I watched from the hospital steps as about 50 Stukas screamed down on the little ships, that immediately put up a dense smoke screen. They gave up after about half an hour, and when the planes had gone, we found that the ships had not been damaged – no planes shot down, and only two men were wounded! Later in the afternoon, the docks were shelled heavily from the long-range enemy guns, known as 'Bardia Bill'. Seven men were killed and 23 wounded in the attack, including two damaged eyes. I had to remove one.

7 July

Over the last week, I received letters on four days running! Mildred enclosed photos of the children, and little notes that they had written for me. Each day there have been raids and machine gun strafing, but surprisingly few casualties. There were no air raids today, but the long range 'Bardia Bill' shelled the town heavily.

I drove out to the perimeter with Major McQuillan and visited various points. I found John Lloyd and Arnold Buntine in their dugouts, and had a yarn. Troops on the perimeter live in harsh conditions compared to ours at the hospital. The blazing sun, heat and dust, together with the strict water rationing, make for conditions of extreme hardship.

9 July

I was woken this morning by bombs whistling down close by! After a busy morning's work, I went for a swim with Captain Tom Steel to 'Waddy Auda', a charming sandy beach near the staging camp. We had just come out of the water when a Hun bomber screamed over very low, followed by a storm of 'ack ack' shells! We took cover, crouching naked behind the rocks! We returned to the hospital at 6 p.m. and were surprised to find *fresh beef* for dinner!

10 July

McQuillan and I went for a swim at 'Anzac Cove', another pleasant little beach, which was just delightful until several Hun bombers thundered over at low altitude and dropped half a dozen bombs that landed just over the hill from us. No damage! After lunch I went and examined a captured German heavy tank, and a crashed bomber, brought down a few weeks ago.

17 July

The weather is getting hot. There has been much long range shelling over the last week. Alan Lendon's 'Majority' was announced at lunchtime a couple of days ago, with speeches and congratulations! At about 10 that night, a nearby building received a direct hit in the bombing raid, and three were killed.

Had another delightful swim at 'Waddy Auda' yesterday before tea. Went to bed early, but slept badly. The bombs were very close at 5 a.m.

The hot weather has brought the flies, which are present in swarms! Also, the whole area is infested with fleas that get in to everything! In an attempt to exterminate the fleas, soldiers occasionally drench their dugout with petrol, and then toss in a lighted match. This often resulted in severe burns!

The dust is everywhere. It coats everything. Blankets, which cannot be washed, are soon blood-stained and thickly caked with dust. Theatre work, care of instruments, and asepsis entails an endless struggle against the all-pervading dust, which is beyond description! It lies in a thick layer on floors, shelves and tables. The fine reddish powder grits in the teeth; permeates the food; lies in one's hair and eyebrows, and creeps into every crevice! A goldfields man told me that after living for years in Coolgardie, he thought he knew all about dust storms – until he came to Tobruk!

General Morshead, the GOC came to 'dinner' at 6.30 last evening – we had fresh beef, onions, and plum pudding! Followed by a bombing raid at 10 p.m.!

This morning six bombs landed close and shook my bedroom. No casualties. A few patients this morning, then after lunch, went out with Alan Lendon to the 11th Field Ambulance at the 2nd Escarpment, where they entertained us to tea. A very delightful occasion that aroused memories of 23 years ago!

31 July
Last night mines were dropped in the harbour, which was immediately closed. Two destroyers arrived, but could not come in and returned to Mersa. Taking our mail with them! The last fortnight has seen a lot of shelling and heavy air raids. A week ago at 6.30 in the evening, the hospital was bombed! Two bombs fell outside the Q Store, and one through the roof of Ward 10, which fortunately was almost empty! Two bombs landed in the courtyard beside the huge Red Cross in the ground, just outside the Orderly room! There were no serious casualties. We found out that a fuel dump of about a million gallons has been discovered, about a mile from the hospital, buried below the surface! This perhaps explained the heavy bombing attacks so close to the hospital for the past month. The enemy obviously knew of it, and wanted to blow it up! The fuel has all been moved now.

I've had a lot of toothache and finally had my last back molar removed after days of pain. A difficult and obstinate tooth!

The daily work routine was punctuated with an invitation to Divisional HQ for lunch, with the General, five Colonels and myself present. They were most hospitable and friendly! I was driven back at 2.30, and had a busy afternoon in the Clinic. Yesterday, I went with Major John Blair in his car to have the evening meal at 5th Field Ambulance. We visited two rear posts of the Ambulance, then the Advanced Dressing Station, which is in a cave on an escarpment, with an excellent view of enemy territory on the western perimeter. John dropped me home at about 11 p.m., just as an air raid commenced, which killed two, wounded several, and blew out the remains of the Mess window. John's car was blown off the road on his way home, but he was not hurt!

3 August
An attack by 43rd Bn and 28th Bn on enemy posts commenced at 3.30 a.m., and casualties began to arrive by 7 a.m. By midday 93 wounded had arrived. By sunset, 120 wounded, and 27 killed. I had four eye injuries to deal with.

11 August 1941
My 53rd Birthday!

At 4 a.m. there was a tremendous dive-bombing attack, and violent ack-ack defence. Sleep was impossible between 4 and 5, with dive after dive, met with a hail of shells. The bombs were not too close.

At morning tea I read the birthday cable that arrived *yesterday* from Mildred, having been sent from Perth on 17 July and stamped in Cairo on 23rd. And it reached me yesterday!

I said nothing to Lendon about my birthday until lunchtime when I stood 'drinks' to all the Mess. He then told me that it was also *his* birthday, and that he intended shouting drinks at dinner! So we were keeping it quiet from each other, and sleeping in the same room! He is 15 years younger than me. The hospital was bombed again in the night, with one casualty, and two ambulance vehicles smashed.

13 August
This morning, as the post closes at 10 am, I decided to write to Pam for her birthday, instead of my usual routine of going round wards 4 & 5 at this time.

While writing, an air raid started, with two bombs falling, one on ward 5, through the flimsy roof, and the other in the space between wards 4 & 5.

Two were killed, and 10 wounded, including Gar Hone who was in ward 5 where I should normally have been! As it was, the last lines of my letter were a bit shaky! *My lucky 13th again!*

Gar had a piece of shrapnel removed from his leg and was evacuated to Base. The hospital was raided several times during the day, but no buildings were hit, and there were no more casualties.

We all feel that the hospital is now being *deliberately* attacked! There is a noticeable nervousness among all ranks and patients!

More bombs fell near the hospital between 2 a.m. and 4.30. The planes kept coming back and dropping more. Some were very close!

15 August

There were the most violent raids from 4 a.m. till daylight. I counted 12 separate dives over the hospital, each met with a terrific storm of ack-ack. Stick after stick of bombs fell, some about 50 yards from us! Amazingly there were no casualties!

At sunset I watched a dive-bombing attack on the harbour, about 20 planes, which were met with a tremendous ack-ack barrage, but I saw none hit. Can't imagine how they escape in a veritable storm of bursting shells and tracer bullets!

22 August

Major McQuillan left for Alex, to be replaced by a Polish MO. Before he left, he presented me with two Italian rifles and some ammunition.

The 9th Battalion leaves the fortress tonight, to be replaced by a battalion of Poles.

During a sunset raid, a Greek ship was hit, with about 10 killed, and a dozen wounded.

The 9th got away that night, 2 hours before the harbour was raided again!

31 August

The last week has been uneventful.

Last Sunday we were swimming near the beach hospital when there was a sudden dive-bombing attack on the harbour! We watched, standing naked on the beach about a mile away, when two returning planes circled around us, but at a respectable distance!

I have spent a few evenings giving anaesthetics for Lendon and Eric Kyle, who arrived two weeks ago, when the CO went on leave.

We heard that Britain and Russia had invaded Iran.

A minesweeper in the harbour was bombed and sunk, with a number of casualties, and the daily air raids have continued, except when the dust storms make them impossible! The weather is still very warm.

4 September 1941

Pamela's 12th birthday! – I celebrated by having a piece of my own birthday cake at afternoon tea, and drank her health with Gerald Moss and the Padré before dinner. The dust is bad, too bad for the enemy aircraft!

11 September

Two eggs for breakfast this morning!!

The hospital was attacked again yesterday, with two bombs landing about twenty paces from my room! One exploded with a frightful din, the other was a dud, and still lies there. No casualties!

The CO returned from leave and brought a lot of mail with him, including a bundle for me!

I have commenced writing a 'review of Ophthalmic work in Tobruk'.

14 September

The hospital was bombed again last night, with one landing in the yard outside the dental surgery, blowing in the window and the door, and taking a large chunk out of the wall. The place was a frightful mess!

Another bomb went through the ceiling of Ward 1 where the desperately serious surgical cases. Head wounds, amputations, abdominal and chest wounds, etc. All are bedridden. The ward was only half full, with patients all up one end. The bomb came through the other end! The patients were covered with debris, but no one was touched. It was a miracle!

30 September

The weather is changing. We have had a few showers of rain, and it was quite cold a few days ago. I wore a tunic for the first time in Tobruk!

I have almost finished writing my 'review', and sorting through statistics.

The withdrawal has started. Already two whole Brigades of English troops have arrived, and the 18th and 24th Brigades of Australians have gone back to Palestine.

A few days ago there was a raid in which 3 were killed and 10–12 wounded. The casualties were from an English Ack-Ack Unit who had just arrived, and were having *a parade to issue cigarettes! In full view of the enemy planes!!*

Went for a swim after lunch as the weather has warmed up again, but didn't go in, as a stick of bombs exploded in the water just as we arrived!

The moon is now getting bright, so no more relief work is expected for another 10 days. Our turn must come.

3 October 1941

Geoffrey's 9th birthday, and a full moon. Bombs very close last night. Didn't sleep well. Read all Geoff's letters before morning tea and toasted him with Lendon before lunch. Went for a walk in the evening and visualised my happy little boy.

Geoffrey's firework display started at 10 o'clock, when we were bombarded with incendiaries! Several landed on the ground near by, and one on the roof of the medical store. The whole of Tobruk was lit up in a wall of fire! There is no question about it, they are *deliberately* trying to set fire to the hospital!

10 October

There was a tremendous incendiary attack on the hospital last night, with blazing heaps of magnesium all over the bare ground. No roofs were hit. I put out one fire on the concrete veranda near our quarters.

A few days ago the CO informed me that I was to command an advance party of 20 who will leave Tobruk by destroyer next Sunday! The next day I went to the docks and interviewed Lieutenant Taylor RNR re chance of getting valises on to the destroyer, in spite of the general order that only baggage carried 'on the person' can go. I spent my spare time in the next two days going through my belongings and packing.

Yesterday I ran into the CO in the corridor, and he calmly informed me that the order for me to command the advance party had been cancelled! 'The ADMS does not wish Specialists to leave with the advance party'. And here I was all packed up, and with the advance party all organised! Kyle is to take my place, and will have the honour of leading the unit out! I am to be 'Liaison Officer' with Divisional HQ, and will be the *last to leave!* Will not get away until 21-22 Oct.

20 October

Today the 4th AGH closed down, and we are working for the RAMC 62nd. Tomorrow we leave!

The last 10 days have been eventful. Kyle and the advance party, with groups from most Australian Units, slipped away in the darkness on four destroyers. There was some shelling during the move, but no casualties. Ten RAMC Officers and 50 men arrived to relieve us, but the eye specialist wasn't among them! The relieving eye man, Major Wallace, was not expected for some days. My luck!

The next morning we experienced the worst dust storm I have seen! The air was so thick one could hardly breathe!

A few days later there was a heavy shelling bombardment of the harbour, before the destroyers arrived. Shells hit the hospital for the first time! Ward 3 received a direct hit, and the wall and steps were destroyed! Again, miraculously, there were no casualties!

The weather was cold last week, with occasional showers of rain. The nights were so cold that I had 2 blankets and an overcoat on my bed! Yesterday the weather warmed up, and I went for my last swim.

Eye injuries still poured in over the last week. Mostly Poles.

This morning I woke early, and with my greatcoat over my pyjamas, I walked up to the escarpment to watch the sunrise.

Looking back at the hospital, bombs had damaged almost every ward over the period of the siege, but there had been remarkably few casualties, considering the onslaught!

Colonel Furnell and Col. Fulton, the new ADMS came to lunch. In the middle of the meal, a stick of bombs crashed down about 100 yards away. The room rapidly emptied! The following stayed to finish the meal! All the Colonels at the top table. At my table, myself at one end, and a Polish officer at the other. My next-door neighbour was under the table! There were several casualties, and one was killed.

That afternoon I did my last operation, to remove the shattered eye of a Polish soldier.

21 October 1941

Farewell to Tobruk!

Last night, there was a little 'Ack Ack' activity in the early evening, but no raid.

The RAMC arrived in force after midnight, and made a hell of a racket, shouting and chattering and banging about! We all lay awake for at least 2 hours listening to the uproar!

I wondered if we would have done the same?

This morning I handed over the Eye Department before lunch, and walked out of my rooms! I sat in the Mess and tried to write a letter to Mildred amid the excited chatter of 3–4 men. Will take it with me and post it in Palestine, and thus give the latest news of my *deliverance!*

Just before 8 p.m. we quietly got into buses at different points around the hospital. Mine started from Ward 5. We moved down to the docks to await the destroyers, only taking with us what we can carry. We stopped about 1/2 mile from the wharf, and marched silently to the waterside in pitch darkness.

At 10.30, the destroyer *Napier* crept in like a shadow. Presently men appeared out of the darkness in swarms, as troops came off to relieve us. Then our turn came. In close single file we staggered along the narrow jetty, over the wreck, and on to the destroyer that was tied up to it. Shortly after, we slipped silently out of the harbour, like a ghost in the darkness!

We all slept on the iron decks, pillowed by our haversacks, and huddled in greatcoats. Sunrise found us dashing along, four abreast, on the rolling blue Mediterranean! The ships were packed with troops, like a swarm of ants.

At 8 a.m. we had breakfast! *Grapefruit, eggs and bacon, coffee and crisp toast and butter!!* I took nearly an hour over it!

During the night, a ship in the convoy had been torpedoed! One of the destroyers had whirled around to go to her aid, and in the process, spilt 12 soldiers overboard! Seven were rescued, and the rest drowned! The torpedoed ship was escorted to safety.

Our destroyers made the journey to Alex slowly, searching for the submarine. Thank God we never found it, and got safely to Alex at sunset.

Athol Hobbs was standing on the wharf to welcome us!

Chapter 22

[1941]

It was pitch dark by the time we reached Amiriya railway siding, as it had been when we were here nearly 5 months ago, heading for Mersa Metruh. We were then given a fairly decent hot meal before boarding the troop train bound for Ismailia. The train was crowded, and with six in our carriage, I sat up all night and arrived stiff and aching, after fitfully dozing through the night.

From Ismailia we went north by train to Kantara, arriving at 9 a.m. for breakfast. I went to the 2nd AGH where I was shown a number of my cases from Tobruk. I had a brief talk with Joe Stubbe before entraining once again, for the next stage to Palestine, which seemed an interminable, slow and uncomfortable trip!

It was 8. p.m. and dark when we arrived at Beit Jerja camp, where I was welcomed by Alan Lendon and Tom Steel, and made comfy in their tent. It was a cold night, and my valise was still in transit somewhere!

Next morning I found my trunk and suitcase, and a great pile of mail! I spent the rest of the day reading, and writing letters home.

25 October
Saturday

I reported to the 1st AGH and had lunch with Armstrong, then met Charlie Foulkes-Taylor, (Red Cross) who very kindly lent me transport. I had two weeks leave!

I went to Gaza, and ordered some shoes, had a hair cut, and then sent the car to pick up Armstrong. We had dinner together at Spinney's and got home again, in the Red Cross car, at about 10 p.m.

On Monday morning, at about 10, I got a lift in the QM staff truck to Tel Aviv and bought a new watch, and ordered some shirts and shorts. After a visit to the dentist, I got back and was invited by Tom Tyrer and Tommy Steel to join them on a trip to Syria, as guests of the Corps Petrol Park! We were to leave immediately.

We dined at Haifa, and reached Beirut after midnight, billeting with the local Corps Petrol Park, which we made our headquarters. For the next week we toured around, drove through snow-covered passes and mountain villages, and visited a Convent where the Nuns did beautiful needlework. I bought some lace mats. The Lebanese silversmiths produce the most beautiful silver lace filigree work, and I bought a cigarette case, brooch and bracelet for Mildred.

We lunched at the French Officer's Club, and wandered through the native bazaars. We got back to camp and found most of the Unit was still away on leave.

7th November 1941

We received news that the 4th AGH is to take over from the 60th General, RAMC and work in Jerusalem. Until then, I have been ordered to 1AGH to relieve Armstrong. This I did for the next four days.

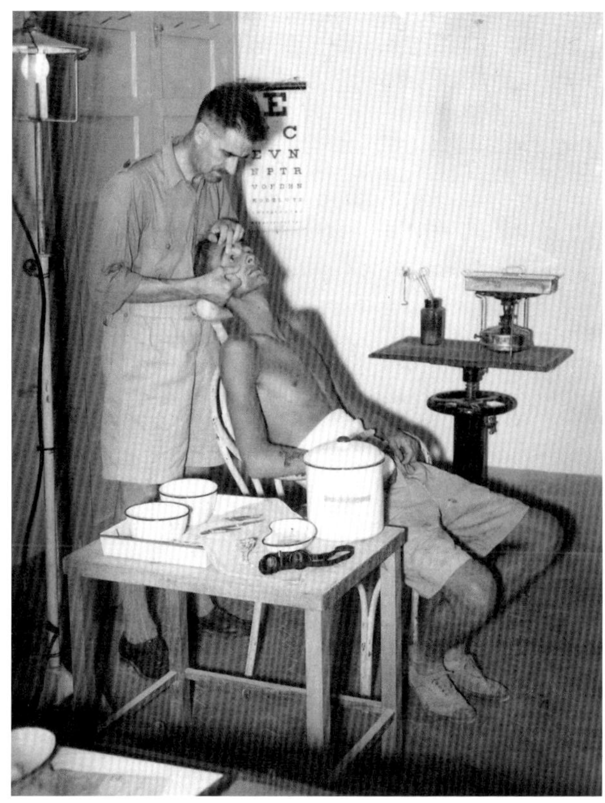

Claude the ophthalmologist in the Middle East, 1942

We discussed Ophthalmic Policy, and in my spare time I finished my monthly report from Tobruk, up to the time of our 'hand-over' to the 62nd Gen Hospital.

11 November

Armistice Day. Worked all day in the Eye Clinic of 1st AGH.

I really disapprove of Armstrong's wholesale operating on *all* pterygia and also squints. Even small pterygia, (not even requiring surgery, in my opinion,) are kept in hospital for four weeks or more as a *routine!* Consequently, the eye ward has 70–80 inpatients!

At 4 p.m. I received orders to return to Camp and proceed to Jerusalem at noon tomorrow, with the 4th AGH advance party. Hooray!

The next day we moved off in convoy at 0900 hrs, and arrived at the 60th Gen Hosp. RAMC at 11. These people have been here since Italy declared war (18 months ago) and are in the Italian Hospital and adjoining Italian Club Sumptuous quarters, with tennis court and beautiful mess room; arched ceiling; high-backed leather upholstered chairs, etc.

I am to take over most perfect and elaborate equipment from Major Wren RAMC, who has lived in Jerusalem for 13 years doing eye work, and has everything just perfect in his department. The Eye Department is self-contained, with clinic, operating theatre and wards, all on the top floor of the hospital, overlooking the city.

The next morning I went carefully over the equipment with Major Wren, then took over and signed for the Eye Department of the 60th. Armstrong wants me to return to Gaza, and do his work while he goes on 'leave', but I got the CO to refuse to send me back there. Hooray again!

(Armstrong takes a jaundiced view of *my* taking over from Wren, whose department he has envied and admired since his arrival in Palestine.)

By mid November the RAMC officers and men finally left, and we occupied the living quarters. Prior to this we had been living from suitcases, and sleeping in an unoccupied ward, like a dormitory.

I was allocated a comfy little room, and settled myself in. The valises and kit bags finally arrived from Tobruk, but my valise was missing! Some had obviously been opened and inspected; mine contained the little Italian rifle. I think it was just too tempting!

The little rifle was a 'cadet' training rifle, designed to fire blank ammunition and was about half the size of the other rifle. I had it repaired in Tobruk by the armourer, and most carefully greased and cloth wrapped. I had also the full sized Italian Carbine packed in my stretcher, with the valise containing the little rifle wrapped around it. The carbine was for Geoffrey when he grew older. Alas! After all my trouble!

For the next two weeks there was little work, and the weather became colder. At the end of the month I received orders to proceed back to 1st AGH in Gaza to assist Armstrong! I tried to get the Colonel to protest, without success.

The next morning, feeling depressed after a sleepless night, I visited the 7th AGH and got a great welcome from Fred Clark and Gerald Moss! I stayed the night, and bunked in Fred's tent with him and Gerald. That evening the three of us had a banquet at a Jewish roadhouse on the outskirts of Jaffa, with much good food and drink.

Next morning, Monday, I watched Bruce Hamilton's Eye Department at work, after which, Fred showed me around his wards.

I got news that my valise had turned up at the kit store, which cheered me up! After lunch I reported for duty at 1st AGH and spent the afternoon assisting Armstrong in theatre. After dinner, I unpacked my valise and found the rifles untouched!

On 8 December we heard that Japan and America were at war! The next day, it was announced that Australia was at war with Japan too! I sat and discussed the situation with Athol Hobbs over lunch.

The mail has been regular, with letters from Mildred arriving frequently, and only taking about 2 weeks in transit.

We heard on the 10th that the bloody Japs had sunk the *Prince of Wales*, and the *Repulse*!

I spent the next weekend with Athol Hobbs in Gaza, where we had a riotous Saturday evening in the Club, and got in to all sorts of trouble! In the process, I lent him £2. We both spent Sunday recovering from dreadful hangovers! Next morning I said goodbye to Athol (and my £2, no doubt) and returned to 1st AGH. The weekend had cost me quite a sum and I was feeling chastened and depressed.

During the week, Colonel Spiers from our Hospital came to dinner, and asked Colonel Adey, CO of the 1st, if he would release me now to return to the 4th AGH. He refused! It seems that I am the bone between these two old dogs!

On Christmas Eve I arranged to return to Jerusalem with Roy Paxton. The weather was perfectly foul with rain, hail, and mud everywhere.

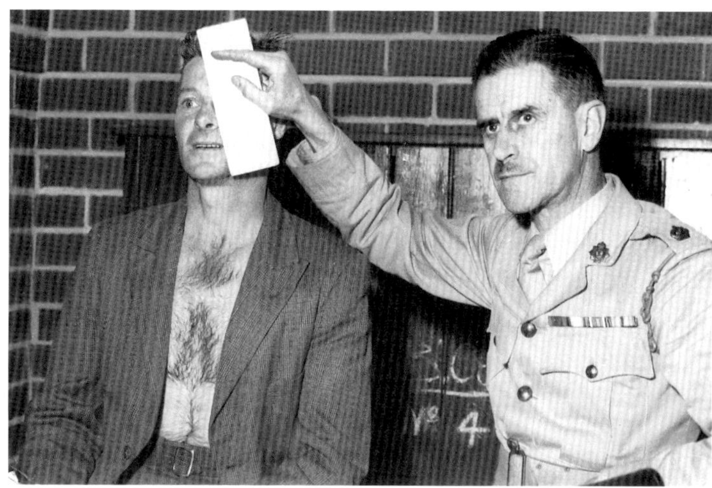

Claude was appointed Consultant Ophthalmologist to the AIF in late 1941; testing a patient in 1943

I woke at 7 a.m. on Christmas morning, and I thought of my little family getting ready for Christmas Dinner at home. I toasted them with my early morning tea. I found letters from home waiting for me, and also a Christmas Hamper from Mildred, and parcels from a few old friends at home!

I spent the afternoon writing letters, and that evening the whole Unit had a slap-up Christmas Dinner in the Picture Hall. The weather had improved, and the Clinic was extremely busy for the next few days.

I had dinner at 24th Bde HQ with Jack Lloyd, now Brigadier, and Arnold Buntine – neither had I seen since Tobruk.

On New Year's Eve, I received a note from Alec Dawkins, with a hint of a Staff Appointment for me! I wonder? We had a few drinks before dinner, and then I went to a vaudeville show with Armstrong, and got home at about 10.30 p.m. Armstrong went on to the Nurses' dance, and I sat down alone and wrote to Mildred until midnight, then turned in, with the distant strains of' 'Auld Lang Syne' floating over from the Nurses Mess.

New Years Day 1942

I had a hard day's work at 1st AGH, and during the evening meal was informed that I have been appointed *Consultant Ophthalmologist to the AIF!*

The whole Mess toasted me, and I replied to the toast.

After dinner I was shown the Order –

> CHANGES IN ALLOTMENT FOR DUTY
>
> The following changes in allotment for duty have been approved by the General Officer Commanding, Australian Imperial Force in the Middle East.
> Consultant Ophthalmologist.
> Maj. C. Morlet DSO, AAMC. Date 23-12-1941. Comment. 'In addition to his present duties'.

Chapter 23

[1942]

The weather is extremely cold, and Jerusalem is under snow! They say it happens every 20 years! I received orders to proceed to Cairo, for discussions with the Director of Medical Services, regarding the supply of spectacles for the army.

After Communion, I spent Sunday pondering over the glasses problem, and reading the notes I'd made from my discussions with Armstrong.

The next day, I waded through the slush of melting snow collecting information and prices of lenses and frames in Palestine, and also from wholesale firms in Australia and America.

On Tuesday morning I caught the train at Jerusalem with heavy frost and snow everywhere. As we proceeded through the desert, the sun came out and the weather became warm and pleasant. We reached Kantara in time for dinner at the 2nd AGH, where I spent an enjoyable evening.

I slept badly in a tent. It was bitterly cold. Next morning I sent off letters and my parcels for the family on a hospital ship heading for home.

I caught the 3 p.m. train for Cairo, arriving at 7.30 p.m. after a comfortable journey, to find myself accommodated on a house-boat, the 'Sudan', which seemed to have every possible luxury!

The next morning I found my way to the DMS's Office, full of anticipation. I spoke first with Alec Dawkins, and Walter McCallum, then finally, with the DMS, General Burston. I outlined my idea for mobile optical workshops to him, and explained the requirements.

Our meeting was quite friendly and nice, but was full of interruptions, and, it seemed, not taken very seriously!

I was then carted off back to Cairo in the DMS's car, and dumped there! I spent a couple of hours interviewing the manager of the Egypt Optical Company, then returned to the DMS Office at 4. p.m. for a further interview. This again was much interrupted, and inconclusive!

I was told afterwards by Alec Dawkins *not* to expect promotion! I was *very* disappointed! I had secretly felt that with my appointment, I would be restored to my previous rank of Lt. Colonel.

I visited the RAMC Base Spectacle Unit in Cairo, hoping to start something of the sort for the AIF, but was met with extreme discouragement! The Officer in Charge, a Lieutenant, said he had combed the Middle East for machines, lenses and frames, and there were no more to be had! I left discouraged! I went on searching, and found 1000 lenses and two edging wheels at Kodak Company, and a cutting machine at Wm. Darby's. Things looked brighter!

I reported my progress at HQ, and continued my search, turning up a whole lot more equipment and frames! I went back to my quarters on the 'Sudan' for a weekend's rest.

12 January 1942
Monday

I picked up Sergeant Morris the optician, and took him around to inspect the equipment. Unfortunately the second-hand edging wheels were no good. My meeting with the Authorities was more productive, and I obtained official authority to spend £400 for establishing an Optical Workshop!

Later that day I found a hoard of lenses, frames, cases, and edging stones in a Jewish den in the native quarter! Over the next few days I spent hours with the Jew, and was able to find almost everything I needed in his den. I revisited the Egyptian Optical Co and Wm. Darby, and am now in sight of completing my job! At the end of the week, I was given authority to spend £1400 on setting up three workshops! I obtained permission to make a flying visit to Alex, as I had been humbugged over some of the equipment, and set out with Col Littlejohn by car. He was in search of surgical instruments, and I was looking for edging stones.

I was successful in finding three good edging stones, and caught the midday train back to Cairo. The next day I went round Cairo with a truck, collecting all the workshop materials.

I reported to the DMS next day, informing him of my complete success, and that we now possessed all the necessary equipment for three optical workshops. General Burston personally thanked me!

I spent the next day resting on the houseboat –my first break for 10 days.

I went to see about the lenses I'd ordered, but Goldenstein the Jew had cheated me! I spent the whole of Friday trying to persuade him to sell at a reasonable price, and finally had success!

After lunch I interviewed Bernstein, then an optician from 7th AGH, and started him and Morris on counting and sorting lenses. On Monday we descended on Goldenstein with a truck, and carried off 5,000 lenses in triumph!

On Wednesday we drove to Tel el Kebir with all our purchases, to find the camp in turmoil, about to embark for Australia, or the Far East! We had a miserable cold night camping in tents with sand floors, and woke in freezing conditions.

Most of the Base Ordinance Depot had moved out, but I managed to arrange for the edging wheels to be mounted, and cabinets made for the lenses. I left an NCO in charge of the work, and drove back to Cairo after lunch to buy more frames and lenses.

I slept well on the houseboat that night.

30 January

I rushed about all morning to finalise the cheque for £520 for the lenses, etc., hoping to get a decent discount. I arrived with the cheque but the old Jew took payment of £520 in 7 days as a matter of course, and would only give me a miserable 1.5% off the frames!

I spent the next morning in HQ, arranging for a trip to Tel el Kebir for the following day. The purchasing was almost complete, after an arduous, and worrying three weeks.

I went for a long walk in the afternoon; but had a foreboding of evil! That evening I sat and wrote my report.

Next morning there was bad news from Singapore, and also from Cyrenaica! I set out for Tel el Kebir to supervise the packing of the workshops, and was hospitably received by Colonel Cornelius, whose hut I am to share.

Somehow I mislaid some important paperwork involving about £600! I got in to a fearful state of worry, and spent the whole afternoon driving the 60 miles to Cairo and back, unsuccessfully searching for it! I lay awake worrying for hours, but finally was comforted by my stable mate Colonel Cornelius, a most happy-go-lucky fellow, who *never* worries! After a couple of whiskies with him, I slept.

Next morning I discovered the papers safely stowed with some instruments that I had brought down from Cairo for packing! Life became worthwhile again! Thank God! If those papers had been lost, I would have been discredited, and branded as unreliable. An unforgivable crime for a Staff Officer!

2 February

Airmail to and from Australia has been suspended indefinitely! Singapore is besieged!

Today I commenced having all the equipment overhauled, checked and divided into three units, then packed in cases to form three mobile optical workshops. The sheds where this was taking place were all about half mile apart, spread out over the desert. I had to walk miles each day in the bitter cold wind and dust.

The weather is miserable, and there is no hot water, except for shaving.

9 February

I arrived back in Cairo yesterday by utility truck, and repaired to HQ with my written report on my activities over the past 4 weeks. I had a long talk to Dawkins and Masters about the establishment of mobile optical workshops, and stayed on for lunch with them.

This morning I went to see Goldenstein again. He now says that he has some low power lenses for sale. I sent for Sgt Morris from Tel el Kebir so he can go and wrestle with Goldenstein!

I was summoned back to HQ in the afternoon. Alec Dawkins had no criticism to offer on my report, and I talked over the new scheme with him.

11 February

It is exactly twelve months since that miserable day when I stood on the deck of the *Mauritania* and waved to three distant and beloved figures on a sand hill at Fremantle. What a long and lonely year!

I spent the whole day bartering with natives and rogues over the price of lenses, and finalised the division of equipment for the three Mobile Workshops, then arranged our departure from Cairo. The 4th AGH sails from the Middle East in 10 days!

I lunched with Alec Dawkins and left for Tel el Kebir with the last of the purchases, and after depositing them, Sgt Morris and I caught the train to Palestine. We arrived back in camp at daylight after a miserable night in the crowded train, and I started immediately to sort out my gear. We are only allowed to carry 100 lbs.

I've decided that the Italian carbine rifle is not worth the trouble, and will give it to Freddie Clark. I know he will appreciate it, and I doubt if Geoffrey will be old enough to care about it for 5–6 years. That evening I dined with Armstrong and explained the Mobile Workshops to him.

16 February 1942

Singapore has fallen! We hear that about 70,000 troops unconditionally surrendered!! A dark day!

A few days later, No 1 Workshop arrived! One of *my* creations! They stayed the night, and the next day we sent them off to Base Medical Depot. No.2 Workshop arrived, and I handed it over to 1st AGH, having first gone over there and explained it all to Bruce Hamilton.

I had a run-in with silly old Wally Summons, who imagined himself slighted, and thought that as CO of the hospital, I should have gone through him! I signalled HQ asking that instructions be issued to Col. Summons – to shut him up. The next day orders arrived for Wally (and a copy to me) so now, I hope, he will deflate!

A week later, I received information that my *whole* scheme for Optical Workshops has been officially incorporated in AIF Orders!!

I feel gratified and proud, as I have now really achieved something!

28 February

Darwin has been bombed!!

We are shocked and apprehensive at the news! No details have been received.

2 March 1942

Wyndham and Broome bombed!!

We are all filled with dread and horror! I now realise that I am to very likely be shut out of Australia until the end of the war. May God watch over my darlings!

Four of us went to the Gaza Club for dinner – to try and cheer up. While we were there we were informed that we embark today week!! Some comfort from that!

10 March

Tuesday

Today we leave! Spent the week packing up, and as the Mess was devoid of furniture and utensils; we ate out of our mess tins.

Last night we had a farewell party in the Gaza Club, with 25 officers and nurses. It developed into a wild night, and I woke this morning with a nasty hangover!

At lunchtime I paid my final visit No 1 Workshop, which is complete and functioning. All our baggage has gone, and we leave at 6 p.m.!

Wednesday

We left Palestine last night in buses, which took us to Gaza Station, where we caught the train. To my astonishment, I got a whole seat to myself. I stretched out, and had a good night's sleep!

We arrived at Suez at midday, and marched to the transit camp, which was very rough and uncomfortable.

We then got the news that we are *not* going to Australia, but to Ceylon instead! What bitter disappointment!

Friday 13 March

My second 'Black Friday' at sea!

Yesterday, Reveille was at 3.30 a.m. We had slept in our clothes for the second night running, and stumbled around in the pitch dark, packing up by torchlight.

We were given a cup of tea but nothing to eat, then marched with full equipment for 4–5 miles to the wharf, loaded up like camels! Day dawned as we marched, and we reached the wharf at 9.30, where we boarded a lighter. We climbed aboard the SS *Westernland* at 10 a.m., where I found I had a small cabin with Matheson and Lendon. At least it had a porthole!

I have been made Medical Officer for the crew of the ship. 200 Dutchmen, 5 Britons, and 200 Lascars and Goanese. We steamed out of Suez at 5 p.m. in wonderfully cool weather, and had our first real news of home.

No Jap landing in Australia as yet, but New Guinea seems to have fallen, also Java, Sumatra, Borneo and Timor! We are steaming towards Aden, so far unescorted. The weather has warmed up.

The Captain, a Dutchman, thinks that the Japs will soon attack Suez, via the Red Sea. If so, thank God we have got out of the Middle East!

Dreadful news of the loss of HMAS *Perth, Yarra*, and ten other warships!

We reached Aden at dusk on the 16th, where the Chief Steward informed me that I am to be served with *free drinks* for the voyage, as I am Ship's Surgeon without pay!!

The next day in Aden was hot and sweaty. We all dressed in tropical shirts and shorts. No one was allowed ashore, and the ship was in a filthy mess with dust from the coal bunkering. That night, the Captain held a cocktail party and dance, with the sweat and the soot! I did not participate, but had a few drinks and went to bed. We sailed at 8 a.m. sharp, with the *Orontes*, which arrived yesterday, and the *Corfu*, an armed merchantman.

We heard the astounding news that General McArthur G.O.C of the Philippines, is to be our G.O.C in Australia! Surely there must then be a huge American force in our homeland? I wonder what is happening?

After five days at sea we are now in the danger zone and zigzag constantly. The enemy is thought to be close. The watertight doors are closed at 3 a.m. The weather is hot and steamy, and I sleep badly, anticipating an attack.

No sign of enemy aircraft or submarines. It is noon, and we are now 265 miles from Colombo. The night passed without incident, and I rose at 4.30 am and packed – to get it over with and be clear of the fetid cabin. On Wednesday 25th March at 1 p.m., we anchored in Colombo Harbour.

CHAPTER 24

Colombo [1942]
21 April

Today our hospital beds, tents and equipment are being unloaded from the ship at last! It has all been sitting there for the past four weeks, just waiting to be bombed. The harbour arrangements are a disgrace and a scandal! When we arrived nearly a month ago, we prepared to disembark, and all our kit was taken off at 9 a.m. At 4 p.m. it was brought back on board and we spent another two sweltering nights on the ship.

When we finally disembarked, we were driven to St Peters College, a boy's school, which is about half way between Colombo and Mt Lavinia, on the Galle Road. As usual, the English troops are still here and we can't take over the place until they leave.

Lendon and I took a ride in an ambulance out to 12th AGH, which is about 15 miles inland from us, and a much cooler climate. We received a great welcome from Gilbert Troup and Geoff Thompson, and stayed for dinner and for the night.

Next morning after breakfast, we returned to the discomfort of the 4th AGH.

The College is close by the sea, and the humidity is extreme. Our clothes are wet with sweat all the time. Swimming in the morning and evening is far from refreshing, as the water is warm and not very pleasant. It is impossible to dry oneself properly with a towel, and we are soaked with sweat again by the time we get home.

Alan Lendon is a good bridge player, and thus is a favourite of the CO and his 2-IC Littlejohn, and lives in luxury with them, having a room to himself! The rest of us sleep in a dormitory of 14 officers! The hospital, having no equipment, is quite inactive, but the Island is being heavily fortified, and women and children are being sent away inland.

We are all bored and homesick with no work to do, and spend the time sitting about writing letters and swimming. All the work is being done by the 12th AGH, and they are run off their feet!

I went in to Colombo and ordered some lightweight shirts and shorts, and have started seeing a few patients at 12th, which relieves the boredom.

Gilbert has received a letter from Tibby, with information that all three of my little ones are now in Katanning, at Kobeelya! Also that brother Jack was wounded in the Darwin bombing raid, on the hospital ship *Manunda*!

On Good Friday I went to Church at 9 a.m. It was simply packed with a chocolate-faced congregation. I stayed half an hour, listening to a sleepy oration by a tired looking parson, and sang a couple of hymns sharing the book with a black man in a white suit.

The next day, Col. Spiers was appointed ADMS for the AIF in Ceylon, in addition to his present role as CO.

In the afternoon we moved to our new quarters, a brick and tile bungalow with a concrete floor, about half a mile down the road from the College. It has no furniture, and 6 of us share it. I have been given a good little room, with a veranda facing out on a grove of palm trees.

I set up my camp stretcher bed, and scrounged a table and chair, which has made it more homely. A school desk and my cabin trunk complete the furnishings.

Our new ADMS then tried to send me to a Field Ambulance, under Lt. Col Fisher, who is 20 years my junior! *Me!* At *my age!* He thought better of it at the last moment and sent a younger man.

On Easter Sunday, Colombo had its first air raid! Out of the 75 Jap planes counted, our fighters shot down 25! We lost 11 planes and two ships were set on fire. Couldn't see much of the aerial combat owing to low clouds, but I saw my first Jap planes! Invasion seems imminent, as 4 Jap transports and a strong convoy have been sighted off the south coast!

On 7 April, I cabled Mildred for our coming wedding anniversary, and then thought about setting up my eye department. In the afternoon, I wandered around the Unit trying to get to know the NCOs and men. I have been appointed Company Officer for the 4th AGH, which at least provides me with military duties, in the absence of any medical work.

On 10 April, our 14th Anniversary, I woke early and lay reading Mildred's old letters, and looking at photos. I did some work in the morning then had lunch with Gilbert at the 12th. He showed me a cable from Tibby, stating 'House let to American Navy. Staying at Esplanade hotel. Mildred with me'.

I cabled Mildred immediately, 'Anniversary Greetings. Address 4th AGH' – to obviate any possible reason for her not replying, and to let her know that I know where *she* is!

That afternoon 60 poor bedraggled survivors from the cruisers *Dorsetshire* and *Cromwell* sunk yesterday were taken to a hospital up in the hills, instead of to us, as was expected.

Three days later I had a cable from Mildred dated a week before. She *still* thinks I am on my way home!

We are having trouble with discipline. The men are playing up, getting drunk and being insolent and disobedient. Three are up for Court Martial. The CO has been ridiculously lenient with the men and rarely supports his officers.

We asked the CO to come on Parade – for a change. This he did, and addressed the men, then gave them Company drill in the sun all afternoon, instead of the planned cricket match!

So now our hospital is unpacked and set up properly, and we are able to function at last. The harbour is full of warships, with 2 aircraft carriers, several cruisers, a battleship, and many destroyers, said to be part of the Atlantic Fleet.

27 April

On Anzac Day there was a church parade at 10.45 a.m., attended by most of the officers and men, and about 50 nurses. The RC Padré officiated, as our Unit Anglican Padré, did not turn up! I gave him a talking-to later!

This evening I was elected Mess President!

Less than 12 months ago I came to 4th AGH in Tobruk shy, self-effacing, and overcome with inferiority complex. Now I am Consultant Ophthalmologist for the AIF, Company Officer of 4th AGH, and President of the Mess!

2 May 1942

At 6.30 this evening, our Mess invited the Officers and Nurses of 12th AGH to a Cocktail Party. Our CO didn't turn up until about 9.30 p.m. when the party was nearly over. The rude old pig! As Mess President, I had to entertain the CO of the 12th for the whole three hours!

When our CO finally turned up, I told him in a fury that the Mess considered that he had deliberately insulted their guests! I then stamped off to bed in a rage! Next morning I woke with a hangover and a nasty guilty feeling about 'insubordinate language'!

By 11 a.m. I was feeling better, and I went straight to the CO and apologised. He was very decent and accepted the apology, and said it was forgotten. (I think I was lucky!)

Brigadier Jack Lloyd came to lunch, then took me out to the 12th. They were all very much under the weather after our hospitality, and very appreciative of our Party!

Meanwhile in Western Australia, after the bombing raids on Wyndham and Broome, there was a growing fear of an attack on Perth. Air raid shelters were dug, including one in the garden at Clovelly, and sand bags were appearing round buildings. Petrol, food and clothing were rationed, and many of Mildred's friends had evacuated to the country.

Claude's Ford motor car had been put on blocks in the garage 'for the duration', with its sump and radiator drained, but Mildred could still drive her Vauxhall – when she had the petrol.

Pamela was in her third year at Kobeelya, and both Geoffrey and Neville were now both at Christ Church Grammar School.

Mildred lived alone in Clovelly, getting the boys off to school each day in the bus, and for the first time in her married life, she was doing the washing and cooking without the accustomed domestic help! She had the added responsibility of looking after the finances and paying the bills, tasks that Claude had always taken care of in the past.

She was sure that Claude was on the way home, and his stop at Colombo was only temporary. She was determined to have their home ready for him when he appeared at the door, as she thought would happen, with little or no notice!

There was no airmail service to Ceylon, and much of the mail was held up by the irregularity of the shipping. The lack of up-to-date information to and from Australia was frustrating in the extreme! Claude sent cables which took 6–7 days to arrive, but could only send three short sentences, and any allusion to location or movements was censored. Somehow, all the information that Mildred received added up in her mind to his imminent return to Australia.

Finally, as letters came in irregular batches, sometimes 2–3 at a time, she realised that Claude had been placed in Colombo indefinitely, and she must organise her life accordingly. As a temporary arrangement, she put both the boys in to boarding school at Christ Church, and moved out of Clovelly, which had become a lonely burden for her.

She shared an apartment in Mount Street, close to Perth's centre, with Tibby Troup who had 'let' her home, and was doing war work by driving for the RAAF.

Mildred and the children with a pet sheep, at Dr Caldwell's house, Katanning, 1942.

Mildred was receiving rent from both the Busselton property, and also from the property in Inglewood, together with dividends from their investment portfolios, and some income from the Practice, now run by Claude's partner, Dr John Day. This allowed her to pay the school fees, and cope with everyday expenses, but with little to spare. Claude remitted most of his army pay to her, and pointed out that army pay was not taxable.

(The Taxation Department at that time was causing great concern to the overseas troops, with demands for money that they had no possibility of meeting! One of Claude's colleagues had been appalled by a Taxation Department demand for £1,100! The general trend however, was to ignore the demands, but sooner or later, it would catch up with them!)

With the increasing fear of attack, or even invasion, Mildred took the boys out of Christ Church, and in the process had an argument with the school's administration, which demanded an extra term's fees in lieu of proper notice! Prior to doing this, she had visited Katanning where she spent Half Term Vacation with Pamela, and at the same time, arranged for little Neville, aged six, and Geoffrey to become boarders at 'Kobeelya' with Pam.

Mildred then returned to the flat she shared in Perth.

She went to Clovelly, then being looked after by the old gardener, and packed up a lot of their effects – silver, linen and good clothing, etc. – into cases and boxes. Some she sent down to Katanning. Other cases she left with friends in Perth. She wrote an inventory of everything, and deposited the letter, addressed to Claude with Perpetual Trustees, who held their Wills. All would not be lost if the house was bombed!

She managed to let Clovelly to some suitable tenants, on a three-monthly basis, and then returned to Katanning, where she rented a comfortable flat attached to the home of Dr Caldwell, a local General Practitioner. She had the Vauxhall shipped to Katanning by rail. The boys then came to live with her, and attended Kobeelya as day students.

The Caldwell family was very kind and helpful to Mildred, and her time in Katanning was relatively peaceful and happy. They had two sons who were good company for Geoff, and in the May holidays, Mildred rented a pony, which they kept in the Caldwell's large garden.

The American Navy had a Submarine Base at Albany, about 100 miles further south, and Naval Officers would visit Katanning from time to time. Parties were given to entertain the servicemen, providing some variety in the otherwise slow country lifestyle.

In Ceylon, Claude sweltered and sweated in the tropical monsoon that he hated. Every day the rain poured down, and every afternoon it was accompanied by thunder and lightning. The palm trees outside his veranda dripped with water, and steam rose from the warm earth. Everything grew mould – shoes, leather belts, damp towels, clothes, everything.

Of all the General Hospitals to be recently moved out of the Middle East, the 4thAGH was the only one that had seen action. It had been shipwrecked on the way to Tobruk, bombed and shelled for 7 months during the siege, and now, when in Claude's opinion they deserved to be sent home, they were dumped in Colombo, while the rest of the convoy had sailed on to Australia! In spite of his hatred of the climate and resentment at being '*stuck in this infernal hole*' he conceded that he was indeed fortunate not to be a prisoner of war like so many of his friends!

Claude's health remained good. With the exception of the CO, who was two years his senior, he was the oldest person in the Hospital, and in the absence of a lot of eye work, he busied himself with other tasks. He was President of the Mess, which occupied some of his time, and was also Company Officer for the Hospital. This was a 'third in command' position, and provided him with military duties such as holding morning parades, and carrying out administration tasks in the Orderly Room. He wrote to Mildred every 2–3 days, and cabled her about once a week, hungrily awaiting letters from home.

Early in May, together with fellow officers Lendon, Rudd and Morton he arranged a three-day leave pass and went to the mountains. They caught the train in Colombo at 6.45 a.m., and climbed steadily all day past rubber and tea plantations, arriving at Nurawa Eliya at 4. p.m. where they settled into the luxurious Grand Hotel, 6,200 feet above sea level in beautiful surroundings. The air was crisp and cool, and that night they sat by a log fire, and had blankets on their beds! The Golf Club was right beside the hotel, and the next morning they hired clubs, paid their green fees and played golf all day. The golf course reminded Claude of Mount Lofty, where he and Mildred had stayed years ago after attending a Congress in Adelaide.

Claude, in his own words, '*played shocking golf, lost 5 balls, and came in at the end of the day in a bad mood, and with aching feet.*' He resolved not to play the next day!

The following morning when the others went out for golf, Claude phoned a tea planter, '*a delightful fellow named Henstock*', who had married the sister of his friend Reg Summerhayes, the Perth architect. They met and had a cup of tea and a chat. That afternoon Henstock took all four on a tour of his tea factory, then to the Hills Club ('*a rather swanky place*') for a drink, after which the four entertained him for dinner in their Hotel. His wife Dorothy and the two boys had just gone to Cape Town for safety, and Henstock hoped to see them '*in about a year*'. After that, the boys would have to go off to boarding school in England. '*At least when this is all over we can all live together without more separations*', Claude wrote to Mildred.

After another 24 hours in the delightful mountain climate they returned on the night train to the 4th AGH and the tropical humidity.

In May an outbreak of Dengue Fever struck the hospital, and of the 24 Officers, only five were spared the infection. All five of Claude's bungalow-mates went down with the disease, which put them out of action for about three weeks; two weeks in hospital, and one in the mountains, convalescing.

Claude was spared, though he considered that a week convalescing in the mountains would have made the suffering worthwhile!

As a result of the epidemic, Claude was landed with extra duty. When the ENT Specialist became ill, Claude, after more than 30 years away from that type of work, took over his duties – after a hasty brush up with the textbooks! The CO went down with Dengue, and many of his duties were added to Claude's burden as Company Officer. As well, he became acting Registrar of the Hospital, an administrative task, and spent the day rushing from one job to the next.

News of the war in Europe and Africa was scanty, but there were rumours that the Americans were landing in England in preparation for an attack on Europe. Also, that the Battle of the Coral Sea had saved Australia – for the time being?

Tobruk had been lost, and the Germans had pushed through towards Alexandria. Things looked grim!

The epidemic of Dengue added two more duties to Claude's already busy life. He became Admitting Officer, and Orderly Officer, and '*I was run off my feet!*'

By the end of May, life was returning to normal. After eight days on his own, his sick friends were drifting back to the bungalow, and Claude was gradually relieved of his extra duties. He concentrated on finishing the 'fit out' the new Eye Clinic, where he had started to see a few patients, and as Consultant Ophthalmologist, he began to organise an Optical Workshop, as he had done in the Middle East.

Gilbert Troup and Geoff Thompson were the only West Australians in the area, but it was difficult to obtain transport out to the 12th and both were both always very busy. When the mail arrived, they would ring, or get together to pool their information about home.

Claude borrowed a bicycle and rode to the Mess each day, and on short excursions, such as to the Zoo, where he took photos to send to the children. He was starting to become acclimatised.

4th AGH
10 June 1942
Wednesday

My own darling wife.
I wrote to you on Saturday hoping the mail would leave the next day, but it is still waiting for a ship I believe. The rumours about mail movement are quite unreliable!

It is evening. Exactly two years ago tonight, Reg Hall mysteriously invited all the neighbours to come in at 7.30 p.m. He had some news for us!

We went, and he produced champagne, whisky, etc., and then informed us that France had laid down her arms! Do you remember dearest? And then, he and Cam Milne had the bad taste to insinuate unpleasant hints reflecting on my French name and ancestry – or so I thought!

Well! Two years have gone by, and for 18 months of them I have been exiled from everyone and everything that makes life worth living to me, doing my small part and making my sacrifices to help my Country. And what has Reg Hall done in these two years?

I am quite well, thank God. Only 5 of us, out of 24 Officers have escaped this raging epidemic of Dengue Fever. All the others are men in their 30s, so your decrepit old man has not proved such a washout in health and capacity for work as his years would lead one to expect!

I've had to do all sorts of jobs in the last few weeks as well as my own, including the ENT work!

Gilbert and Geoff Thompson are coming for lunch tomorrow, which will do them both good. They have both been here for 9 months now, working very hard, and both look thin, and have become listless and morbid. This rotten equatorial climate has got them down! They are awfully lucky to have each other in the same Unit, and when I go there, we talk of WA and our own people and the good old days all the time.

I am so thankful that all my darlings are nearly 200 miles from Perth, and 100 from Albany, as we all agree that Fremantle, and probably Perth too, is certain to be raided or shelled before too long!

Thursday evening
We had a good lunch, and the three of us went to the pictures in the afternoon, which I haven't done before. The theatre was nearly empty, and we sat in the front of the 'dress circle' under the 'punkah', which was cool and comfortable. We saw an English comedy, and had a good laugh, which did us all good!

Afterwards we sat and chatted, and visualised cold wet weather in WA, and in Katanning you must be enduring the coldest winter you have ever experienced dearest! I only hope you don't get one of those awful colds when you lose your voice, that beautiful sweet voice that I used to call the 'silver bell' when we were engaged. What I wouldn't give to hear it tonight!

It's getting insufferably hot writing here, dearest, although I am stripped to the waist. Horrible little flying ant things keep settling on my bare chest and back, so I think I will stop now and go out on the veranda in the dark and lie on my bed.

Goodnight my sweet girl. I hope you are all snuggled up and sleeping soundly. XXX

Friday
Good morning darling.
It's 6.30 am, and I am writing this in bed, with the pad on my pillow. The sun is just getting up, and a church bell is ringing in the distance. Not a leaf is moving in the forest of dripping palm trees beside my veranda, and the air is full of bird sounds, with the murmur of the sea in the background.

I've been lying here gazing at the palm trees since it began to get light, thinking of all the wonderful happy years we have lived together, and the peaceful mornings when I used to wake, and find you sleeping beside me, and I would listen to the motor launches chugging by on the river, and peep out over our green lawn to see the sun rise over the water. And then you would open your eyes and smile at me, as a patter of little feet would come running in to our room, in time for morning tea, and granita biscuits.

Well darling, those days are gone. They could not last forever, and here we are both exiled from our dear old home, and separated by nearly 3,000 miles of ocean, and yet I know that we are not separated in spirit, for we think constantly of each other, and our lives are really in constant touch.

The sun is up now dearest, and a squadron of Hurricanes has just thundered low overhead. I must stop now.

Sunday afternoon
My darling girl, a bunch of letters was handed to me, with one from yourself, and one from Pamela.

You poor darling! The school holidays must have been real slavery for you with the three children in that little flat, and the washing and cooking to do, especially on that beastly wood stove and all. What a pity you couldn't have got them in to a boarding house like the one at the Porongurups.

To think it has come to this, after all those years with two maids living in, and practically never without any help at all, except for a day or so … Well dearest, the holidays are over now, and you must be about exhausted!

Pamela drew me a plan of your 'lovely flat' (as she put it) at the Caldwells, so I have a clear idea of it all. But the bed sitting room at the end of the passage must be cold with no fireplace. I hope you've bought a couple of radiators!

I think its splendid that you have the Theobald's pony and no doubt the children had a glorious holiday with their bikes, and the pony and freedom, *and* the greatest blessing of all, their own darling mother.

On Tuesday afternoon Dr Theobald came to see me. I showed him over the hospital, and he invited me to stay with him in the hills where he has his practice. I told him that you had his children's pony for the holidays, and he reassured me that it is a quiet and gentle one.

It is interesting that I should come across him here, isn't it?

You are right Mildred dear, to stay where you can watch over the children. They are so young and sweet, and too good to be brought up in the cold hard atmosphere of boarding school with no home influence. Besides dearest, they will so quickly grow up, and you can't get their childhood back again to enjoy after the war.

Gilbert tells me that Tibby thinks you will go back to live in Perth after the holidays are over. I suppose its natural that you will get restless and bored in the country, when you have always lived in the town. God knows we all get restless and bored enough *here*, wasting our lives in exile in this filthy climate! But if you were in Perth when the raids start, which I feel certain will happen in the present circumstances, you may not be able to get away. Roads will be blocked with accidents, and bridges and culverts down, and railways out of commission! You must stay near the children darling, for their sake and for mine! I couldn't feel happy knowing that you were all separated at this time.

Let Geoff go to the State School if necessary. Why not? It would be a saving in your expenses, and everyone says they teach them well, and he will have you to come home to. The war can't go on forever! Kobeelya have stated his age as 10 in his report. But he is only nine! You should mention this to Mrs Strugnell.

I am sending you another £20 at once in case you need it. Be sure to remind Langoulant that remittances from me are out of military pay and are free from income tax!

I suppose it would be better to sell the Busselton place. I hope you won't *give* it away! Remember what we paid for it and the improvements we have put in. I suppose we should sell it while there is someone in WA with enough money left to pay for it! It is probably looking a little shabby by now!

It is 6 p.m. and I must get dressed for mess, and post this.

I hope you are keeping Neville with you this term. I don't like him being separated from you at the age of six. Be sure to tell me if you have received the parcels of tea. I have sent two boxes of 5 lbs each.

Must stop now darling. Goodbye my dear sweet girl.

From your Claude

By mid-June, Claude's melancholia deepened. He felt completely cut off from his family, and despaired of ever getting home again, and watched with envy and frustration as his younger colleagues were promoted.

He wrote to Mildred, '*I am getting old now. They can have their promotions and decorations. I hear that Joe Stubbe is now a Lieut. Colonel, and Lindsay Male a full Colonel. Tom Louch and Don Cleland are now Brigadiers! Ah well! With the exception of Tom, they are all young men compared to me, and young men always rise up in wartime. If they last the distance!*

In the last war I was a Lieut. Colonel before I was 30 years old! You can't keep on doing it dear, war after war. This war is not being fought by my generation, but by the one after mine.

If only they would give me an honourable discharge from the service, like they did to Hubert Parker, that is all I ask of the army, after two years service abroad, and at the age of nearly 54. You and I would be able to watch the war wear itself out, living happily together, and with a clear conscience that we had made our sacrifice, with the best of them. I think we deserve it my dearest, don't you?'

Towards the end of June, orders came to pack up the 4th AGH ready for transport! It was to be empty in seven days, but no destination had been given. Claude drove out to the 12th to tell Gilbert and Geoff, but they had already heard the news and were green with envy.

Claude withdrew all his army pay, and spent the next week going round the shops buying gifts to take home. He bought silk underwear and stockings, and jewellery made with zircons and other beautiful precious stones.

The CO announced that there would be no more mail service out, and any suspicion of a coded message in a cable would prevent it from being sent. (In his letters to Mildred, Claude had carefully explained a code he would use if they received 'marching orders') So much for that idea!

He continued his shopping spree, and purchased more tea, which he packed and sent to Mildred, sending a couple of bland cables, with a 'watered down' version of his code, which was not understood!

Claude wrote his report on the 'Eye Work' in Ceylon as the hospital was being packed up. At the end of the week, the 12th entertained them to a farewell Cocktail Party that was a riotous success, and provided them all with bad hangovers!

They received instructions about travel, with the hospital staff being divided among several ships. As their departure approached, bad news came from the war in Africa! The Germans had taken Mersa Metruh, and were only 80 miles from Alex. They had taken huge numbers of prisoners, and vast hoards of munitions were in their hands. It seemed that the end of the Middle East was in sight. *'Thank God we are half way home!'*

The first contingent boarded for departure, but Claude's party had their boarding postponed, then confirmed, then postponed again! He called on some friends at sundown to say goodbye, and ruefully noted that he was only offered a cup of tea!

On the eve of departure, the RAMC and Indian Medical Officers took over the Mess, to the good news that Alexandria had not fallen as expected!

At 10 o'clock on the 7th July, they boarded the *City of Canterbury*, at anchor in the harbour, where Claude was to share a small cabin with Matheson, the Registrar. At least it had an electric fan!

The *City of Canterbury* was an 8,000 ton coal burner, small but comfortable, with narrow decks and a tiny saloon. It was capable of carrying 1,500 troops, but there were only 1,350 aboard. All around them ships were filling up with troops and stores, preparing for the convoy home.

The following afternoon, Claude was required to perform a 'Short Arm

Parade', which involved inspecting the penis of each of the 280 troops, looking for signs of VD! *'This I did reluctantly in the humidity, heat and stench of the fetid troop deck. Me! An* ***eye specialist****! I nearly fainted!'*

They remained at anchor for five days of heat and boredom. On the fifth day a load of mail from Australia arrived, with five letters from Mildred and school reports, some from the children, and a statement from Langoulant, his accountant. These he devoured for the rest of the afternoon. It was rumoured that they would sail the next day.

Monday 13 July

This morning the atmosphere is charged with suspense! At noon the great warships filed out of the harbour, and after a thunderous blast on its horn, the 30,000 ton *Athlone Castle* led the convoy out. With bands gaily playing, one by one the ships weighed anchor and moved out in an imposing procession! We are the sixth ship in the line, and a stately cruiser stood outside the harbour entrance and watched as her family filed by. It is a huge convoy!

Thank God it has come at last! *'May He watch over these eager thousands, and bring us safely home to our wives and loved ones.'*

Wednesday

We crossed the equator at 10 a.m. in squalls of rain. There are 16 ships in the convoy, surrounded by a cordon of warships of various sorts, and we zigzag about every ten minutes, but always making south. Matheson and I have slept on deck for the last few nights, as the cabin is just hell when closed down.

We have had instruction in Bren gun firing and Boat Drill, and it is rumoured that we will reach Melbourne about 7 August. As the days pass it is becoming cooler, and we can now sleep in the cabin.

An American cruiser took over from the *Gambier* that has accompanied us so far, and for the first time, I can see the 'Stars and Stripes' flying on an American warship, cleared for action! At the end of the first week at sea, the HMAS *Kanimbla* took over from the last of the English escorts. Goodbye to the British Navy! In future we fight for *Australia*, with America!

22 July 1942

Shortly after daybreak we were awakened with the ship's alarm! Fire had broken out in the forward hold! We mustered on deck with life jackets, while the crew fought the blaze. It took two hours to extinguish, and a lot of hospital equipment was lost! Fire on a crowded troop ship could have been a dreadful disaster! We had a very narrow escape!

The weather continued to improve, and on one beautiful calm day, the Yankee cruiser sent up *four* reconnaissance planes! It continued to do so for the next few days, winching them back on board when they returned.

We estimate we are getting close to Fremantle. A Catalina flying boat from WA flew out and had a good look at us, then returned.

At 2 p.m. on the 27th the Australian destroyer, HMAS *Vendetta*, and another warship joined us. The Convoy was then split, and 6 ships escorted by 2 warships veered away east towards Fremantle. A really majestic sight!

The remainder of the convoy put on speed and headed south towards the Bight, accompanied by *Vendetta*, and the American cruiser *Phoenix*.

As we turned east in the Bight, the *Duntroon*, the *Manoora*, the *Westralia*, and a Dutch destroyer joined us. Aerial reconnaissance had spotted a Japanese submarine, which had immediately submerged! We were ordered to sleep in our clothes with life jackets handy. The weather was now bleak!

Six days later, on Monday 3 August, with no further incident, and sleeping uncomfortably in clothes each night, we anchored in Port Phillip Bay. It is rumoured that we will go to camp in Seymour, with no leave for ages! Oh my God! After all this!

We waited at the wharf all the next day, and were then entrained for Seymour, where we arrived in freezing weather and pitch darkness. There was no telephone link to Perth, so the next day I sent telegrams to Mildred while I waited for information regarding my leave. Nearly all the officers and men had been granted leave and had already gone, with only a couple of us now left in camp – until four officers arrived with 30 men – and 100 VD patients! Not only was the camp miserable, muddy and cold, it was now crawling with VD!

The next morning I received my leave pass, and boarded the crowded troop train at Seymour station, where I had a quick lunch in the restaurant. I settled in for a cold uncomfortable night, sitting up fully dressed in the crowded cabin.

I woke with cold feet and a headache. We had stopped at a siding outside Adelaide, the Showgrounds I think, then marched a mile to camp where we had a shave and a shower, then a plate of slushy stew.

The train was even more crowded now, and I sat uncomfortably in the cramped cabin to Port Pirie. There, we changed on to the 'Trans' train, which had no restaurant car, but I got a sleeper, with no bedding. I had the lower bunk and unrolled my valise and stretched out – at last!

We reached Kalgoorlie on my 54th birthday, and changed again onto the narrow gauge train to Perth – *almost home!!* After an endless, uncomfortable night we pulled in to Perth station at 8 a.m. – exactly 18 months to the day since I sailed from WA!!

I found my own darling wife waiting for me at the Esplanade Hotel.

Is it only a glorious dream? – *Peace and comfort at last!*

[Claude's diary ends here]

Claude and Mildred stayed at the Esplanade for a few days, during which time brother Jack arrived in Perth on his way east. He had recovered from his wound, and they had a great reunion.

When Jack left, Claude and Mildred caught the train to Katanning, where all three children were now boarding at 'Kobeelya'. The slow journey started at 8 a.m., and took all day in wet cold weather. They arrived at 7.30 p.m., just in time to go to the school and see the children before bed.

The next day was Sunday, and in bright sunny weather the whole family had a wonderful day together, with a happy reunion luncheon in their hotel. Claude delighted Geoffrey by presenting him with the tiny Italian rifle with its little folding bayonet, which made him the envy of the other little boys in the boarding school. He promptly managed to break a window by doing a 'bayonet charge' on the draped blackout curtain in front of it! At the request of the Headmistress, Claude took the rifle back to Perth with him, to be given at another time!

On Monday, after packing all Mildred's bags and paying the bills, they returned by train to Perth, ending Mildred's six-month country sojourn. After another night in the Esplanade Hotel, Claude collected the Vauxhall from the garage, and loaded in the baggage.

They visited the hospital to see Mildred's mother, whose health was declining, then, in glorious sunshine, they drove to Mosman Bay and arrived at Clovelly at noon, to be greeted by their old neighbours. That evening, Reg and Linda McKellar Hall entertained Claude and Mildred, together with neighbours and friends, to a merry dinner party.

Claude was given a month's leave, and with Pamela remaining at Kobeelya, and the boys back at Christ Church, they had happy time together. They had help in the house, with Mrs Laker, who lived close by, coming in each day to do the chores. The Ford V8 was made functional again, but with only 3 gallons of petrol per month on the ration, they used the cars sparingly.

At the end of his leave, Claude reported to his new posting at the 118th AGH based at Northam, where he was to spend many months. Every second weekend he was able to go to Perth on the train, and he spent time at Hollywood Repatriation Hospital organising Ophthalmic services for Returned Servicemen.

Mildred, meanwhile, looked after the home, with Mrs Laker's help, and got the boys off to school each day on the bus.

Whilst Northam was only 60 miles from Perth, telephone calls were still 'long distance' and only three-minute duration, with extensions. They were also expensive! Thus Claude continued his custom of writing frequently.

Darling
I have just hung up the telephone after an appallingly short 6 minutes talking with you. It is delightful being able to speak to you and hear your voice.

Your last question was about the car. I put 3 gallons in it, and you should get 17–18 miles to the gallon, so when it shows a little over 50, you will be nearly out! I will try to arrange a bit more from John Day when I come down at the end of the week, but I will have to drive up to the to Tivoli Garage to have it put in as John leaves all his ration tickets there. Please remember to tell Langoulant that, up to date, I have used 6 gallons (two lots of 3) of John's petrol. I would like to get in first, so he can make the adjustments before John speaks about it!

... Also ask Langoulant how on earth the Taxation department arrived at our assessment of £1080 last year when the taxable income was less than £2000! Anyhow I know that the next assessment will be on a taxable income of £1400, so surely it can't be anything like as much again.

I can't see how we can ever save enough out of income to pay £60 a month and still keep Pamela at boarding school and dress and feed everybody...

For the first time in their married life they were feeling financially threatened. Claude's meagre army pay, together with the other supplements was barely enough to make ends meet. The Taxation Department served him with a demand that was far in excess of anything anticipated, and Claude was under great pressure! He had a life insurance policy that was nearing maturity, having paid in to it for the past 23 years, but had grave concerns about using any of the money to pay taxation demands. Eventually, the Busselton and Inglewood properties were sold, and this money, together with a large amount of his life insurance reluctantly went to the Tax Department!

Mildred for her part had endured 18 months alone with the children in a threatening war environment, with her share of domestic and financial worries. It was starting to tell.

Claude continued to travel to and from Northam, dividing his time between his clinic at the 118th AGH and Hollywood Hospital. His old Unit, the 4th AGH, had moved from Seymour to Queensland, and had set up their hospital at Redbank, a few miles south of Brisbane. Claude received a number of letters from his old colleagues, wishing him well.

At home, life started to return to normal, and with the resumption of the school year, Pamela caught the train back to Kobeelya, and the boys returned to Christ Church, but at the end of first term, Pamela returned to Perth to resume school at St Hilda's. Claude felt that the family had been split up for too long.

By mid 1943 the tide of war had turned in Europe, and the Japanese had been halted in their push to Australia. The Battle of the Coral Sea had destroyed the Japanese plan of attacking Port Moresby from the sea, and the land war in New Guinea was gradually going against the Japanese.

In August 1943 Claude was posted from the 118th to become the first 'Medical Director and Adviser in Ophthalmology to the Director General of Medical Services' (but still with no promotion!). His duties included the supervision of all Ophthalmic Services across Australia, which mostly involved travel to Sydney, Queensland and the Northern Territory.

On more than one occasion he visited his old Unit, the 4th AGH, at Redbank and noted that an optical workshop of the type he had designed was working efficiently there.

In March 1944, Claude received his discharge from the Army, and gratefully returned to his home to pick up the threads of his previous life.

Claude Morlet photographed during the Second World War

Chapter 25

Claude resumed his practice in St George's Terrace with John Day, and had his old Ford V8 thoroughly serviced, and spray-painted a smart cream colour.

Neville and I attended Christ Church, and would be dropped off there in the mornings by Father on his way to the city, and then catch the bus home after school. At the end of the day, usually when it was getting dark, Dad would arrive home, and as he came up the steps to the front door, Mum would caution us, 'Don't talk to your father till he's had a drink'. He always looked very tired.

In the weekends, sometimes we would hire a row boat from Waite's (later Smith's) Boatshed at the bottom of the street and Dad would row the family along the river shore to Chidley Point. There we would have a picnic and swim in the river. We had picnics by the ocean too, at a secluded little place he called 'secret beach' where we would sit in the shelter of the rocks and eat our sandwiches.

In the home we had Mary Sunley, a lovely, large red-faced Yorkshire woman, who 'lived in', and did the cooking and the chores. She was a diabetic, and I recall watching in awe as she injected herself with insulin!

That Christmas, after a marvellous traditional dinner cooked by Mary, I remember her joining the family for a glass of beer, and her giving a Yorkshire toast. ' 'Eres to me, an' my 'usband's wife, – an' not forgettin' myself!' We all loved Mary!

In 1945, Neville and I started at Hale School in West Perth, where the new headmaster of the school was Dr Arnold Buntine, whom Father knew in Tobruk. Father travelled to work each day in his car, and he would take us with him and drop us off at school on his way to the city. This must have rated as one of the most nerve-wracking events of our childhood. Father's bad driving was legendary! He always travelled at high speed, and would pass a slower vehicle that he considered was not driving correctly, then turn in his seat and shake his fist at the hapless driver.

Our route to the city took us past Claremont Railway Station, where from the street, one could see the large 'railway clock' on the wall. As we drove by it was our job to call out the time, so that Father could adjust his speed appropriately so as to have us at school on time. We were invariably running

Claude and Mildred enjoy a picnic at Chidley Point, 1944

a little late, which prompted a sudden burst of speed, and we would thunder along past the Show Grounds, to arrive with a few moments to spare before the school bell rang. We would try to think up reasons for us to catch the bus to school.

In May the war in Europe came to an end, then on 15 August, Japan surrendered and the war was over.

Father decided that he should have a boat. After discussing the idea with his old friends Gilbert Troup and Fred Clarke, it was agreed that they would join forces as partners and buy one. After watching the newspaper advertisements, they finally decided on a rather ancient and run down 16-foot centreboard sailing boat, that they inspected lying heeled-over in shallow water in the river near Fremantle, its hull covered with weed and barnacles.

Claude was a member of Royal Freshwater Bay Yacht Club, near his home, where I had become a Cadet Member and an enthusiastic junior sailor. The boat was towed up the river to the Club, and passed over to the shipwrights who endeavoured to make something out of it. It was cleaned inside and out and given a fresh coat of paint. Floorboards and side seats were installed, and the yacht was ceremoniously named *Cygnet*.

Finally it was ready to sail, and lay on a mooring close to the east shore at the Club. It had 'quarter decking' that ran back to the mast, and around the sides to the stern. The bowsprit was gleaming with fresh varnish, like the other spars, and all the standing and running rigging had been replaced. The two sails – main and jib – had been overhauled and repaired by Beaver the Sailmaker, who made the best out of a bad job!

On a sunny Saturday afternoon in the early summer, with the Yacht Club in full activity, a man with a dinghy deposited Father, Gilbert and me on the yacht, where we set about preparing to sail. By the time we had got the boat rigged, the afternoon sea breeze had strengthened, and the sails were flapping violently. Our mooring was in a group of boats, and when commanded to do so, I cast off the mooring rope.

We charged through the anchorage with the sails filled, Father clutching the helm, and Gilbert looking anxious. As we passed too close to a moored yacht, our 'main sheet' that controlled the extended main sail, caught on a deck fitting of the yacht, and we were tethered – with sails filled and heeling dangerously!

By this time we had come to the notice of the spectators on the Club lawn who gleefully watched the drama unfold. Father bellowed at me to get over the side and release the rope, so I jumped into the water and pulled myself hand over hand along the rope then climbed up on to the other boat's deck. After a struggle I managed to release the snagged main sheet, and like a startled bird, the *Cygnet* and its two hapless occupants surged off, leaving me marooned on the offending boat. The crowd roared with delight!

I sat cold, shivering and miserable and watched as father wove his way through the racing fleet, then out into the middle of the river, where they pulled in the sails and prepared to 'go about'. As they turned into the wind, the main sail crashed down, with the heavy gaff narrowly missing the intrepid sailors! There was a roar of laughter from the spectators, and I cringed with shame. Ultimately they made their way back to the Club under the jib, and tied up to the wharf.

At that point, Claude set out to rescue his son whom he had left stranded, and, sculling the heavy Club dinghy with one oar, he rounded the end of the jetty and battled into the brisk sea breeze, heading for his boy.

The spectators watched delightedly as the next saga unfolded. The elements finally overpowered Claude, and he drifted helplessly across the river towards Claremont, a mile or so away! It all ended satisfactorily as Claude was rescued by a launch, and I was collected and returned to shore. Little was said as we drove home, but I remember standing under the hot shower recovering, and vowing I would never go sailing again with them!

Of course I did, and over the next few months we collided with a couple of spit posts, and transgressed most of the rules of sailing. Gilbert bravely accompanied Claude as we cruised around the bays and they drank glasses of beer, pitching the empty bottles or 'dead marines' as father called them, over the side. I don't remember Fred Clark ever coming out on the *Cygnet*.

The next summer, father decided to take his boys camping in the yacht. Gilbert was invited, but wisely declined, owing to another commitment. After much careful planning, we set out early on a Friday morning heading for the Canning River, with myself, Neville, and a neighbour's son, Binkie Frayne, a lad of about seventeen. Binkie was a competent sailor and had gallantly agreed to accompany us. The boat was loaded up the night before, with clothing and provisions all arranged by mother, who was rather anxious about the whole thing.

The next morning we arrived at the Yacht Club to find a stiff easterly breeze blowing. The problem we faced was that the Canning River opened in to the Swan about six miles due east of our position, and that was where the wind was coming from! Undaunted, we pulled up the sails and butted our way 'close-hauled' into the wind and waves. We were soon wet through, and made remarkably poor progress, as the boat could not sail well close to the wind. We tacked from side to side, but made little progress forward. It wasn't until mid-afternoon that we reached the Canning River, at which time the breeze had almost completely died out.

Fortunately, Binkie had brought his father's outboard engine, which we fitted on to the stern bracket, and after much tugging of the starting cord, the little engine spluttered into life and we proceeded slowly up the river. By late afternoon we found a suitable place to stop, and set up camp on the deserted riverbank.

Claude demonstrated his bushman skills by cutting saplings to make beds, while Binkie and I unloaded the boat and set up camp. With hurricane lamps lit we sat by the fire and had our supper of tinned food. Little Neville, who was only nine years old, was exhausted, and was tucked in to his bush bed by father. No sooner were we all settled down for the night then we were startled by a piercing scream from Neville. A large Sergeant ant had bitten him! Of course we had no first aid kit, so father rubbed whisky on the sting from his flask, interspersed with a few nips. Nev was ultimately consoled and we all had an uncomfortable and restless night.

The next day after bacon and eggs and billy tea, we all felt better – except Neville, who wanted to go home. He had a painful bite on his leg.

We lasted another 24 hours then packed up and started the long sail home. By the time we reached the Swan River it was mid afternoon, and the wind was blowing strongly from the southwest – where we were heading! Once again we close-hauled the sails and beat into the wind and waves.

The sun went down, and the breeze dropped. We were somewhere off Dalkeith, about half way home, and becalmed in the pitch-black moonless night. Binky's outboard engine stubbornly refused to start, and was rendered even more useless by his attempts to repair it by torchlight on the deck. Something important fell overboard, and that was that!

It was about 11 p.m. when we finally drifted in to shallow water and ran aground. Claude decided to go for help, and we were to remain in the boat. Unfortunately the torch batteries were almost exhausted by this time, and Claude groped and floundered across the flat ground towards the lights he could see higher up on the escarpment. He heard voices and called out. 'Where are you?' The voice answered 'Over here!' Claude stumbled towards the voice and promptly fell into water! He was in the notorious 'Hot Pool'. This did not improve his humour, but with directions from the bather, he found the steps that led up to the buildings of 'Sunset', a home for old men.

Mildred was woken by the phone, and drove over at midnight to rescue the shipwrecked sailors. How the boat was returned I cannot recall, but we never went camping in it again!

CHAPTER 26

When the school year of 1946 started there was a shadow of gloom over our house. Mum and Dad argued a lot, and Mum always seemed unhappy. In an effort to revitalise her interest in their home, Father had arranged for Edna Walling, the great Melbourne landscape gardener, to draw up plans for Clovelly. This entailed lots of photographs and a detailed survey of the property. Finally it was done and the plans were finished, but unfortunately by then Mother's health had deteriorated, and they were never put into effect.

Clovelly in 1946 – photographed for Edna Wallings to draw up landscaping plans

At the end of the first Term, I was invited to go to Rottnest Island for the May holidays by our neighbours the Smiths. Roland Smith owned a beautiful launch named *Pollyanna*, and his son Tony and I were friends. We spent happy days fishing and cruising around the bays, and one late afternoon, we were anchored at Green Island on the south side of Rottnest, in company with Roland's brother Gordon, in his launch *Nokomis*, just about to cook our crayfish. It was sundown when a truck drove down to the beach nearby, and Jim Starke, the Island Administrator, called Roland in. They talked for a while, and then he returned to the launch. I was told that my mother was sick, and that I must go home immediately.

I was transferred to the *Nokomis* and we set out for Fremantle, some 14 miles away. I remember that the sea was smooth as glass as we ploughed along on that still, moonlit night. Binkie Frayne met me at the wharf in Fremantle, drove me up to St John of God Hospital. There I found Mother sitting up in bed, and we talked for a while. I had no idea what was wrong with her. The next morning she was taken to the airport and flew to Melbourne. I never saw her again.

Mother stayed at a guesthouse in Eltham, in the country near Melbourne, and Claude flew over to see her a couple of times. She wrote letters to us, telling how much she missed us, and that she wanted to come home, but was not well enough. It was about 3 July when Father gathered the three of us in his bedroom after breakfast and told us the unbelievable news that Mother had died!

He then put us all in the car and drove us up to Yanchep, a quiet resort, where we hired a row boat and paddled around the peaceful lake, trying to come to terms with our grief. He sent us all back to school the next day.

After that followed a succession of housekeepers, while Father struggled to keep the home under control. The first was a drunk, and Pam and I watched in horror as she staggered round the kitchen preparing dinner, dripping blood from her cut hand into everything!

On Sundays, father and I went often to Communion at St Luke's Church, and each evening he would kneel beside his bed to say his prayers. His great faith gave him the strength to go on.

Pam finished her schooling at St Hilda's at the end of the year, and Father sent her off to Melbourne for another year's 'finishing school', as he put it, at Toorak College in Frankston.

Claude's practice was still busy, however he and John Day had fallen out, and the partnership was dissolved.

In that year, Dr Lindsay Male came to live with us. He had returned from overseas as a full Colonel, having spent a period of time after the war with the Red Cross in Greece. His personal life was in tatters after an unpleasant divorce, and he had been in no hurry to come home. He and father got on famously, and he was great company for us all. At that time I was doing a lot of horse riding, and he gave me his beautiful leather riding-boots, which fitted me perfectly.

Towards the end of the year, my father and I were out walking one day, when he told me that he was sending me to school in Victoria. He had wanted to send me to his old school, Melbourne Grammar, but as neither he nor his brother Jack had paid their 'Old Boys' subscriptions, they would not accept me! Instead, I was enrolled as a boarder in Geelong College, where father's friend Arnold Buntine was now Headmaster, having moved on from Hale School. I was put on the 'Overland' train, and changing at Kalgoorlie, Port Pirie and Adelaide, I was eventually met on Spencer Street Station in Melbourne by Claude's sister, my Aunt Lucile.

In 1948, Claude became the President of the Ophthalmological Society of Australia, and as such he was to host the Congress that was to be held in Perth. His eastern states colleagues travelled by sea, rail and air to join him, at the Inaugural Meeting in that city, where the welcoming cocktail party was held at Clovelly. Unfortunately, Claude was not present, as he was in hospital with pneumonia!

However he did hold another cocktail party, in the summer of 1949. He had shaken off the gloom of the past, and invited all his friends to join him for the great party. It was held in the lovely garden of Clovelly, which was illuminated with floodlights. He had employed staff to serve food and drinks, and the evening was a great success.

At the end of that year, I finished school, and returned to Perth. By then, father had sold his Ford V8 and had purchased a new Jowett Javelin, with a revolutionary style of engine. He had previously taught me to drive in the Ford, in the process of which I managed to collide with the gatepost, making him very angry. However, he allowed me to drive the new car, which was at that time the epitome of British design and luxury.

Father had a tow bar fitted, and decided that we should have a caravan holiday. He hired a caravan, and with the family aboard, we set out for Moore River, about 70 miles north of Perth. At that time the area was virtually uninhabited, apart from a couple of farms, and access was by a sandy bush track.

We arrived without incident, and descended into the river valley, setting up camp beside the water. There we stayed for two days, swimming and fishing, and sitting round the campfire at night. On the morning we were to leave, we packed the car and caravan, and all climbed in. The track out of the valley was rather steep, and the little Jowett, with only four cylinders, made very heavy weather of it. We children were ordered out, and walked anxiously beside the car as father revved up the engine. With the wheels spinning, and groaning under the strain, the little car made slow progress up the incline. Finally we reached level ground and were allowed into the car again, only to become hopelessly bogged in the sandy track.

Father was furious! He walked to a nearby farm, and eventually returned with the farmer in his truck. With a chain he connected us to the back of the truck, and we started off again, but after only a few yards, the truck itself also became bogged! The farmer then walked back to his farm, and returned with a large tractor. With this in the lead, pulling the truck, then the car with the caravan, the procession moved slowly to firm ground. By this time it was mid-afternoon, and we were all tired, hot and hungry. It was quite dark when we finally pulled in to Clovelly, and I recalled as I was going to bed, my father sitting with a stiff whisky muttering 'Never again!'

In 1950 I commenced Medicine at the University of Western Australia. At that time, only the first year was catered for in WA, after which medical students went on either to Adelaide or Melbourne University.

It was during my first year that, sitting at dinner one evening in Clovelly with Pam and father, that I asked a question that had puzzled me for the last four years as I grew up: 'What exactly did mother die of?'

Pam and father looked at each other, and then after a long pause, I was told that Mother had committed suicide! Previously I had been told vaguely of 'a stroke' or something. Such was Claude's secretive nature.

When I look back on the time of her death, it was all shrouded with mystery. Mother was cremated in Melbourne, but the ashes were not brought home. Instead, they remained in a Melbourne cemetery next to Claude's Mother, Mary Alice. There was no Service of Remembrance, nor any other token of mourning. Little wonder that for years I really thought she would come home one day.

At the beginning of 1951 I set out for Adelaide to continue my medical course, not knowing that I had left Clovelly for the last time. During that year, without mentioning his intention, Claude sold the house to a stock-broker, for the sum of £16,000. He wrote and told me when the deal had been done. He was part paid with an exchange of houses, a small place in Queenslea Drive, Claremont; with some cash, and with a large parcel of shares that within a few years became worthless.

After the grandeur of Clovelly, Claude's new home was indeed humble! Pamela was by then nursing at Princess Margaret Hospital for Children, and was given the second bedroom in the house, while Neville occupied a small balcony room opening off father's bedroom, which he used as his bedroom/study while he completed his education at Hale School.

When I returned from Adelaide at the end of second year Medicine, there was no bedroom for me, except a tiny cupboard-like room, opening off the closed-in back veranda, with a single bed and space only for a small chest of drawers. However it was of little concern to me, as I considered that I had now 'left home'.

Fom then on, Claude lived quietly in Queenslea Drive looked after by housekeepers, who came and went. He drove to the city each day and saw patients, and returned each evening to have dinner with Neville, who was now at university studying French as a major subject. Neville had spent one year in St George's University College, but returned home to be with father.

Pam completed her nursing training and then became an air hostess with Australian National Airlines. She moved to Melbourne where she shared a flat with other 'hosties' and visited father on her flights to Perth.

Meanwhile I continued my studies, living in St Mark's University College in Adelaide. Among my friends in Medicine was Michael Hobbs, Athol's son. We roomed close to each other in College, and travelled to and from Adelaide together on the train. I came home in vacations, and spent time with father, who was now in his mid sixties.

Claude regularly had lunch at the Weld Club which he regarded as a second home, and where he had a great number of friends. He spent his Saturday afternoons in the summer on his friend Athol Hobbs' launch *Nereid*, otherwise referred to as the 'Gin Palace'!

Nereid was a Thames River Boat, brought out to Perth by Athol's father, General Sir Talbot Hobbs, and was a beautifully maintained craft with a varnished hull, a white awning and polished brass. Each Saturday in those later years, Athol's old friends gathered on board and chugged around the river following the yacht races. Needless to say a good deal of drinking went on in the process, and at the end of the afternoon, they were usually a little 'worse for wear'.

I well remember one such occasion when father had arranged for me to collect him at the end of the afternoon. The boatshed was located in Freshwater Bay, about 25 yards off the beach, and accessed by a narrow catwalk that had a handrail on one side. There were a few yards of handrail missing at that time, and as I sat waiting in the car, father emerged from the shed and made his way unsteadily along the catwalk. He reached the gap in the handrail and took a couple more steps, then after swaying perilously from side to side, he fell in to the shallow water. I had great difficulty keeping a straight face as I rescued him.

The *Cygnet* consortium had long since sold their little boat, and had found a new venture for their summer holidays. Each January they rented a beach cottage at Rockingham, about ten miles south of Fremantle, and there, the three of them, and Fred Clark's wife Lou, spent a fortnight swimming and fishing.

I drove down to visit them on one occasion with my girlfriend, Elisabeth, and we were treated to an excellent fish lunch. Father took us out to the

Claude (centre) fishing with friends Fred Clark and Gilbert Troup, at Rockingham

enclosed back veranda where there were enough bottles standing in rows to set up a grog shop! He showed us, with great seriousness, which belonged to Gilbert, which were Fred's, and which were his.

Claude came to Adelaide while I was a student to attend a Conference, and I had great pleasure showing him around our University College. During the visit he looked up some of his old Army friends, including Alan Lendon, who was at that time one of my teachers in Medical School.

By then he had sold the Jowett Javelin, as it seemed to always have something wrong with it, and had replaced it with a smart pale blue Morris Minor. He was far from satisfied, however, as it was, in his view, grossly underpowered. He sorely missed his V8!

Father was delighted when I became engaged to Elisabeth in my final year of Medicine, and declared that she reminded him of Mildred. We spent a lot of time with father when I was home on vacation, and the three of us would go out for meals together by the seaside at Cottesloe, to his favourite restaurant, the 'Seacrest', whose owner was an old patient of his.

One of the problems at Queenslea Drive was the presence of possums. They would scamper around in the roof at night, keeping Claude awake, and leaving damp patches on the ceiling. Among Claude's old friends was Dr Percy White, a delightful man with a wonderful sense of humour. They would often sit together on the veranda sharing a bottle of whisky as they chatted. One evening when home on vacation I came in and found Claude at the top of a stepladder, with Percy below, holding it steady. Claude had his head through the manhole, with a torch in one hand and his trusty old .45 revolver in the other – he was possum hunting! After much persuasion he came down, and I pointed out that a .45 calibre bullet may well travel across the street and injure or even kill someone, and that would surely put him in prison. He finally saw reason. They sat and resumed their whisky, planning other forms of assault on the possums.

Later on, Claude bought a possum trap, and was greatly delighted when he finally he caught one. He then took the poor caged creature down to the back of the garden, and dispatched it with the revolver! Shades of his Jackaroo days.

By that time I had discovered a hole in the ceiling over the enclosed back veranda, and concluded that a bullet must have caused this on another occasion. After some agonising I took the revolver one day when he was out, and under cover of darkness, dropped it from the Fremantle Bridge into the fast running tide of the Swan River. It would never be found. The problem was solved, but I don't think Father ever really forgave me.

CHAPTER 27

At the end of 1955 I had graduated in Medicine, and returned to Perth. Pam was engaged, and was living in Melbourne. Her fiancé Terry was a charming Anglo-Irishman, and an officer in the merchant navy. They married in February 1956. Neville was slogging along at University, completing his degree, and still living at home with Father and the daily housekeeper. It was a fairly happy arrangement.

In April of that year, Claude received the tragic news that his brother Jack had died. At the time he and Nora had been living in Ringwood, Victoria, where he conducted a General Practice. His well-known mood swings had become more of a problem, and in a severe bout of depression, he had committed suicide. Claude was devastated.

I was then an Intern at the Fremantle Hospital, and in May of that year, Elisabeth and I were married. Together, we kept a close eye on Father, who was delighted to have more of his family around him again. We had happy Sundays in the winter sitting by the fire with him having afternoon tea, and his favourite – hot buttered crumpets with honey.

He had new friends too, Elisabeth's parents, Harry and Violet Elliott, who were most kind to him, and often had us all round for Sunday lunch.

As I was in need of a motor car, Father offered to sell me his Morris Minor, which he did – for £400! He then bought a new Holden that was more to his liking. Unfortunately I found that the gearbox of the Morris was ruined, and I had it replaced at great expense.

In April of the next year, Nigel, our first baby arrived, and two weeks earlier in Melbourne Pam had Sally, their first daughter.

At the end of that year, I decided to take on a job with the North West Medical Service. We were to go to Roebourne in the Pilbara District, but considering the extreme heat of summer and our new baby, we postponed our departure until the end of the summer. We started our new life there, and were visited by Father that winter, when he stayed with us for a couple of weeks. By this time he had given up surgery, and passed all his operation cases over to Drs Tim Yates and Graham Raad.

I had asked him to bring some eye equipment with him when he visited, and I well recall him one day on the veranda of my hospital trying to test a young boy for glasses. It turned out to be a difficult case, and as I stood leaning on the veranda post watching, I thought to myself that ophthal-

Examining children for trachoma, on the verandah of the Roebourne Hospital, 1958

Claude with Elisabeth and Pamela having afternoon tea by the fire at Queenslea Drive, 1956.

mology was a rather dull corner of the profession, compared to the life of excitement that I was living, flying around the country with the Royal Flying Doctor Service!

He came again the following winter, and brought Gilbert Troup with him. They had a wonderful holiday together, and on one occasion, went fishing at Point Sampson, returning at the end of the day like two excited schoolboys with a large fish. I was far from amused, as the fish was neither cleaned nor scaled, and they had transported it in my beautiful soft leather travel-bag, which was now full of slime and scales.

We returned to Perth at the end of that year, and I recall us standing on the roof of the Mercantile Mutual Building, where Claude's rooms were located, as we watched the Opening of the Narrows Bridge across the Swan River. It was Friday, 13 November 1959. A lucky day, Claude had said.

Father had decided to give up his city rooms. He was now 71 years old, and found that travelling to and from the city was stressful. As Pam had left home, he converted her bedroom into a consulting room, and continued to see patients there. His housekeeper doubled as a receptionist.

Elisabeth and I moved to Northam, taking over a General Practice with the intention of buying it and settling down. Our second child Andrew was born in May of that year, and Pam's second child, Prudence, was born two days before. Claude was delighted to have four grandchildren, and often drove the 60 miles to stay with us for weekends.

It was on one such occasion that I told him that I intended to specialise in Ophthalmology, and I was somewhat taken back when his face clouded and he told me that I should stay put in General Practice, where I would make much more money!

At the end of the year, when we had finally decided to go to Melbourne so that I could study Ophthalmology, I was having lunch with Father at the Weld Club. One of Father's Ophthalmic Colleagues asked me over a pre-lunch drink, 'Well young Morlet, what are you going to do now?' I replied that I was about to start training in Ophthalmology. He then coolly said. 'Well there really isn't room for another Ophthalmologist in Perth'. I was astonished! I caught Father's eye and he gave a little wink. The wheel goes round.

We left for Melbourne in January of 1961, and a few months later, Neville decided to go to Europe to continue his studies in French. His ship called at Melbourne on its way east through the Panama Canal, and we had a day together. Neville was nearly 25 and needed to get away from home.

And so Claude settled in to a lonely life at his little home, with Mrs Clarke the housekeeper watching over him, and his few patients to see. He chose not to retire completely, which was a wise decision; he would get up each morning and put on a suit to see his patients, and then go to the Weld Club for lunch. He had an interest in life.

His sister Lucile's daughter Janet Elder now lived in Perth, having come out from England to take up an appointment as Senior Chest Physician at the Sir Charles Gairdner Hospital. Janet and Claude got on very well, and she spent a lot of time with him in the last years of his life.

He came and stayed with us on a couple of occasions during the years that we spent in Melbourne, and on one occasion, his stay corresponded with the 'Rats of Tobruk' reunion. Full of happy anticipation, he drove off in a taxi. Well after midnight he appeared at the front door, propped up by a couple of fellow 'Rats' who had obviously had 'a good evening' too, but as they were some 20 years younger than Claude, they had weathered it better!

Meanwhile Pam's marriage was on the rocks. Terry turned out to be a hopeless alcoholic, and whilst he was charm personified when he was sober, he became violent and vicious when drunk. Pam finally left him and with her two little girls fled to Perth. She had met John Rigg, who was kind and supportive to her in her troubled times, and who accompanied Pam to the West.

Claude in his sixties

Claude was outraged that Pamela should be 'living with another man'! It was in total conflict with his lifelong early Victorian principles. He would not allow John in the house, and some very harsh words were spoken. Some time later, when Pam and John returned to Melbourne, and when her divorce was finalised, they married and lived happily together with the girls, who took on John's family name.

By this stage, I had finished my postgraduate studies at the Royal Victorian Eye and Ear Hospital, where Claude had trained just before World War 1. I had decided, however, to go further with my study and sit for the Royal Australasian College of Surgeons Fellowship. I sat for the 'Primary Exam' in mid 1964; however, in company with the majority of the candidates, I failed.

I then decided that we should go to UK to further my studies, but owing to the high cost of travel, with two children and another on the way, I successfully applied for a temporary position with the Northern Territory Department of Health as Ophthalmologist.The job was well paid, and I could save money for our trip.

Our baby daughter Karen Elisabeth (or 'Kate' as she was called), was born in Darwin Hospital just before Christmas that year, and at the end of the wet season we moved to Alice Springs, to carry out a research program in the desert. While we were there, I received news that Father had broken his hip! Apparently he had got out of bed without turning on the light and had fallen. He was unable to reach the phone, and lay on the floor until morning when the housekeeper found him.

As soon as I heard the news I caught a plane to Adelaide, then another to Melbourne, to connect with a direct flight to Perth. It was a long day! I visited Father in Royal Perth Hospital, where he had undergone a surgical repair of his hip, but found him incoherent, and mentally wandering.

A few days previously, Mildred's brother Carlton had died, and after another visit to the hospital, where Father's mental condition had not significantly improved, I accompanied my cousin Dallas to her father's funeral, and then caught a plane back to the Alice. The only glimmer of light came from reading Evelyn Waugh's *The Loved One* on the plane.

When Claude was sufficiently recovered from his operation, he went to a convalescent hospital in South Perth until he could walk comfortably, and care for himself. Surprisingly, he made a quick and excellent recovery from his fractured hip, and returned to Queenslea Drive, to the care of his daily help.

Meanwhile I had booked our passage on a Port Line steamer, which carried 12 passengers and general cargo, sailing from Fremantle to UK. I was to be Ship's Doctor. In November we arrived back in Perth, to find not only had Father fully recovered, he was once again seeing patients in his Consulting Room at home.

While we waited for the ship, I took him to the Weld Club for lunch once or twice a week, and we had lots of long chats. I had told him that we would come back to Perth as soon as I passed my Fellowship and that he could live with us, and we could set up practice together. I remember thinking at the time that he had been somewhat non-committal about my suggestion!

On these terms we left Australia, and after a long slow journey on the old steamer, we landed at Hull, in Yorkshire. As soon as we were settled in our hospital accommodation in Huddersfield, Yorkshire, I rang my old friend Michael Hobbs, who was working in Oxford. His first remark was, 'I'm sorry to hear about your old man.'

'What? Is he dead?' I replied aghast, having been out of communication for some six weeks.

'No', he replied. 'He's got married.'

I nearly fell off the phone!

Chapter 28

Claude and Jacqueline marry, December 1963

Claude had married Jacqueline Wright, an elderly spinster. She was an intelligent woman, who had in the past been Secretary to the Governor of the State. Claude had been secretly 'courting' her for some time, and would park his car a block away and walk to her place – in case the neighbours recognised his car!

Pam had told me that she thought he had a 'girlfriend', as she had picked up the phone one day at his place, and had accidentally overheard him talking to a woman on the other extension. However I thought this was unlikely, as he had never mentioned her in our long lunch conversations.

Looking back at that time, Claude was in a terrible dilemma. His strong and determined mother had brought him up with her strict Victorian morals and religious convictions, to believe that remarriage was disrespectful to one's dead spouse. As children we grew up with the 'hallowed memories' of Mother, and Father's often-stated conviction that he would never marry again. It must have been with great difficulty and embarrassment that he finally told Pam and Janet of his intentions.

Elisabeth's mother told us that he took Jacqueline around to their home one evening to break the news, and when Harry opened the front door, Claude with a defiant expression blurted out 'We are getting married!' Harry and Violet were speechless! Our plans for the future needed revising, as we certainly would not be having Claude to live with us!

Life was difficult in England as Junior Registrars were poorly paid, and the prospect of two or more years study there, with the children growing up and needing education, did not look attractive. I wrote and made some enquiries in Melbourne where I had done my training, and was rewarded with an invitation to return there and join the Postgraduate Teaching Program in my old hospital. Once again we set sail on a Port Line ship, with me again as Ship's Doctor, but this time heading for Melbourne.

We had seen Neville occasionally in England, and he had come up to the North and stayed with us for a long weekend in the summer. He had completed a degree at the Sorbonne University in Paris, and was now teaching in London. When we left England, he saw us off at Liverpool Station. We reached Melbourne and heard good reports about Claude and Jacqueline. She was 'looking after him very well'.

I worked as a locum for Dr Jim McBride White, a Collins Street Ophthalmologist, and started study for my Australian Fellowship Primary, which I passed in August of that year, and then set about studying for the second part of the Fellowship.

One month later, we received the tragic news that our brother Neville had died in London! He had been found dead in a bath. Although the inquest found that he had indeed drowned, it failed to determine exactly what had happened. There was neither alcohol nor drugs in his blood. The Coroner gave an open verdict. It seemed just a tragic accident. It was a terrible irony that he should drown in a bath when he had been a champion swimmer, and held a gold medal for lifesaving. Poor Father was inconsolable. His little Neville, for whom he had been both mother and father since the age of ten. He just could not accept it.

Claude and Jacqueline visited Melbourne the following year, giving us all an opportunity to meet his new wife. Claude, for his part rejoiced at seeing his five grandchildren again.

Twelve months later, I passed the Fellowship examination and joined Jim McBride White in his practice. I was appointed a Consultant at the hospital, and I was extremely busy with my work. We had bought a beautiful home in Kew, and the boys went to nearby Trinity Grammar, while little Katie attended pre-school at Ruyton. We seemed to be well settled.

Claude went on Consulting until 1972. Jacqueline was also his receptionist, and each morning he saw a few patients. He assured me towards the end, that only a few old patients came to see him, together with some old nurses and nuns, whom he would never charge a fee.

In the process of going through Claude's old papers, Jacqueline came across the diaries he had written of 'The Honeymoon' in 1928, and also the 'Leave in Paris in 1917' where he described his flirtation with a French girl. Both of these Jacqueline burned!

I was surprised when Father told me that he very rarely went to Church now, even though Christ Church was only a short walk along Queenslea Drive. He said that Jacqueline did not believe in 'church'.

In the winter of 1972 he became ill and was admitted to Sir Charles Gairdner Hospital. He was diagnosed with cancer of the oesophagus, and treated successfully with radiotherapy.

I flew to Perth to see him, and found him sitting up in hospital frail, but cheerful. He had no more obstructive symptoms, and had a bottle of Scotch in his bedside locker that he shared with old friends who visited him.

I stayed a few days then returned to Melbourne, and we continued to write to each other regularly. He came home from hospital briefly, but in October, he was re-admitted, very short of breath. His lungs had been damaged by the radiation.

In a very shaky hand he wrote to me.

Sir Charles Gairdner Hospital
Nedlands
Tues 24 Oct 1972

Dear Geoff
Your welcome letter has just arrived! I am still bedridden and am writing this with considerable difficulty. I shall be thinking of you all camping again on Melbourne Cup weekend, and only hope you get good weather.

We are terribly short of rain too, and water restrictions are expected any moment.

I was getting on fine, and learning to walk around my bedroom when I had another fall about five days ago. It was on the right hip, which is the artificial joint. It was X Rayed immediately, but no broken bones were found, but I've got a big haematoma in my gluteal muscles, and pain on any hip movement. So the walking lessons have ceased for a week or two!

I am very comfortable here, and Jacqueline comes in to see me each morning and evening, also Janet pops in daily.

Elisabeth's parents have just been in, and are both looking very well, but Harry is still having trouble with his foot.

We also are having lovely weather and my room has a balcony.

This is a marvellous hospital, with all the latest 'mod cons' and I am putting on weight.

No more now old boy, but love to you all, from us both.
Dad

A week later, on 1 November 1972, Claude passed away. He had a couple of visitors at the end of that day, and they chatted over a whisky. He then had his dinner, and peacefully went to sleep. He was 84 years old.

I flew over for the funeral. It was a cremation, preceded by a simple non-religious service. Sadly, Jacqueline had finally taken him away from his lifelong deep religious principles.

I stayed a few days to help Jacqueline sort things out, and then returned to my family. All my links with Perth seemed to be severed. Two years later however, on a freezing cold wet Melbourne day – the first day of summer – we became acutely homesick, and felt that the children would be better off growing up in Perth's wonderful climate. So we sold our lovely home in Melbourne, and returned to Perth to live.

We often visited Jacqueline, who continued to live at Queenslea Drive, and our boys would go round and do gardening for her on the weekends. Jacqueline died on 23 June 1979, at the age of 76. Her ashes lie with Claude's in the Memorial Rose Garden at Kattakatta Cemetery.

In about 1989, Clovelly was sold again, for a price 'around a million', and then knocked down. The house was half demolished when Elisabeth and I went to have a look at the ruins. Everywhere we walked, memories of my childhood came flooding back. On one wall there was a graffiti scribble – *'No ghosts here.'* If only they knew!

I picked up a piece of jarrah floorboard from our parent's old bedroom, where both Pam and I were born, and gave it to an old Dutch patient of mine who was a wood carver. He returned it to me with the word 'Clovelly' inscribed, and it now sits on the bookshelf over my desk.

After Jacqueline died, 'Queenslea Drive' was sold, demolished, and replaced with modern units, while a most elegant home now occupies the large block looking across the Swan River where Clovelly had stood for sixty years.

And so, in one small corner of this earth, a tiny chapter of history came to a close.

Lythrum Press
ADELAIDE

www.lythrumpress.com.au